Capture the Dream

Capture the Dream

The Many Lives of Captain C.P. Krishnan Nair

Bachi Karkaria

JUGGERNAUT BOOKS
C-I-128, First Floor, Sangam Vihar, Near Holi Chowk,
New Delhi 110080, India

First published by Juggernaut Books 2022

10 9 8 7 6 5 4 3 2 1

P-ISBN: 9789391165598
E-ISBN: 9789391165604

Typeset in Adobe Caslon Pro by R. Ajith Kumar, Noida

Printed at Thomson Press India Ltd

To my grandsons: Kahaan, master chef, and
Kabir, master cool

Contents

Foreword

When I first met Captain Nair in the early 1980s, he was in his 60s. In the first half an hour of our interaction, the thing that struck me most was his amazing passion and optimism for life. Always upbeat, at an age when most of us would plan to slow down and dream of blissful days of retirement, here was a man ready to defy all odds to keep changing his life's trajectory, while creating milestones along the way.

A former army captain, he joined his wife's handloom enterprise and created a flourishing business, developing and marketing handloom textiles like fine lace for home décor and the famous 'Bleeding Madras' fabrics – something I related to immediately having been called the 'Madras Monsoon' on the world tennis stage! The success of this business paved the way for huge fabric and garment exports from India.

The unstoppable Captain Nair then embarked on his next venture with equal passion and energy – to create the magnificent Leela Hotels. His interest in the hotel industry was inspired by his love for India and its famous hospitality tradition. He realized that the India of his dreams would need world-class facilities, the kind he had experienced during his stay at some of the finest hotels in the West. He saw it as an opportunity to showcase the resplendent culture of India. Here was a chance to contribute towards the building of a nation by creating world-class hotels and resorts. He was sure that luxury could be translated into exquisite interiors and beautiful gardens that would recreate the unique grandeur of India, putting the country on the world tourism map.

To my mind, Captain Nair is proof that if we dare to dream, we can transform the course of our own destiny through creativity, hard work and passion. I recall spending so many evenings with him in his lovely suite at the majestic Leela Hotels, where he would share his future thoughts and dreams for India's growth. Today, he lives on through the masterpieces he created, always an inspiration to all of us whose lives he touched.

This book is a small gesture of admiration, appreciation and love.

December 2021 **Vijay Amritraj**
Los Angeles, California

Introduction

'And one man in his time plays many parts.'
– William Shakespeare, *As You Like It*

Those who live till the age of ninety-two often have a ringside seat as history unfolds. Some even manage a role in shaping some of the drama. But there are a few who dare divide their world into several stages, and stride across each of them with a performance to remember. Captain C.P. Krishnan Nair was one such serial player.

Leftist and capitalist. Freedom fighter, rationing overseer, soldier. Promoter of humble handloom and manufacturer of Scottish lace. Finally, and most remarkably, the hotelier who redefined luxury. The child who could only get rice gruel for breakfast went on to dine with kings.

This is his story.

1

A Birth that Almost Wasn't

'In the midnight shadows of a forest clearing, bounded on one side by a moonlit paddy field, on the other by the darkness of a rubber plantation and a green canopy of coconut palms, lit only by a bonfire and a carpet of flickering camphor lights, a large crowd has gathered . . . They are waiting and watching for the moment when, once a year, the gods come down to earth, and dance . . . For 20 minutes now, a troupe of six, sweat-glistening, half naked, Dalit drummers have been raising their tempo. The insistent beats they are rapping out on the goat-hide chenda drums is getting louder, faster, more frenzied. The first of the dancers has just been "seized by the gods".'

– 'The Dancer of Kannaur', *Nine Lives*, William Dalrymple

In that rapt crowd sits a skinny five-year-old, holding on to his mother with clammy hands. She brings him every year to the sacred ritual that is unique to this part of Kerala's northern Malabar coast. The sight of the gaudily painted Theyyam dancers pirouetting, shimmying and leaping around in a trance with swords unsheathed would terrify even an uninitiated adult.

However, with lullaby and legend, Madhavi Amma has ingrained in her son the power of the community deity, Muchilot Bhagavathi, who is now ready to possess the dancers. Despite the fanged, red-painted face and huge red-gilt mirrored headdress flashing a myriad reflected light, little Krishnan is not afraid. Subconsciously, he is being rooted to his Vaniya culture as firmly as the sentinel palms to the land. Like their fruit, he will be carried across a sea of continents and careers but will remain moored to this core of his being.

Yet, C.P. Krishnan Nair may not have been at all. Infant mortality was a fact of life in 1922, even in India's big cities. Modern medicine was unheard of in Kunnavil, a village in Kannur district, Kerala. When she was pregnant with him, Madhavi Amma often gazed upon her belly bump with dismay. Her fourth had died immediately after birth just months earlier, and she dreaded a repetition of that trauma.

She had collected a bunch of herbs and already pounded them ready to swallow when her friend Mani Amma fortuitously arrived and flung away the abortive mush. Not only did she save the unborn child, but also put him to her breast soon after he emerged. She was also nursing her own infant.

Gregorian calendars being as unknown as pre- and postnatal care at the time, the new baby's date of birth was determined by a totally extraneous event: the marriage of the son of the nearby Victoria Weaving Mill's owner. Madhavi Amma had gone into labour just as the groom was being welcomed with drums and firecrackers, and that's what determined 9 February 1922 as the fifth child's date of birth. He would be one of seven siblings who survived from nine pregnancies. Back then, no one knew the enormity of tiny Krishnan's escape into the world.

2

Just Another Village Childhood

Kunnavil is a pin-sized dot of a village some distance from Kannur, the main cantonment town of the eponymous district. Krishnan's parents owned 2 acres of land there and had built a thatched hut amidst palms which provided shade and income. Madhavi Amma, who came from farming stock, sold the dried kernel as copra or crushed it for oil. Her husband, Appu Nair, was a cog in the revenue machinery, accompanying the village headman to collect taxes. You might call him a peon if you were being blunt. Still, this job cushioned the harshness of his lowly Vaniya caste, even in this region's rigidly stratified system. He was empowered to enter any house in the course of duty. His monthly salary was Rs 9, not princely, but not a pittance. Like an obedient member of a matrilineal society, he would hand over most of it to his wife.

Salary day was also boys' day out. Fathers and sons would go to town – literally. They would walk 10 km from the village to big, bustling Kannur, which explains why the child would remain so fit into adulthood. The trip combined business with pleasure. Their first courtesy call would be to the main coconut oil trader, 'Meeshakkaran' (moustachioed) Kunhiraman. Little Krishnan looked forward to this because his precocious charm was rewarded with a shiny Re 1 coin – a gesture which also indicated the regard the dealer had for Madhavi Amma, his industrious supplier.

In his Malayalam autobiography, *Krishnanleela*,[1] released in Kovalam on 25 July 2011 by Kerala chief minister Oommen Chandy, Captain Nair records that more than the rows of administrative buildings in Kannur, he was awed by its many greens 'which lay spread like the skies. Municipal Maidan, Fort Maidan were the trademark features of Kannur. Large assemblies and protests to do with the freedom struggle took place in these venues. If one were to put one's ear to the ground here today, one might hear the old rumbles again. However, now the maidans are all in pieces and resemble a mutilated body. Kannur developed slowly and when this happened the first victims were what constituted the heart of the town.'

These sentences reveal how the child is father of the man. Nature would remain the alluring call on all his travels, and Krishnan became not merely the observer, but also the creator in his seventies – lush gardens were a signature touch in the hotels he built, signifying one among his many passions. It was in Kannur's expansive green spaces that he attended political rallies that inspired his teenage slogans as he fought for freedom from social inequalities.

The boy Krishnan looked up to his father, but his heart belonged to his amma, who doted on him more than any of his three elder siblings. He was probably considered even more special because like the fourth child, the sixth had also died at birth. As 'Kochukrishnan' lay on a mat with its distinct Malabar weaves, she would croon him to sleep. He was lulled by her hymns to Muchilot Bhagavathi but would listen wide-eyed to the songs about the mythic warriors from northern Malabar. These ballads were enshrined in a collection of medieval Malayalam ditties called *Vadakkan Pattukal*, though the simple village woman was unlikely to have heard of this tome. Madhavi Amma had imbibed them in the same way that they had been passed down for four centuries: as part of

---

1 *Krishnanleela* by Captain C.P. Krishnan with Thaha Madayi (DC Books, 2007). All quotes unless otherwise indicated are from the English version, *My Leela, My Life*, translated, updated and recast by T.C. Narayan in 2011.

the strong oral cultural tradition that binds rural communities everywhere in the world.

Thrilling to the martial arts prowess of Aromal Chekavar and Thacholi Othenan, the child cast himself in these heroic roles. Not in his most fanciful dreams would he have thought that he would become something of a Malayali folk hero himself, acquiring a larger-than-life reputation as a creator of wealth and jobs.

Gently shaking her tiny warrior awake, Madhavi Amma would spoon out the traditional breakfast: last night's rice mixed with fresh buttermilk, diluted with the water in which the rice had been boiled, all of it spiked with the brine of pickled limes. The older Krishnan would write in his autobiography that this humble gruel 'accounted for the brawn and brain of every North Kerala child of my generation'. Previous and successive ones too.

When he was a little older, he helped by sweeping the area where she dried the coconuts, happily munching on the slivers of copra that flew from her blade, as lethal as the *urumi* swords of his *kalaripayattu* heroes.

~

Madhavi Amma had grown up in Kootali in a place surrounded by perfumed trees. Her home was in the benign shadow of the Muchilot Bhagavathi temple, where her father was a *komaram*, one who knows and understands the deity. In an age still unmarred by the human–wildlife conflict, elephants from Coorg often landed up in the forests surrounding their home. Madhavi Amma passed on her love for these intelligent, gentle giants to her son. Krishnan's second school was in paddy-rich Etakkad, not far from Kootali. On weekends, she would take him to see the lumbering visitors, let him stroke their trunks and play with their calves.

Eight decades later, he would gaze at her faded photograph and softly whisper, 'Amma, this naughty son of yours, Krishnan, who grew up on that morning gruel is approaching 90 years of age. I would still love to go back to our old home and see the elephant that lost its way. But those elephant tracks, those forests and the trees that exuded fragrance have all gone far, far away!'

3

Protectors, Celestial and Secular

In the New Testament, Jesus Christ tells the Pharisees, 'Render unto Caesar the things that are Caesar's and unto God the things that are God's.' At a less lofty level, for Krishnan's community of Vaniyas, Muchilot Bhagavathi was 'God' and Valiya Raja was Caesar. The two protected them and dominated their religious and secular existences, respectively.

In many old cultures, king and god are interchangeable. Lord Rama is both the king of Ayodhya and the seventh incarnation of Vishnu, the Preserver. In the West, the king couldn't quite say he was God, but found an excuse via the doctrine of the divine right of kings. Institutionalized by King James I of England (1603–25), this doctrine declared that a monarch's word was absolute and his deeds unquestionable because he derived his authority from God. He was therefore not accountable to some earthly parliament. Latter-day dictators have suffered from the same delusion.

With due reverence, let us start with the fanged, red-faced goddess of the Theyyam dance that so riveted devotees.

In Hinduism, as in many tribal structures, there are what are called 'little traditions'. Not those of the grand pantheons but smaller, more personal deities. Like Bon Bibi in the Sundarbans, Muchilot Bhagavathi was the more accessible guardian spirit of the Vaniya community that was concentrated in Kannur. Her legend is a metaphor of the continuing injustices of gender and caste. This is her story.

Uchila, a girl from the Namboodiri Rayaramangalam family, was in fact a divine maiden who had taken human form. By age sixteen, she had acquired fame as a Vedanta scholar. On the auspicious day of the star Pooram, the date of her marriage was fixed. In front of a lamp with seven wicks, the astrologer spread out the cowries on a golden platter and announced the auspicious time after reading them: 'After seven Mondays, on the eighth Monday after dawn.'

The day after this pronouncement, the ruler of Perinjallur, Pacha Nambi, himself arrived. He had been sent a message on the traditional palm leaf by the Perinjallur Scholars Assembly, which declared that if anyone in his domain had mastered the Vedas, that person should appear before the experts of the Udayamangalam Debating Assembly.

When they saw Uchila among them, her scholarly debating opponents were enraged by the idea of a woman besting them, and not a little envious. They tried trapping her with devious questions. To one of them, 'What is the greatest of all pleasures?', Uchila had fearlessly replied: 'Sensual pleasure.' Her rivals had been waiting for an opportunity to discredit her, and they did what male chauvinists have always done: they declared that this reply could only have been given from personal experience. They proceeded to maul her character till the council of Brahmins finally banished her from her village.

Despondent, Uchila walked away. Visiting all the temples on her route, she reached the sanctum sanctorum of the shrine of Payyannur Perumal and poured out her despair. A disembodied voice intoned, 'Uchila, you are a divine maiden. You have served out the term of your curse and you are free to return to the home of the gods. You must enter a sacrificial fire to do this.'

Uchila filled a pit with embers and stood inside it. A Vaniya passed by carrying a pot of coconut oil, and she asked him to pour some into the pit. The embers leapt into flames, and Uchila soon turned to ash. The man cowered, filled with fear and guilt. But Uchila materialized in her true form and said, 'Abandoned by my villagers and my ruler, it was your oil which enabled me to reach my home with the gods. I shall forever be by your side. You are from Muchilot, so build me a temple there and I shall henceforth be Muchilot Bhagavathi.'

The little boy, whose faith in the deity was seeded with gentle bedtime stories and frenzied Theyyam dances, would in later years refurbish the Katalayi temple in Kannur dedicated to the goddess, adding a large dining hall, special facilities for women, and capacity for a thousand oil lamps around it. It was a token offering for the spiritual anchor the temple had given his parents, and the inner harbour it provided him in tough times. Or simply when he was a thousand miles from home.

Muchilot Bhagavathi's secular counterpart was the Valiya Chirakkal Raja, also referred to in other texts as Chirakkal Rama Varma Thampuran. The seniormost male of the matrilineal Chirakkal branch of the Kolathiri dynasty of what was once the feudal state of Kolathunadu in northern Malabar takes on the title of 'Raja'.

Descended from the Cheras, Pandyas, Cholas and the Ay (known much later as the Travancore Royal Family), this was one of the major, totally independent political houses which came into prominence in Kerala after the disappearance of the imperial Kulasekharas or Perumal rulers by the twelfth century AD. While the British had de facto colonized large swathes of India, such pockets were still the domain of local lords.

The Vaniyas' celestial and earthly protectors would come together mystically in the 1940s during Krishnan's first job as an army radio officer in Abbottabad. But this boy from a remote Kerala village would never have made it to this strategic post without the education he received, and it was the Raja who made that possible in a way more tangible than the blessings of the goddess. We will hear these stories at their appointed hour.

4

Willingly to School

Krishnan's formal education began at Kunnavil Elementary School, three fields away from his hut. No one really raised eyebrows when his age was 'adjusted' by a few months to meet the admission requirement – that was the norm in those easier times. On the very first day, Pacha Krishnan Master, both class teacher and headmaster, asked his five-year-old wards to memorize a verse, 'God, the very core of Vedanta, rules his kingdom forever, just as the benign, all-pervading sun does over the vast sky of our mind.'

In later years, Captain Krishnan Nair would delve deep into Sankaracharya's Advaita philosophy, internalizing the wisdom of many Vedic scholars. But, till the very end, he could recite those lines dinned into him on the first day of school. Attribute it to his innate spiritualism – and maybe some of it to the mnemonic powers given by that childhood breakfast gruel.

Pacha Krishnan Master was a disciple of the area's fearless social reformers, Vagbhatananda Guru (1885–1939) and Narayana Guru (1856–1928), who was also known as the 'Father of the Kerala Renaissance'. The latter had taken up the work of Thycaud Ayyavu Swamikal (1814–1909), also called Sadananda Swami, who was the first to hammer against the iron frame of caste taboos and untouchability. Pacha Krishnan would talk to his primary school students about spiritual enlightenment as well as the courageous movements of these masters.

Krishnan was no stranger to discrimination. Kerala had always been shackled in caste hierarchies; its history bequeathed it a unique demography where the combined population of the two minority communities, Christians and Muslims, together equalled that of the majority Hindus. There were always clashes, opportunistic as well as ideological. The Vaniyas are an old Nair sub-caste in northern Malabar, found mostly in Kannur district. They largely belonged to the Vaishya varna, but in Malabar, all castes other than the Brahmins or the royal Varmas were classified as Shudras, even if they were in traditional Kshatriya or Bania occupations.

Kunnavil Elementary School was exemplary in not making caste distinctions, and in that it was also an exception. As someone from the lower strata, the boy sensed the dominance of the Brahmin Namboodiris, and in his secondary school even found the audacity to confront it. Again, it was his innate belief in equality – arguably bolstered by his father's administrative job which enabled a lowly Vaniya to walk into any house.

Into the midst of this high-minded stuff sashayed the bright and beautiful Padmavathi. She too attended the same school as Krishnan, but there the similarity ended. Her father was the local physician, Appa Doctor, whose name was corrupted to 'Appu Dercer'. Their two-storeyed house, with its glistening tiled roof, was only two fields but a planet away from Krishnan's thatched home. Despite his declaration that he wouldn't dare look at any girl's face and always kept a respectful distance, Krishnan was undoubtedly smitten. By his own admission, even decades later, he would often find himself wondering what happened to the beauteous Padmavathi. And even Maya, who will be waiting at the next scholastic milestone. But that is a different story.

Here's a detour. Decades later, Krishnan would smart every time he had to land in Calicut or Mangalore and then drive three hours to Kannur, or make an even longer journey by train. That thorn had a subconscious genesis. On 15 October 1932, a date that made aviation history, J.R.D. Tata had piloted the first-ever flight of the Tata Air Service from Karachi's Drigh Road aerodrome to Mumbai's Juhu airstrip via Ahmedabad. The aircraft was a single-engine De Havilland Puss Moth and it carried 25 kg of 4 anna airmail letters. What has been left out of all the breathless accounts of the historic flight is what Captain Nair would record in his Malayalam memoir.

He recalled that from Mumbai, JRD flew south to Kochi. To the utter disbelief of locals, the little plane landed in Kannur's Fort Maidan. Along with other children, Krishnan had raced to see this strange bird and the equally strange person who emerged from it. It was 'as if the celestial pushpaka vimana of the epics had flown straight out of myth into reality'.

It's a great story, but research has failed to show up any such flight path of the Puss Moth. However, a number of amateur fliers did begin whirring about the district later, and perhaps the young lad believed that one of them was the much talked about JRD.

Regardless of that case of mistaken identity, that night, the ten-year-old Krishnan had a dream. He was travelling in a plane dressed up as that stylish pilot. 'A bewitching dream which repeated itself until dawn.'

Of course, it came true, and not only in the thousands of air miles Krishnan Nair would clock up. Years before he passed away, Kannur got an international airport, thanks to his lobbying. Fort Maidan was redundant. We'll come to its twenty-year-long history when we show how deeply he always remained a 'Kerala (and Kannur) boy'.

Captain Nair would reminisce in *Krishnanleela*: 'Dreams are what fuel our life's journey. I learnt this lesson as an industrialist. No vehicle moves forward without fuel. Neither does life.'

5

Caste No Bar

From Kunnavil Elementary School, Krishnan went to Oorpazhassikavu Higher Elementary School, not a scant 'three fields away from his house', but in the picturesque hamlet of Etakkad. It was close to his uncle's house, so that was where he stayed. He didn't get homesick because on holidays and even most weekends he'd spend time with his mother, and those elephants.

As a studious child, or what would later in schoolboy slang be called 'an enthu cutlet', Krishnan endeared himself to his new headmaster. This man was more easy-going than the spiritual reformist Pacha Krishnan. He often took the precocious Vaniya lad home and fed him ghee payasam which was, in the simile of his memoir, 'as sweet as the verses of poetry he taught'. However, the pervasive bitterness of caste intervened one day. Happily, it was the kid on the oppressed side of the barrier who ended up with the more pleasant taste in his mouth.

A few 'twice-born' Namboodiri families lived in his uncle's locality, and naturally treated everyone else with contempt. Despite her caste legacy, Madhavi Amma had instilled in her son the ideal of all humans being created equal. So the eleven-year-old was ready to defy the intractable rule that if any lower mortal came across a Namboodiri on the road, he had to obsequiously let him pass. Finding himself in this situation, Krishnan refused to heed an arrogant Brahmin who ordered him off the footpath. The boy held his ground, audaciously saying, 'This road is meant for everyone. If my presence bothers you, please feel free to step aside yourself.'

In another mansion close by lived a beautiful Namboodiri girl. This was Maya. Unlike the doctor's uppity daughter Padmavathi, she would shyly try to make small talk with Krishnan. He gave her the cold shoulder, though again, in later years he would admit, 'I have often thought of her as I did of Padmavathi.'

Captain Nair would eventually shed that old diffidence and unabashedly charm every woman. Harsh Goenka, in his tribute in the *Economic Times*, mentioned that even when he lay with his organs packing up one by one, he 'managed to enchant the Kerala nurses' at Breach Candy Hospital'.

6

The Verse That Powered a Future

Oorpazhassikavu School ended with the seventh standard, and with it the education of every low-born Vaniya boy. However, even by age twelve, Krishnan had made it clear that he was ready, willing and, to a degree, even able to confront ironclad caste strictures. He pestered his mother to get him admission into the high school in Kunnavil. Madhavi Amma went to Sanku, the son of a local leader, and did some pestering of her own. Sanku succumbed, and the Dalit boy walked into Raja High School. Overseen by the Chirakkal Valiya Raja himself, it had reputed teachers and alumni who had done the school proud.

By the way, little Krishnan was so impressed by Sanku's illustrious father, Thunoli Sankaran Nair, that he once asked his mother: 'Why did you name me Krishnan and not Sankaran?' He naively believed that being called 'Sankaran' automatically bestowed power. Recalling this in his memoir, he wrote: 'It took a long time for me to realize that it was not the name, but his goodness that brought him the regard of all around. Good people are respected. I used to tell myself that I have to grow up to be a good man.'

At Raja High School, Krishnan again worked his way into the affections of the headmaster, Rairu Nair. Not only did he speak respectfully, as he had been taught, he also reached school early and cleaned his classroom and other common areas. He was soon elevated to class monitor.

In the very first year, he got to see the august Chirakkal Valiya Raja. He was the chief guest on the annual day. Twelve-year-old Krishnan was bowled over by his regal looks, bearing and personality. 'Is this Bhishma Pitamaha himself?' he wondered, equating this apparition with the great Kuru warrior from the Mahabharat.

The Raja stood up to deliver his address. His wise words were laced with verses from Rabindranath Tagore and other Indian greats. They suffused Krishnan with such emotion that he found himself drawn to the dais as soon as the chief guest returned to his ornate seat.

Making his obeisance, he poured out the Malayalam verse that had spontaneously risen to his lips:

Our gratitude to you,
You with the energy of a thousand rising suns and moons,
You with the cool image of the moon,
Who has graced us with your presence to bless us
To you who gives us the wealth of learning, of knowledge,
to you our greetings.

He bowed again and turned to go back to his bench. The Raja called him back, and, to his utter amazement, actually embraced him. 'What is your name, son, and who is your father?' he asked. The stunned Krishnan just about managed to reply.

An even happier shock was to follow. The Raja turned to the headmaster and said, 'I will bear all expenses for tuition, books, even clothes, for as long as this bright boy chooses to study. Let him educate himself to the fullest. I can tell that he has a great future.' When Krishnan fell at his feet, the ruler made him stand back up and said kindly, 'Come and meet me on your weekly holiday.'

Neither benefactor nor beneficiary knew then how far that gift of education would take Krishnan Nair. Or how many royals he would interact with, right up to the emperor of Japan. And all because of a verse that sprang unbidden from a bedazzled boy.

7

College, Set in a Diamond Ring

With that auspicious windfall of the first year, Krishnan breezed through Raja High School. Having got on this trajectory, he had no intention of slouching off it. He wrote to virtually every college in Kerala. But, uncharacteristically for this *payyan* for whom neither poverty nor pompous Namboodiri had come in the way so far, this time it turned out like that sad babu joke, 'Apply, apply, no reply.'

What was he to do?

Doing nothing was not an option. He had no intention of staying at home, trapped in the karma of a Vaniya. He had broken the mould, and he wasn't going to just stand around looking desolately at the pieces of his life. He would philosophize as a successful adult, 'It is easy to shrug at fate and fritter away your years, but it takes guts to take charge of your life. When you sit idle, your spirit weakens and dies.'

So, young Krishnan, like all enterprising Malayalis, decided to leave Kerala. Kannur was still part of the Madras Presidency, and its residents looked to that capital when they wanted to move up in life. His brother-in-law was already working at Madras Transport. Praying that he wouldn't get another rejection, he tried the Government Arts College there. This time he got admission, but it turned out he didn't have any money for train fare, let alone the fees. What he did have was his benefactor.

Or did he? His heart sank as he saw the Raja's face fall as soon as he was ushered in to meet him. Having sensed that the young man wasn't here just for a courtesy call, the Chirakkal ruler came straight to the point. 'Look here, Kochukrishnan, I know I had generously offered to fund your entire education, but ...' here he hesitated before forcing himself to admit that he was in dire financial straits himself. Krishnan was equally embarrassed. To be honest, he felt equally sorry for himself at this unexpected barrier to his ambitions.

But mythology and history confirm that a royal promise is carved in stone. As Krishnan stared in disbelief, the Raja eased the diamond ring off his little finger and said, 'Go to Bapalal's in Madras and meet the owner. Tell him I have given it to you. You'll get what you need to complete your education.' Krishnan took the proffered ring, getting in a flash the full measure of a generosity which was as unhesitating as it was unconditional.

Borrowing the train fare, he arrived in Madras, and went straight to the high-end jewellery store. Such establishments were usually too lofty to take back a used item, but as soon as the elderly owner heard the Valiya Raja's name, his proud features softened. 'Did he really tell you to meet me?' Krishnan related the whole story. Bapalal unlocked his safe and counted out the staggering sum of Rs 4500. Accepting it with humility, Krishnan deposited it at the post office.

The money covered his entire college education. The journey that had begun with a short verse concluded with a diamond ring.

8

Seeing Red

The soil of Kannur is red. Literally and ideologically. In the 1950s, Anglo-Indian teachers in the rest of India would wow their young wards with a long-drawn-out 'Nam-boo-diri-pad' to tell them about E.M.S. Namboodiripad, the country's first communist chief minister in 1957, and also the world's first democratically elected communist leader. It was arguably also the first time that those kids would have heard of Marxist politics. Decades later, Jyoti Basu would make West Bengal the 'Red Fortress', but Kerala, and specifically Kannur, had been at the forefront.

The egalitarian ideology enraptured our thirteen-year-old Vaniya lad. The Raja High School Students' Union was formed, and Krishnan became its first secretary, anointed by no less than the firebrand A.K. Gopalan, himself a Kannur boy who would stride around with his pristine dhoti doubled up to his knees. AKG was originally a teacher, but his participation in the Khilafat movement had been something of an epiphany, turning him into a dedicated full-time social and political worker. At the age of twenty-three, AKG joined the Indian National Congress, and, three years later, the salt satyagraha. His consequent arrest brought another turning point: AKG was introduced to communism in prison.

His comrade in transforming the Malabar unit of the Congress Socialist Party into the Kerala unit of the Communist Party of India (CPI) in 1940 was P. Krishnan Pillai from Alleppey. His political dedication is encapsulated in the way contemporary reports say he proposed to his prospective wife, Thankamma: 'Life with me will be difficult, different. My wife should stand by me, the party and its cause. Then alone will she be happy.'

AKG and Krishnan Pillai galvanized the youth of Malabar, uniting them for the first time in a common cause. Both had visited Raja High School to mobilize support for the struggle against the British Raj. Krishnan would treasure that memory till the last, recalling in his autobiography how the great AKG interacted individually with each boy and how he 'asked me many questions'. Perhaps his bold answers along with 'my better physical stature persuaded him to give me the responsibility of managing the Students' Union'.

Without wasting time, Krishnan requisitioned a shop in Chirakkal belonging to Appukuttiettan of New Star Weaving. When he had walked in there accompanied by leaders of that stature, the owner asked the young boy, who had just entered his teens, 'Are you planning to make this a political venue?'

Krishnan replied, '*Sar*, all this is only to win our freedom, *elle*?'

There was no further argument.

Inspired by the charismatic duo of Krishnan Pillai and AKG, the students signed up en masse. Krishnan was among the 300 who marched shouting slogans to the local Vilakkumthara Maidan in response to a call by Krishnan Pillai. They were promptly arrested, but the police soon let off these underage revolutionaries.

In 1938, student leader Krishnan had gone as a volunteer with his hero AKG to the historic Haripura session of the Indian National Congress presided over by Netaji Subhas Chandra Bose.

This Gujarat venue had been selected by Sardar Vallabhbhai Patel. Lined up were fifty-one bullock carts decorated in the colourful local style of the Vansda state, which was ruled by Maharajasaheb Shri Indrasinhji Pratapsinhji Solanki at the time. Santiniketan's celebrated artist Nandalal Bose had created a set of seven posters at the request of Gandhiji. If all this wasn't enough to establish the importance of this Congress session, J.B.H. Wadia of Wadia Movietone Studio immortalized it with a full-length documentary.

Krishnan, now sixteen, had sat enraptured amidst the frisson of nationalistic fervour. He ended up being more than a spectator. His autobiography records this little-known footnote. Once, during those days, Netaji was wracked by a fever which had everyone most anxious. When the news reached him, the young volunteer told AKG of a remedy he had learnt from his mother. It involved putting a cloth soaked in breast milk on the fevered brow of the patient. AKG conveyed this to Netaji's brother, Sarat Chandra. Apparently, the vital ingredient was found, and Netaji was soon back on his feet and the podium.

AKG appealed to the impressionable Krishnan because he was 'the people's warrior', concerned only about their hardships and humiliations. Krishnan's admiration grew when his senior Kannur compatriot became one of the sixteen CPI members of Parliament (MPs). After the historic split in 1964, over conflicting loyalties to the Soviet Union and China, AKG was among those who led the breakaway CPI(Marxist) (CPI[M]).

Many decades later, Prakash Karat, then general secretary of CPI(M), asked him about his years under the tutelage of this party father figure. Captain Nair, now a capitalist entrepreneur, replied with residual awe, 'AKG was one whose greatness radiated from him.' And what he would remember about Krishnan Pillai was that 'behind his forbidding, almost abrasive look, lay a really gentle person'.

Krishnan also revealed in his autobiography what the CPI(M) stalwart Jyoti Basu had said to him while he was a guest in one of Krishnan's hotels: 'If AKG had been your chief minister in place of EMS, no other party would have come to power in Kerala for the next 30 years.'

Krishnan went on to write:

> Jyoti Basu's observation is correct . . . the entire political history of Kerala would have been different. AKG was not a mere revolutionary but also . . . a great political strategist . . . The Kisan Sabha under his leadership could have brought about a transformation in agricultural productivity. Instead of wasting one's life as an intellectual, AKG considered it more pragmatic to mobilize people for an activity that brought direct benefit to them . . .
>
> In my estimation, the only leaders whom I see as AKG's equals are Subhas Chandra Bose, Jawaharlal Nehru and Jayaprakash Narayan. AKG never saw his followers as his political slaves. Neither did he use them as tools with which to build his image. He saw them as colleagues and equals and treated them as such. There has never been a leader in Kerala after AKG to match him.

Communist leaders were forced underground during the freedom struggle, and even just after Independence. In 1948, the CPI was banned after it passed a resolution known as the 'Calcutta Thesis'. It propagated an armed struggle against the Indian state. While hiding in a worker's hut, Krishnan Pillai, forty-two, succumbed to snakebite.

Krishnan had an underground encounter of his own. When he was an undergraduate in Madras, he heard a furtive knock at the door of his tiny room. When he opened it, AKG rushed in and went on to stay there for a couple of days, telling his protégé to put a deceptive lock on the door whenever he left for college.

Krishnan would spot him once more at Madras's Egmore Railway Station. He waved excitedly, calling out to him by name. AKG at once signalled secrecy, putting his finger to his lips.

And here's a less-glorious aside. In April 2021, Kolkata's The *Telegraph* exhumed the 'rancour and romance of those years in hiding' while reporting on an accusation by T.V. Balram. The Kerala Congress member of the Legislative Assembly alleged that the iconic AKG had committed *bala peedanam*, the literal translation of which is 'child torture or torment' but it can also mean paedophilia. Balram spiced this up further, claiming that the communist titan had had a 'love affair' with a minor in the 1940s, when he was 'a married and middle-aged man', and a decade later had made her his second wife.

The *Telegraph* continued, 'What has given the allegation a political overtone is Balram's attempt to insinuate a parallel with the charges of sexual exploitation against former chief minister Oommen Chandy and other Kerala Congress politicians . . .'

The *Telegraph* continued that, to back up his allegation, 'Balram has cited AKG's own words in his autobiography and a report headlined "Love in the Time of Struggle" in *The Hindu*, published on 20 December 2001. *The Hindu* story clearly says that the marriage followed a decade-old love affair. From what we know, Susheela was twenty-two years old when she married AKG in 1952.

'Going by that, one only needs to calculate how old she was when the affair started.' Balram had posted this on Facebook in Malayalam. Kolkata's *Telegraph* report added, 'AKG wrote in his autobiography that he had unsuccessfully tried to dissuade Susheela from falling in love with him and had waited till she turned an adult to marry her.'

AKG's own Kolkata connection lies not in communism, but in coffee. He founded the cooperative that launched the Indian Coffee House chain, including the celebrated one on the city's totemic College Street. 'A lot can happen over coffee,' as made famous by the tag line of India's own Café Coffee Day.

9

Into the Army with the Kindness of Strangers

Krishnan returned home from Madras in 1942 after completing what was known as the intermediate qualification at the Government Arts College. He wanted to go on to a proper graduation, but the diamond ring had exhausted its lustre. He couldn't count on his mother either, not that he wanted to. What he did want was to fly into the wide world and fulfil his responsibility as a son to support his parents.

So, like many young men without money to match ambition, he decided to join the army. There was also a more immediate goal. Madras had lived in fear of a Japanese attack during 1942–43, and in October 1943 a lone Japanese reconnaissance plane did bomb the city. There were even legends that had sprung up from the time of World War I, when the German cruiser Emden shelled Madras in 1914.

Making his way to Bangalore, Krishnan pressed his only shirt, and with an equally ironed stride, marched into the recruiting office. Not unlike the callow Mohan Singh Oberoi at the gilded gates of Simla's Cecil Hotel some twenty years earlier, young Krishnan Nair boldly asked the colonel in charge, 'Can you give me a job?' He didn't forget to suffix the request with a sharp 'Sir'. Just as the Cecil's British manager had been impressed by Oberoi's self-confidence and well-polished shoes, the British Indian Army officer called our Kerala lad for an interview. We will find more parallels in the trajectories of these two remarkable hoteliers as we go on.

Krishnan not only got the job, but an advance pay of Rs 120 as well. He bought two sets of trousers and shirts, and sent the rest to Madhavi Amma, who was overcome with joy. Her little Kochukrishnan had received his first salary, and he had not forgotten the mother to whom he owed it. Part of it was earmarked for Mani Amma, who had prevented his life from ending before it even began.

From steamy Kerala in the south of India, Krishnan was blasted to the snowy crags of the North-West Frontier Province. His first posting was to Abbottabad. Major James Abbot (1807–96) had set up this capital in Hazara district, and commemorated its beauty in what a critic in the *Guardian*, UK, would damn as 'one of the worst poems ever written'. Abbottabad is now in Pakistan – it won latter-day notoriety for being the sprawling hideout of Osama Bin Laden.

But our story is set in 1942, during World War II. As a civilian wireless officer employed by the British Indian Army, Krishnan had to deal with the cryptic messages of the Allied army, and perhaps even those of the Axis powers, and send the text to headquarters. This grim duty was mostly in the night hours, and with hardly any breaks. So he rarely had a breather, let alone the time or mood to appreciate the breathtaking Himalayan panorama beyond his cubbyhole.

However, getting to Abbottabad was a journey in itself – an inner one as well.

~

Unable to find a simpler rail route, Krishnan travelled from Bangalore to Madras to Delhi to catch the evocative Frontier Mail to Abbottabad. The advance given to him was all gone, and he didn't know that the Madras–Delhi leg would be long. So he sat with a tummy as empty as his pockets, getting more desperate as the hours and landscape rolled by. However, once again, like the deus ex machina in an ancient Greek drama (or his own Valiya Raja), a benefactor appeared to save the day.

His co-passenger was a kindly gent and fellow Nair named Karunakaran who was travelling to Peshawar. Having observed the twenty-year-old starving all the way, he asked him to share the tiffin carrier he had wisely brought along. Embarrassed, Krishnan politely refused the lunch, but by dinner time, he had dropped all pretence at formality.

Not only was the older Nair extremely gracious, he also tucked a Rs 10 note into Krishnan's pocket when they parted ways. Overcome by the gesture, Krishnan mumbled, 'Sir, you must give me your address. I shall return this money as soon as I receive my first salary.'

Karunakaran smiled and replied gently, 'You don't have to return anything. Sometime or the other you might encounter someone in the same state you are in today. Please offer him the same assistance.' He gave Krishnan an embrace but not his address. Krishnan didn't forget Karunakaran, or his pay-it-forward advice.

More impactful was what awaited him at his destination.

~

Apart from decoding and transmitting messages at the wireless office, Krishnan would listen to Netaji's speeches broadcast from Singapore via his show 'Azad Hind Radio', through which he also pumped up the demoralized cadres of the Indian National Army. The young officer recalled that there were ten such speeches. The first was when he anointed Gandhiji as the 'Father of the Nation'. The second was addressed to the people of India. 'So illuminating were those speeches that I would wait expectantly for them every night.'

As his heart thrilled to that commanding voice, Krishnan may also have recalled his mother's 'breast milk remedy' which had helped revive Subhas Chandra Bose at Haripura. For Krishnan, Netaji would always remain the tallest hero of the freedom movement.

In 1997, as chairman of the Netaji Centenary Celebration Committee in Mumbai, he would help organize a grand reception for Netaji's half-German daughter, Anita Bose. Dr P.C. Alexander, as governor of Maharashtra, delivered the keynote address. It was an inspiring, detailed speech, and Captain Nair (now the daring hotelier) distributed 1,00,00 copies of it to all the schools in Mumbai. In the course of his own speech, he said, 'Netaji is the second Rashtrapita,' the second Father of the Nation.

That same year, he would return to this slice of his impressionable youth after a Pacific–Asia Travel Association (PATA) conference in Islamabad, thanks to the efforts of Shirin Wajlis, its Pakistan director. Recalling that visit, his long-time secretary, Asha Dokre, who usually accompanied him on his many trips, said, 'After travelling some distance on the road to the Khyber Pass, we were given additional security by the leader of the Tribal Force as we were to cross No Man's Land by jeep. On one side were the mighty Himalayas – stark, bare, rugged and gigantic. And on the other side miles of barren land, dotted only by cacti. We reached an outpost on the Pakistani side. After a lovely meal of white basmati rice, lamb and vegetables cooked in spices, the Commandant helped us view through binoculars the mountain ranges and explained the Durand Line. In the distance we could see the villages of Afghanistan.'

The party proceeded to Murree, Natyagalli and the chairman's old Abbottabad. 'He was overcome to see that the white horses he used to ride, the age-old banyan tree where he would sit, and the post office from where he sent money orders to his mother were all still there. Nothing had changed even after 50 years, and the place was as it had been. Even the names of some of the villages were the same.' Asha remembered only the familiar-sounding ones 'like Kishanganj and Anand Nagar'.

10

The 6'5" Inspiration

After his first stint there, the Abbottabad experience turned out to be as revitalizing as a mountain stream for Krishnan. It was quite unlike anything he had ever known, even after he had drunk deep from many oceans. It was the place where a twenty-one-year-old Krishnan happened to meet Frontier Gandhi in his own domain. His secretary's brother was a colleague in that wireless department, and Krishnan entreated him for an audience. It turned out to be more like a darshan, for Khan Abdul Ghaffar Khan's Murree office was like an ashram. It was thrice as rewarding because he also met Frontier Gandhi's brother, Khan Abdul Jabbar Khan (Dr Khan Sahib), who was chief minister of the North-West Frontier Province, as well as Sheikh Abdullah, the Lion of Kashmir.

The vibe that the young wireless officer had with the savvy Sheikh would be transmitted into the next generations. His Malayalam memoir states that he found Farooq Abdullah and then his son, Omar, 'totally secular and possessing the same charm as the natural beauty of the Kashmir valley'.

Krishnan recorded that 'Khan Abdul Ghaffar Khan, who was more than 6'5" tall, also had a mind as lofty as the skies'. The young Keralite developed a fraternal bond with his sons, Wali and Gani, once going on a tortuous but thrilling trip to the Khyber Pass with the former in his MG car.

What Captain Nair would chuckle over till the last was how he once 'shocked' their mother. He was staying at Frontier Gandhi's Peshawar home when the sons told her, 'Ammi jaan, we should invite our guest to eat with us.' The begum, taken aback, said, 'Will he? Isn't he a non-believer who does not touch beef?'

They smiled mischievously and watched their mother's eyes widen in disbelief as the young army officer joined the family, sitting cross-legged around the dishes arranged on the white *dastarkhwan*, and tucked into the beef kababs with gusto. After that, the Khan and his begum would lay out an elaborate Pushtoon meal whenever Krishnan was in Peshawar.

'What is truth?' was Frontier Gandhi's constant question, which he answered himself: 'Love is truth. Truth is god.' Then his face would glow with a beatific smile, 'like that of a divine messenger', Captain Nair would recall. He added, 'I still see him standing in front of me, his eyes gleaming brightly.'

Some years later, he met Gandhiji at the Wardha ashram, where he spent ten days. Whenever the Mahatma had time, which wasn't often, Krishnan would listen carefully as he spoke about his involvement with the freedom struggle, always doing so with a 'Do what needs to be done; do what is right' expression.

Krishnan's other takeaways from that trip were that the ashram had no hierarchies. And that the food was as different as it could be from the other Gandhi's dastarkhwan – dry chapattis, boiled onions, an ungarnished daal, a cup of curd and half a salted lime. The last two must have reminded him of his childhood breakfast. Nair would later remark that it was impossible to keep pace with Mahatma Gandhi. 'His ideals also were way ahead of everybody else's.'

His memoir also records Krishnan's take on Jinnah, whom he met much later: 'In dress and behaviour he was very refined. In real life he did not appear to be the person he has been made out to be in history. He struck me as a secular person and treated me warmly. Anybody who has met Jinnah will find it difficult to forget the force of his personality.'

However, no one matched up to Netaji. Captain Nair wrote, 'Truth to tell, our generation was inspired more by Subhas Chandra Bose than by Gandhiji. His famous slogan stirred our spirits: "Give me your blood and I shall give you freedom."'

~

Krishnan Nair began his professional journey in the Himalayas, and right at the start there was a momentous course correction. He had been nurtured in the primitive religiosity of a rural community, but the ethereal mountains awakened in him a higher spirituality. The young man took time off to visit Haridwar and Rishikesh, where he met Swami Sivananda, who had renounced life (and an established medical practice) as Dr Kuppuswamy. He slept in the open on the banks of the Ganga as it made an icy journey from its source at Gangotri. The young Kerala lad was so taken up by this guru that he built him a makeshift hut, and begged to be his disciple. The seer knew that sitting 24x7 in a meditative padmasana was not for this energetic man. He told him that his 'destiny lay elsewhere'.

That is how the wannabe yogi was set on the path of karmayoga. He would continue to drink from the spiritual font of Swami Chinmayananda, the Dalai Lama and other evolved beings.

11

Chirakkal Interlude

Before we leave Abbottabad, here's the promised story of how the Vaniyas' secular and celestial protectors came together during this posting. Krishnan's angel of academia, the Chirakkal Valiya Raja, fell ill and was rushed to the famous Chennai surgeon Chintan Nambiar, who advised a major operation. With the entitlement that rulers are heir to, he summoned his protégé to his side, telling him to bring along his father, Appu Nair. The tortuous journey – from the high Himalayas to the southern tip of India with a detour to a remote Kerala village – took several days. Remember, this was in the 1940s.

After the surgery was over, the patient remained comatose for a while. An anxious twenty-four hours passed with no change in his condition. But then, the Raja suddenly regained consciousness and said to Krishnan, 'Your Bhagavathi saved me.' The goddess had apparently appeared before him, placed her hand on his head and repeated, 'Only good will happen, only good will happen.' The recovery was as complete as it was sudden.

In thanksgiving, the ruler ordered a ritual Kaliyattam dance to be performed at the deity's modest Katalayi temple, entrusting all the arrangements to her devotee father and son. It was a historic event, the first in which the ruler would directly participate. People from even the surrounding areas made the journey and thronged the venue with fervour.

However, it threatened to be a non-starter. Three of the Raja's advisers dissuaded him from even attending the event. The crowd and its expectations grew apace as the hours went by. Finally, only the shocking news of his absence arrived. On hearing it, Appu Nair fainted. The son was equally distraught. However, as if heralding his later prowess at surmounting hurdles, he decided to go himself to persuade the ruler.

He was barred at the palace gates, but he created such a right royal fuss that the noise reached the ruler, who sent for him. Stripping off his shirt and tucking it under his arm since one had to appear bare-bodied in that august presence, Krishnan walked in. With folded hands, he appealed to the Raja to be present at the Kaliyattam. After all, it was in thanksgiving for his recovery – and on his own orders. The Chirakkal Raja said, 'Shuppamani, Sankaran Nair and Nambiar advised me not to, but my Kochukrishnan has come, so I shall listen to him.' The grandee accompanied him to the event, adding one more link in Captain Nair's golden chain of memories.

12

The Prawn Pickle Password

You know the Chaos theory of how a butterfly flapping its wings in Madrid can cause a typhoon in Manila? Well, sometimes the outcome of a small act can be far-reaching in the most beneficial way. Especially when it involves a mother's love.

Madhavi Amma, from her village of Kunnavil, decided to send a taste of home to cheer up her Kochukrishnan, lonesome on his ownsome. A bottle of her spicy prawn pickle would be just the thing. It helped that he had been transferred from remote Abbottabad in 1946 to the Delhi wireless office, where she even had a Kannur connection. Not just any connection, but the doubly powerful Kanakkamma, a no-nonsense Nair matron powered by matrilineal authority plus her status as the wife of V.P. Menon, the political reforms commissioner who powwowed with viceroys and nationalist leaders alike.

Perhaps the savvy mother had more than a cure for homesickness in mind. Getting her son into the ambit of one of the most influential figures of the time could well have been the agenda steeped in that innocuous jar. So, on Kanakkamma's next visit to her native Kannur, Madhavi Amma handed her the prawn pickle, asking her to please pass it on to her son who could be contacted at the army's telegraph office. She also diplomatically gave Mrs Menon a sack of the local fragrant rice she loved.

Thus it was that Krishnan Nair got a message asking him to meet V.P. Menon 'as soon as possible' at his residence. Flummoxed, he caught a tonga and arrived at the grand mansion, made more daunting by the presence of a tennis court and a cluster of British officials. He was escorted into the formidable presence of the chatelaine herself. She handed him his mother's pickle and even offered him lunch. Too intimidated to accept, he did his *namaskarams*, and was ushered out.

As he reached the gate, a Rolls Royce purred in. It stopped, the window slid down, and a head popped out, saying, 'Krishnan!' It was the redoubtable V.P. Menon himself, returning from his routine meeting with Lord Wavell. The younger Nair was asked to get into the car, taken back inside and ordered to have lunch. VP had a piercing gaze that brooked no refusal. It had felled personages loftier than this young man clutching a jar of home-made prawn pickle.

Completing the surreal afternoon, he was driven back to his army office in the Rolls by a uniformed chauffeur at the wheel. It was a portent – Captain Nair would go on to own a vintage Rolls in his fleet. In the Kannur of his childhood, he had known only two cars: one belonging to the owner of Victoria Weaving Mills, the other to 'Appa Dercer', in which he'd see the beauteous Padmavathi drive past.

His commandant happened to be standing in the portico when the regal automobile rolled in. He was so taken aback to see his junior officer emerge that he actually stepped up to him and, to Nair's equal shock, shook his hand. The look he got from his impressed superior told him that a quick promotion was entirely possible. The VP magic – and Madhavi Amma's calculation – had already begun working. But young Krishnan had already decided that his future was plugged into something worthier than wireless transmitters.

~

To understand the enormity of the afternoon triggered by a humble jar of prawn pickle, we need a refresher course on VP's awesome orbit. Tom

Wolfe once wrote, 'The trouble with fiction is that it has to be plausible.' However, as so many trajectories tell us, real life doesn't obey this diktat.

Vappala Pangunni Menon (1893–1965) grew up in Ottapalam, also in north Malabar. Thanks to Kerala's historical association with Christian missionaries – the apostle St Thomas himself had arrived in the fabled port of Muziris on the Malabar coast in AD 52 – it had an English school to which Menon was sent. However, the boy who would become its most eminent alumnus decided to drop out in the fourth standard.

Geeta Doctor, reviewing a biography by VP's great-granddaughter Narayani Basu, wrote:[2]

> As the stories of the time had it, he had run away from his impoverished home in Kerala . . . There are unconfirmed stories about how he had worked as a factory hand and a coolie; of how he had nearly converted to Islam at one point but had, at the last moment, decided that even if he had no qualms about renouncing his religion, the idea of renouncing his foreskin was too much of a sacrifice.

After lowly jobs in Bombay, VP made his way to the colonial summer capital of Simla and managed to track down a Cannanore/Kannur connection – Kothieth Anandan, from a prominent Thiyya family, who worked in the reforms department. When he asked him for a job, Anandan rolled his eyes and said, 'You have studied only till the fourth standard, and don't even know how to type.'

With the self-confidence that had got him out of the Ottapalam rut, and thus far, young Menon replied, 'No problem, Sar, I'll learn typewriting in two months, and be back.' Sure enough, he did and he was. Anandan took him on as a clerk. He worked hard and learnt faster, seizing every opening and kicking down any barriers in his way.

Anandan was married to Kanakkamma – yes, the same lady who had

---

2 Geeta Doctor, 'VP Menon's Biography: Was the Man Who Charmed the Princes Really the Architect of Modern India?', Scroll, 29 February 2020.

ferried Krishnan's prawn pickle from Kannur. On his death, she married his clever protégé. Strangely, she had arranged VP's earlier marriage to a Kerala Christian. They had two sons before she left him and returned to her native place, alone. There is a spicier account that says VP was the one who ditched her to marry Kanakkamma, creating quite a frisson in Delhi's Malayali network. The second wife also had a daughter from her first marriage. 'No problem, Sar,' again. It became a happy family of 'yours' and 'mine'; there were no 'ours' to complicate matters. Later narratives would discreetly gloss over the respective children's 'step' status.

By sheer force of will and not a little disdain for obstacles, the runaway boy from Ottapalam rose to rub shoulders with Gandhiji, Nehru and, most of all, Sardar Patel. He was constitutional adviser and political reforms commissioner under three viceroys: Linlithgow, Wavell and Mountbatten. His early adversities were the furnace in which his steel was tempered. Apart from his survival instincts, it had honed in him the two weapons of negotiation: persistence and cunning. These characteristics were indispensable when, as Sardar Patel's right-hand man, he cajoled and threatened 565 pompous and petulant princes into joining the Indian Union.

From Narayani Basu's biography,[3] we learn how, during VP's first stint at the Round Table negotiations in London in 1930, the prince of Sarila advised him never to be afraid of looking straight into the eyes of the British administrators who were in command and speaking his mind. He also learnt the importance of dressing impeccably.

Here's Geeta Doctor's wry comment:

> Obviously, the tailors of Saville Row in London, who accoutred many a noble savage in their impeccably cut suits, have a lot to claim in transforming a lowly Malayali Menon into a person of distinguished appearance. That – and his fondness for Cuban cigars, an ability to

---

[3] Narayani Basu, *V.P. Menon: The Unsung Architect of Modern India* (Delhi: Simon and Schuster India, 2020).

quaff the best whiskey, take part in tiger shoots – went a long way in establishing his reputation as a friend of the princes.[4]

Menon later became a founding member of the rightist Swatantra Party.

Captain Nair always referred to him as 'Uncle VP' – as it seems did all his Kerala protégés. Among them was K.V. Padmanabhan, undersecretary, Constituent Assembly Secretariat 1947–49, who later joined the Indian Foreign Service (IFS). He was Geeta Doctor's father; her mother, like Kanakkamma, was also from Kannur. So let us wrap up this foray into Menon's mind-boggling life with the reviewer's amusing footnotes. They also tell us how 'Uncle VP' could open the doors he did for Captain Nair.

Geeta's earliest memory is from the wedding of the beautiful Meenakshikutty, daughter of Kanakkamma from her first marriage. The child was most awed by the sonorous 'announcement of the arrival of the Maharajas, their gorgeously attired consorts and their heirs who had just signed away their titles, their privileges, their 21-gun salutes and their vast estates to the Indian Union, with the promise of what would prove to be an illusion: privy purses. And here they were being met and greeted as equals by the extraordinary man who had persuaded them to do so.

'Each one of them brought gifts for the bride that were a sight to behold . . . There were diamonds, emeralds and rubies set in the most gorgeous of necklaces, waistbands and bracelets.'[5]

Geeta's later recollections are from 'the time we would visit them when they had retired to Bangalore . . . "Uncle" was always happy to see us, and greeted my dad like a long-lost son. Mrs VP sat in one corner of the grandly appointed drawing room, and just watched us. When she felt that she had done enough to scare the daylights out of us, she would ask us to go and take a look at the birds. The Bangalore household had the most gorgeous aviary filled from floor to ceiling with nesting canaries in all the shades of turquoise blue, citrus green and yellow and every combination of colours in-between.'

---

4 Doctor, V.P. Menon's Biography.

5 Ibid.

Geeta wondered in retrospect if 'Uncle VP's early morning visits to his aviary reminded him of those colourful princes'. She added, 'Certainly, he was the cat that the Sardar had set amongst the canaries.'

~

As we saw before we got so carried away by 'Uncle VP's' power and personality, Krishnan had made up his mind to leave the army. Not just that. Inspired by his visit to Gandhiji's ashram at Wardha, he wanted to return to Kerala and help uplift its villages. There might also have been the residual effect of the socialism of his youth under the influence of AKG.

So, steeling himself, he announced his intention to Uncle VP, who looked at him as if he'd lost his mind. 'Why?' he demanded, and then, softening his tone, offered, 'Okay, if you don't like the army, I can help you find a place in the civil services or the police.' Menon had been watching this bright young lad and, together with the Kannur connection that his beloved Kanakkamma shared with Krishnan's mother, had developed a paternal interest in him.

Even at that age, Krishnan stood unshaken in resolve. 'No, I must go back and do constructive social work,' he said.

'What social work?' scoffed VP, suppressing his disappointment.

When the young man idealistically quoted Gandhiji that the upliftment of the villages was the only way to 'save India', VP exploded, 'Get lost! I can't help you if you are determined to go back and ruin your future.'

13

Next Stop, Ration Shop

The end of World War II was in sight when Krishnan had been seized by the urge to do something more socially relevant than transmitting messages in the army. He arrived in a Kannur still in the throes of starvation and the diseases that came with it. Well-documented is the Bengal Famine of 1943, estimated to have killed up to 3 million people – six times that of the British casualties in the war. Not as well-known is the Malabar famine, perhaps because it claimed 'only' 40,000 lives.

The Bengal Famine has been proved to be 'man-made', caused not by drought, but by the supreme callousness of Winston Churchill. Cynically, the British prime minister turned down urgent pleas for the export of food to India, fearing it would reduce stockpiles in the UK and take ships away from the war effort. Satyajit Ray's *Ashani Sanket* (1973) captured how the Bengal Famine was a result of British policy. Amartya Sen also came to the world's notice for his thesis on this subject, and he indeed won his 1998 Economics Nobel Prize for his work on the causes and prevention of famines.

What hasn't received the same chronicling is that faraway Malabar too was felled by what was happening on the borders of Bengal. Burma (present-day Myanmar) was the rice bowl of undivided India, cheaply feeding the Malabar region and the states of Travancore and Cochin with 3,00,000 tons of the staple grain. Then the war blasted into South East Asia, with Japan bombing the airfield of the Burmese city of Tavoy, and finally marching into the capital Rangoon (present-day Yangon) at the start of 1942. The British had to beat a retreat that was as hasty as it was ignominious – and one with far-reaching consequences. The inflow of rice into these south Indian principalities was reduced to a trickle of 10,000 tons, a situation made worse by the hoarding practices of unscrupulous traders. Lord Huntington had informed the House of Lords in 1943 that rice 'now costs 950% more than the pre-war price'.

The irony was that this region had always been rich in produce, but it was largely cash crops such as coconut, areca, cashew, etc. Now, even these plantations couldn't be tended by a population wracked by starvation and its aggravating handmaiden: gastrointestinal disease. Perhaps not to the numbing degree that was seen in Bengal, but here too multitudes dropped like flies on the street. Here, *The Communist Manifesto*'s 'spectre' of famine haunting Europe[6] wasn't just a metaphor.

Krishnan was stunned to see his verdant native district so devastated. As a result of his smart intervention, he was pitchforked to a critical post: chief executive of the Producers cum Consumers Cooperative Society (PCCS) of the Civil Supplies Department of Kannur. Statutory rationing had been enforced in 1944, and his job was to ensure the fair distribution of essentials such as rice, kerosene and sugar.

Ten wagons of precious rice arrived from neighbouring Andhra, but no one was available for their unloading. Activating old contacts, Krishnan arranged for a random gang of labourers, who emptied the wagons and carried the sacks to the warehouse. R.P. Kapur, Indian Civil Services (ICS), district food reorganizing officer for Malabar, came to know of this hands-on initiative. He summoned Krishnan and gave him charge of the wider operation.

Krishnan soon cottoned on to a supervisor siphoning off rice to the

---

[6] Friedrich Engels and Karl Marx, The Communist Manifesto (1848).

black market and making false entries in the stock register. His stern reprimanding of the devious fellow almost cost him his life. The vengeful cheat bribed a couple of labourers to knock Krishnan down with loaded bags of rice during an inspection of stocks. It could have been fatal. It was the supervisor who got the sack. And was arrested to boot.

Krishnan's foray into the cooperative movement would teach him more lessons in uncooperative behaviour. After corruption, he had to deal with partisan favouritism. The president of the local Congress committee did not approve of a non-partyman wielding so much power; more to the point, he wanted to install his own stooge instead. Captain Nair's autobiography records that Kapur put paid to his ploy with a firm 'Krishnan is doing a great job. His organizational abilities are reflected in the bottom line, so what is the problem?' However, disgusted by these machinations, and with no intention of wasting his time dealing with political intrigue, Krishnan handed over charge to the favourite, and left the Kannur PCCS.

He moved to the regional Madayi cooperative society, which had several districts in its territory. He stayed in the temple town of Eripuram, fascinated by its trees and intriguing rock formations. He would even take an energizing dip in the sacred pond every morning.

One day, the civil supplies commissioner, Mr Jacks, walked into his office as part of the routine 'surprise inspection' of all PCCS offices. It was 8 a.m., and the day's work was yet to begin. Jacks barked, 'Mr Krishnan Nair, please give a tally of the cash.' To which came the response, 'Rupees thirty-eight thousand three hundred and thirty-nine, Sir.' The posse of accompanying officers was as taken aback by the precision of the declaration as the promptness of the reply. Krishnan unlocked his safe and handed over the bundles. They were laboriously counted, found exact to the last unit, and tallied with the register.

A stunned Jacks exclaimed, 'How did you keep the account so up to date? I have never seen a cash book maintained so meticulously.' Krishnan was chuffed at being complimented by the commissioner himself. He had punctiliously stuck to the rules: tally the takings every night, distribute rice, kerosene and sugar according to the prescribed quota, then securely store the surplus rationed stock. He made no unofficial distribution, thus becoming the bane of black marketeers wanting to make an easy buck from tragedy.

It didn't stop at praise. Jacks continued, 'You must come back to Kannur. The PCCS there is riddled with corruption, and the officer who took over from you is just lost. I'm ordering you to take charge there again.' It was a vindication as sweet as the payasam his headmaster had once fed him.

In those three years under his charge, the Madayi PCCS made a profit of Rs 3 lakh. At that time, the tons of used rice sacks were also a source of revenue. They would be auctioned to big traders who would export them to countries such as South Africa. Buyers hoping to circumvent the bidding process would approach Krishnan with wads of currency. On one such occasion, Krishnan threw a bundle of cash in the face of a persistent briber and stormed out.

He went back to Kannur as the chief executive. But not for long.

14

The Bugle Calls Again

Our man was something of a rolling stone, not comfortable with moss. While walking through the rock formations of Eripuram on his Madayi posting, he would be reminded of the craggier landscape of Abbottabad. Before he realized it, his memories grew into an itch to return to the army.

Fortunately, the means to scratch it appeared in the form of an advertisement in the local papers inviting candidates for the post of short commission officers. Excited, he applied, got called for an interview at the Southern Command, and was selected. But delight had to wait upon patience. It was months later, when he had moved out of the Madayi society and returned to the Kannur one, that he received the official order to report to Poona.

Here the drill was somewhat more strenuous than transmitting messages. It involved sweating it out, not merely stirring to the speeches of Netaji on Shonan Radio. One wrong step, and he would be ordered to run round the parade ground with both arms holding his rifle over his head. There were days when, exhausted and sore with aching deltoids and blistered soles, he wondered if he had over-romanticized the army. But he soldiered on and graduated with flying colours. In 1947, he was assigned to the Maratha Light Infantry division as second lieutenant.

After four years, he received orders to proceed to a posting in Belgaum, on the Karnataka–Maharashtra border. General Kuldip Singh Brar arrived on the same day as the junior. The coincidence proved fortunate. The general sized him up, and asked him to command the battalion parade, a task usually assigned to an officer of longer experience. Brar, impressed by Krishnan's performance, promoted him to lieutenant. He also appointed him as his aide-de-camp (ADC), and soon enough gave him the rank of captain, which he would proudly bear for the rest of his life.

When the general became chief of the Western Command, Captain Krishnan Nair moved with him to Bombay. He was given a room on the ground floor of the iconic headquarters, Gun House. This was where all the visiting C-in-Cs would stay, so the ADC got to meet the likes of Generals Thimayya, Chowdhury, Rajendrasinghji and Cariappa. He would accompany the last-mentioned Coorgi general to Goa and tuck another memory under his belt.

But it was from his own boss that he learnt the spit and polish of military administration. Meanwhile, Mrs Meena Brar became his social etiquette mentor. She trained him in a range of niceties, from the correct way to converse on the telephone to doing the balancing act at official parties. Of course, her ward could handle situations stickier than cocktail canapés.

Despite all these opportunities, his congenital itch began again. Captain Nair told his boss that he wanted to leave, but General Brar, like V.P. Menon before him, kept telling his ADC not 'to talk nonsense, young man'. Then fate threw him into an encounter with Morarji Desai, the chief minister of Maharashtra at the time.

Whenever protocol forced the ascetic Gandhian to attend a function at Gun House, General Brar's ADC had to attend to him, and ensure that Morarji's strict dietary requirements were taken care of. Mercifully, not his preferred drink. The chief minister wouldn't touch fripperies such as cashew nuts or sweets. The ADC made discreet enquiries with Morarji Desai's household, and mastered the complicated art of catering to simple needs at elaborate defence parties. He was rewarded with what passed for a smile on that stern visage.

Our man wasn't going to be content with a smile. He waited for a suitably opportune moment that wouldn't seem like he was exploiting a powerful acquaintance. He then mentioned to Morarji a subject which he knew was equally dear to the Gandhian: he said he would like to promote the handloom sector back in his native Kannur.

'Are you a Congressman?' asked Chief Minister Desai.

Krishnan replied truthfully, and with no hint of opportunistic sycophancy, 'Sir, I am a Gandhian and a socialist.'

'Achcha, okay, I can arrange this but on one condition. No going back to Kannur. Mumba Devi does not easily permit anyone to leave Bombay. Stay on and fulfil your mission here.'

This threw Krishnan off guard, but, regaining his composure, he expressed the practical difficulty of finding accommodation. Real estate in this city was still to reach skyscraper prices, but the Rent Control Act made landlords prefer keeping flats empty rather than give them to tenants who would pay a pittance plus be impossible to evict.

However, this was the chief minister, right? Morarji put D.S. Bakhle, ICS, on the job. The powerful revenue secretary found Krishnan a flat on the tree-lined Vatcha Gandhi Road, off the arterial Hughes Road. Besides being spacious, it was just a chant away from Gandhiji's own Mani Bhavan. Now, leaving the army was a fait accompli. So Captain Nair once again returned to civvy street. Though by no stretch did he hang up his boots.

Here we must mention that the accompli had an accomplice. Someone more influential than chief ministers in Krishnan's scheme of things. His bride, Leela.

In place of Captain Nair's earlier room, the newly-wed couple had been allotted a villa in the Gun House complex. Incidentally, this was the heavily guarded accommodation given in retirement to Lieutenant General Brar, who in 1984 had led Operation Blue Star – one of the world's most hotly debated military operations in which the army had marched into the sacred Golden Temple to flush out Sikh separatists. He had continued to need security personnel. Several attempts were made on his life in India, and in 2012, while holidaying in London, he survived an audacious knife attack by four men seeking vengeance for that 'defilement'.

In those easier days, the general's little boys, nicknamed Bulbul and Trippy, would often run through the small gate separating the villa from the main Gun House, and jovial 'Krishnan Uncle' would happily horse around with them. They were equally fond of Leela Aunty. The special rapport notwithstanding, it was Leela who insisted that he leave the army instead of wasting his life 'saluting all and sundry'. He resigned in 1952. From the time she was a young bride till the companion at the end of his life, Leela would remain his guiding force.

15

Enter, Leela

'God moves in a mysterious way, His wonders to perform.'[7]

These are the first lines of William Cowper's poem based on Jesus telling his disciples: 'What I do thou knowest not now; but thou shalt know hereafter.'

Who would have thought that detecting a stolen bag of rice would lead Krishnan to his life partner, soulmate and Influencer No. 1?

Azhikode was the oldest panchayat in Kannur district, and A.K. Nair its first head. The choice had been a no-brainer, for the owner of Rajarajeshwari Weaving Mills combined business acumen with high-mindedness. The local talk was that his earnings would need several carts to carry, but he wore his wealth as lightly as his fine *melmundu*. He ploughed his profits into the spiritualism and reformist thinking that were Azhikode's markers through history.

A.K. Nair lived simply, looked after his workers, set up social and educational welfare organizations and was involved in a seminal biography of Brahmananda Sivayogi. Reformers and intellectuals from all over Kerala were frequent visitors to his home. His economic clout was evident

---

[7] William Cowper, 'God Moves in a Mysterious Way', 1773.

in the Kannur Chamber of Commerce which he had established and served as chairman several times. His motto was 'Work hard and keep your hands and head strong.'

After this preamble, we need to recall Shankuettan 'Sanku', who had helped Madhavi Amma get Krishnan into the prestigious Chirakkal Valiya Raja School. Shankuettan lived a mile or so from Rajarajeshwari Weaving Mills, and Krishnan would often go to meet him when he had quit his first army stint in Abbottabad and joined the cooperative movement. Just as he had noticed Padmavathi and Maya on their way to school, the girl leading a gaggle of her classmates caught our Krishnan's eye. Perhaps she had more of an effect because her good looks were complemented by an authoritative air. Leela was, after all, the eminent A.K. Nair's daughter.

Krishnan's first encounter with her illustrious father was less than propitious. As chief executive of Kannur's PCCS, he was tipped off on rice being siphoned from the ration shop in front of Rajarajeshwari Weaving Mills. Its own premises had been rented from A.K. Nair. So Krishnan arrived there at 7 a.m. to conduct a surprise inspection.

Checking stocks against the register, he found the tally one sack of rice short, and booted out the dishonest shopkeeper. Since the fellow was a tenant of the mill owner, Krishnan expected the senior Nair to be incensed. Quite the contrary. The principled gentleman commended him for punishing what was legally and morally wrong.

The incident may or may not have come up in his mind when, several years later, he accepted the upright officer's 'bid' for the hand of his youngest daughter. They were married on 20 April 1950. By then Krishnan had left the cooperative sector and Kannur, had rejoined the army, and was now ADC to General Kuldip Singh Brar (chief of the Western Command).

This 'Krishnan–Leela' would turn out to be as joyous as the mythic one in the groves of Vrindavan. It was also prescient that her favourite elder brother, Ravindran, had changed her given name, Sumathi, to Leela, because, as the autobiography states, 'there already was a Sumathi Vakil in that area, and two Sumathis would be too confusing'.

It was a match not only approved of by the stars but actually ordained by them. Before finalizing the proposal, Krishnan's father had asked a renowned local astrologer if the horoscopes were compatible. He took one look at the charts and cried 'Siva! Siva!' in amazement. They were a perfect match. The girl's chart showed that her birth had multiplied the prosperity of the family hundredfold. And would do so thousandfold for her future husband. The astrologer also foretold that the boy was destined for greatness, adding that he would 'own many vehicles and would feed thousands'.

In the meantime, here's an incident about grumbled feeding. Remember how the Chirakkal Valiya Raja had promised to underwrite Krishnan's education, and even parted with his diamond ring to pay for his college fees? Well, such generosity (that too towards a low-born Vaniya) hadn't gone down well with his son, Chirakkal T. Balakrishnan Nair, who later became a noted historian. A month or so after Krishnan's wedding, with both contempt and exaggeration, Balakrishnan had thundered in a speech, 'A capitalist invited 4000 people to his daughter's wedding feast. This is at a time when there is no ration rice available. Where did he get all this rice?'

The well-known socialist P.M. Kunhiraman Nambiar was also present on the dais. When this remark reached the already no-nonsense Leela, she declared, 'If these two happen to come to our house they will not get even a drop of water.' Later on, Kunhiraman realized that Krishnan too was a socialist at heart, and the two became good friends. So much so that when he was a house guest of the couple in Bombay, Leela's hospitality extended well beyond that 'drop of water'.

The stars were right, the bond between Krishnan and Leela deepened with the years. Wives tend to be left behind as men advance across the chequerboard of corporate power. This was far from the case here. He named all his ventures after the wife who had set them on track. He would grow to value her care, her caution plus the authority she had exuded even when she strode to school all those years ago in Azhikode.

As he would tell his sons, Vivek and Dinesh, when they grew into men, 'Love is not just an attitude. It is a strong tonic. It invigorates us, drives us forward.' Leela would live on for seven years and a day more after the passing of the man who had been her soulmate for sixty-four fulfilling years.

16

Failing Uncle VP

Despite their inglorious parting over Krishnan's determination to give up his first army job in favour of Gandhian ideals, Uncle VP did not give up on his protégé. Years later, as part of his drive to industrialize his home state, he passed on three of his pet projects to Krishnan Nair.

Although this Keralite threw himself into them with characteristic fervour, none of them took off.

One was a high-tension insulator-manufacturing unit in Matayikunnu using local clay. The second was a mill in Cochin to convert waste steel into pure steel. The third was the most interesting – it involved the popular root cassava or tapioca.

V.V. Giri, as governor of Kerala (1960–65), had sanctioned 100 acres of land in the Travancore area to convert cassava into laundry starch. Krishnan asked Rajmata Vijayaraje Scindia of Gwalior to be the chairperson of this proposed venture, Cassava Industries. She readily agreed. Royalty may be starchy, but it didn't do laundry. The Rajmata was more interested in the by-product that would be attained in the manufacturing process: cattle-feed. She was a devotee of the cowherd-god Krishnan, and extensively promoted cattle welfare.

So how did a Kannur commoner connect with the Rajmata of a Hindi heartland state? Once again, he had Uncle VP to thank. VP had known her husband, Maharaja Jivajirao Scindia, from the time he was corralling the princes into the nascent Indian Union, and had forged long-lasting relationships with several of those royals. When VP visited Bombay, he would stay at Krishnan's house on Vatcha Gandhi Road. The Scindias, who had their palace on the Haji Ali seafront, would always drop in to talk of old times and new. The friendship soon extended to the affable host and sharp hostess.

The maharaja loved Leela Nair's prawn curry, and insisted on sending over his main *bawarchi* to master it. The traditional way to cook it is in an earthen *chatti*, and Mrs Nair wondered how this lowly vessel would go down with the royal cook. The problem was solved when he told her that his kitchen used such vessels too because several of Gwalior's traditional dishes called for the earthy flavour they imparted.

The friendship continued after the maharaja's early death in 1961 at the age of forty-five. As we said earlier, the Rajmata had agreed to be the chairperson of Cassava Industries and Krishnan its hands-on managing director (MD). A technical collaboration was sought – and agreed to – with a Milwaukee-based company owned by Robert Eihleen and his wife, Laura, an American Airlines stewardess he met on a flight and instantly fell in love with.

So Nair and the Rajmata took off to the United States in 1965. They stayed at New York's Waldorf Astoria, where a grand reception had been organized by the Eihleens, who also owned the top-selling Schlitz Beer. Krishnan thought there was another business opportunity there. There wasn't. Remember, these were still the prim socialist decades.

It was a lavish evening, more so because tandoori chicken from Delhi's famed Moti Mahal had been flown in on Air India. The royal Gwalior pennant fluttered outside the legendary hotel. The press couldn't have enough of the 'two Maharanis' – the Rajmata's daughter, Usha Raje Scindia, had joined them.

And here's an anecdotal gem. They hadn't brought along any of their heirloom baubles. No problem. A call was made to the bespoke jeweller

Harry Winston, who arrived in person with a selection to be worn for the occasion. Stars on Oscar night are not the only ones in borrowed rocks.

During this visit, the lights famously went out in New York. The Rajmata, stuck on some vertiginous floor of the Towers – the premium luxury residences at the Waldorf Astoria – was beside herself with anxiety over Usha Raje, who was out on the town. Manhattan was plunged into darkness, and she feared the worst would befall her precious daughter. She kept praying to the Krishnan idol she always carried with her. Krishnan tramped the dark streets till he located Usha Rani, and the two of them trudged up all those endless flights to her suite and her relieved mother. The next day, the trio were flown on Eihleen's private plane to Milwaukee.

Despite all this effort, the project came a cropper. Like much else the world over, the problem was politics. This is where we must go back to the Anglo-Indian schoolteacher's intonation of 'Nam-boo-di-ri-pad'. Young India's first elected communist government led by the fiery EMS made news across the world. Catching the headline as he sipped his morning coffee, Eihleen turned red. No, no, not ideologically. Quite the opposite.

He was American, and McCarthyism's 'A Red under every bed' witch-hunt wasn't too distant in the past. The hoped-for cassava collaborator dashed off a short letter to Krishnan Nair: 'Our company does not wish to work in a state within the control of a communist government. I regret to drop out of this project.'

No machinery, so no industry. The 100 acres given by V.V. Giri were regretfully returned.

But here's a more satisfying story from that US trip. Irritated by a guy who kept making condescending remarks about Indians being 'cow-worshippers', Krishnan Nair shut him up with this statement: 'We consider the cow to be our mother, because, like her, she gives us milk. In fact, the cow has the upper hand because it is her milk, not that of the human mother, which the world has with its tea and coffee.'

Meanwhile, if you are wondering about the yucca plant from faraway Brazil taking root and becoming such a staple in Kerala, here's how that happened. A great famine had gripped Travancore during the reign of

Ayilyam Thirunal Rama Varma (1860–80). He tried to find ways to assuage the terrible hunger of his people. His younger brother, Vishakham Thirunal Rama Varma, was a keen botanist, and he imported saplings of this versatile tuber.

Swathes of it were planted in the royal fields. The shrewd ruler put up signs saying these were his property and very tasty, so no one should dare steal them. Not surprisingly, tapioca grafts surreptitiously appeared all over the state. It became an acceptable and cheap substitute for rice. Cassava with fish curry is such a favourite that it is even served in London's feted restaurant Rasa, established by Chef Sreedharan Das, who introduced the city to 'the authentic taste of Kerala'. Captain Nair's granddaughter Samyukta would do her bit for it via her stylish restaurant, Jamavar, in London's Mayfair district.

And what of Uncle VP? Did he despair again and wash his hands of Krishnan Nair? No, he had seen his potential, and he wasn't going to let three setbacks make him stop backing a winner, and certainly not a fellow Keralite. The Malayali network is as strong as it is wide.

17

Coconut Husk in a Mercedes

Think Kerala, think coconut palms – among nature's most multitasking, 100 per cent recyclable creations. However, think Mercedes, and it is unlikely that the image of a steaming bowl of Malabar curry will spring to your mind and salivating mouth. Here's the connection.

After the kernel or copra has been extracted, the coconut shell isn't thrown away. The humble, wiry husk is as much of a money spinner as the rest of this cash crop. As coir, it makes coarse ropes, but married to rubber, it goes into comfy mattresses – and the foot mats in a Mercedes salon.

Krishnan, cradled in Kannur's coconut groves, had seen his mother preserve the husk after she extracted the copra from which she made a living. Rough coir ropes and mats were so much a part of the landscape that he barely noticed them.

It took a visit to West Germany in 1957 before his eyes opened to coir's potential. He realized that the mats in the Mercedes cars in which his delegation was taken around had rubberized coir foam mats. India was already exporting spun coir fibre, and his entrepreneurial brain began ticking. It got even louder at his next stop, the Austrian town of Linzer, home to the traditional latticed Linzer torte. But it wasn't this shortcake topped with fruit preserves and sliced nuts that had triggered his mental salivation; it was the fibre foam-making machines he saw on sale.

However, private-sector imports were complicated in those early socialist decades when only the public sector sat at the commanding heights of the economy. Who else to help overcome bureaucratic hurdles than the resourceful Uncle VP?

By 1965, Krishnan Nair had set up India's first fibre foam factory, with the support of his brother-in-law, Ravindran, and named it after both men's favourite person. Leela Fibre Foam, with Uncle VP as chairman, produced rubberized coir mattresses, cushions, pillows, travel kits, railway/bus seats and air filters for refrigerators.

He located it at Baliapattam, where the biggest industries at the time were clay tiles and wood processing. The decisive factor for Krishnan was that it was in Kannur district, a scant 7 kilometres away from the eponymous town. Also called Valapattanam, the locality spans just 2.04 sq. km. The Kalarivathukkal temple, where the child Krishnan was taken to witness the famed Muchilot Bhagavathi Theyyam, and the Kakkulangara mosque established the town's secular credentials.

It had a grander past. Historically, it got its name (*valya* means big and *pattanam* means town in Malayalam) from the Valapattanam river flowing through it, the main channel for trading ships. It was once the capital of the medieval Mooshika dynasty, and also finds mention in the journals of the fourteenth-century Arab traveller Ibn Battuta as well as the sixteenth-century Portuguese official Duarte Barbosa, who referred to it as the 'residence of the King of Cannanore'.

The inauguration of the fibre-foam factory was a grand affair. The Rajmata of Gwalior was invited to be a board member. The chief guest was the Congress strongman S.K. Patil, who was then the railway minister, and earlier known as the 'Uncrowned King of Bombay'. The minister and the Rajmata travelled by train to Kannur in specially attached saloons. However, that made the train too long to fit into what was then the modest Cannanore Station. So, in honour of the country's railway minister gracing a small Kerala town for the first time, the platform was extended to accommodate the extra length.

This wasn't the visit's only benefit. At the civic reception, Patil turned to Krishnan and asked magnanimously, 'What is it that Kannur wants from me?' Seizing the moment, Krishnan mentioned a particularly urgent need of the town's residents. And that is the origin of the underpass that Kannur still finds so useful.

18

A Leg-Up For Handlooms

Was it a comedown from ADC (and principal staff officer) to the chief of the Western Command to be tramping up and down Bombay carrying an armload of swatch catalogues and negotiating prices? Conventionally, yes. Quitting the army and returning to Kannur in 1952, Krishnan had joined his father-in-law's business, Rajarajeshwari Weaving Mills. Not as an employee, for that would not have been culturally correct, but as a sales agent getting a commission on the orders he bagged. Krishnan's gusto in promoting handloom was woven into the skein of his DNA.

His guru Swami Sivananda, who had thwarted him from becoming a yogi, had instilled in him the essence of karma *kanda*: 'Do your duty.' Spinning and weaving were the traditional occupations of the Saliyar/Saliya/Chaliyan community, an Other Backward Class (OBC) community, like his own Vaniya – in fact, the original name of the weaver community came from the word 'spider'. The people who did this work had been using primitive looms, and Krishnan considered it his duty to take up Gandhiji's idea of bringing this ancient skill up to speed and to wider markets.

And consider this. The Indian basics are *roti*, *kapda aur makaan* – food, clothes and a home. Arguably, thousands go without the first for a day or more, without the third for considerably longer. But clothing is literally the barest necessity; human dignity itself gets stripped without it.

When Krishnan had returned to Kannur to take up Mission Handloom, he realized that the industry didn't need attention only in his native region. In 1952, he sought a meeting with Captain V. Nanjappa, ICS, the textile commissioner of India, to discuss its problems and potential. Setting up a national handloom board wasn't easy because the 1956 reorganization of state boundaries was still on the anvil. Once again, the still-influential Uncle VP was tapped. This resulted in their seeking an appointment with the prime minister.

Here is the insider information.

Their contact felt that Pandit Nehru wouldn't take kindly to the idea because he wanted to 'upgrade' the handloom industry to power looms with their greater scope for production and employment. Krishnan's plan was to make weavers switch from their primitive looms to frame looms, which at the time were brought only by the Basel Mission, and distributed to those who converted to Christianity.

Sure enough, Pandit Nehru turned down the first request for a meeting. So, Krishnan and representatives from Uttar Pradesh, Andhra Pradesh, Tamil Nadu and West Bengal tried Home Minister Govind Ballabh Pant. He agreed to meet the delegation – at six in the morning. He warmed to the notion of scaling up the handloom sector, put a call through to Nehru, and got them an appointment for 4 p.m. the same afternoon.

Krishnan's delegation not only softened the prime minister's stand, but also convinced him to impose a 1 paisa cess on every yard of fabric emanating from the textile mill industry. This would add up to the then grand sum of Rs 300 crore, which went into 'modernizing' the hand-operated looms. Decades later, in 1992, the All-India Handloom Board would emerge from that meeting, powered by the redoubtable Pupul Jayakar.

In 1957, Krishnan went on his first trip abroad – to what was still

West Germany. He was part of an Indian trade delegation invited by its federal government. The commerce secretary, K.B. Lall, couldn't lead it as planned, but in his place went the textile magnate Lala Bharat Ram of Delhi Cloth Mills. The visit, specifically Krishnan's stay at Kempinski Hotels in major cities, would hold a key to a different future, but we will open that door in its own time.

The delegation consulted with the Chambers of Commerce of Berlin, Bonn, Hamburg and Munich to understand how they handled their large ventures, and gauge what kind of a collaboration was possible. There would be a cherry on the torte. At the time, Indian handlooms exported to Germany were subject to ironclad quotas. Krishnan seized the opportunity to put a case to the federal minister for economics for an exemption. To everyone's surprise, Herr Ludwig Erhard agreed.

Naturally, a surge of exports followed. Krishnan was again included in the next trade delegation to Germany. More cherries. Riding on his rapport with the federal minister established during the last visit, Krishnan made another presentation, this time to remove the export duty on Indian handlooms. With consummate skill powered by passion and warmed by genuine feeling, he pointed out how this cottage-based industry provided a livelihood for the poorer sections of the population. How India was trying to prop up these threatened, ancient skills. How their craft had been smothered, first, during colonial rule, and then by competition from large mills. How could they compete when in the time a handloom produces 8 yards of material, a mill disgorges 1000?

Germans had taken to these fabrics in a big way, so, argued Captain Nair, exemption from export duty as well would ensure food in the huts of the poor, increase employment and earn eternal gratitude – 'good kaar-ma' as the West would learn to say. While expounding on this, the image of the indigent weavers of Malabar and Madras flashed through his mind, and his eyes welled up. The Teutonic race is famously unemotional, but this seemed to have a profound impact on Herr Erhard. He said as much while acceding to the request.

Krishnan came home crowned with victory – and with a lesson tucked into his waistband. As he would record in his autobiography: 'The hallmark of a good negotiator must be his evocative line of persuasion, winning the empathy of the other side.'

19

Let It Bleed

Millennials, or even their moms, may never have heard of 'Bleeding Madras'. But this was the catchy name of a fabric which caught on with the world's trendies in the Swinging Sixties. It had a gobsmacking journey from a south Indian village to salons worldwide, not unlike our protagonist's own trajectory. Like him, the tale is an example of the SWOT (strengths, weaknesses, opportunities, threats) analysis long before it became a management mantra. But the story goes beyond mere similarities. Captain Nair is the story.

His marriage to Leela had made him change tack from managing wartime rations to selling textiles. Remember? Along with his daughter's hand, A.K. Nair had handed over the sales agency of his Rajarajeshwari Weaving Mills to his son-in-law. It was in this capacity that Krishnan first displayed his marketing chops. He based himself in Bombay, targeting the crammed, chaotic lanes of the historic Mulji Jaitha market, considered to be Asia's largest textile trading hub. He would periodically return to Kannur to collect more samples.

His skills managed to earn him a fair amount. Not princely, but more than his army pay. It enabled him to give a fairly good life to his beloved Leela and their two sons, Vivek, born on 3 January 1952, and Dinesh, who emerged on Christmas Eve three years later. But the commission didn't always come in time, even though it was from his father-in-law's mill.

So here's a little story. Leela was pregnant a third time, and decided to have the baby in Bombay instead of at her parental home. The delayed commission meant there was no money for the nursing home. Too proud to ask his father-in-law, Krishnan went to a customer he was quite close to. R.K. Seth readily tided him over. The infant girl didn't survive beyond a few months, claimed by smallpox. Krishnan kept his indebtedness to Seth in his memory, and returned the favour two decades later, when the cloth merchant fell into dire straits. By then, the modest sales agent had become India's biggest exporter of ready-to-wear to the US.

His experience in selling handloom and power loom fabric made Krishnan realize the importance and potential of India's ancient and once globally coveted weaving tradition, prompting him to suggest a board for the promotion of handloom to Morarji Desai, then the chief minister of Bombay.

This led to, first, the All India Handicrafts Board and, much later, a similar body for handlooms, both of which would be taken to unprecedented heights by Pupul Jayakar, the czarina of rural arts, crafts and textiles. For Krishnan, from there it was a logical step to take 'Made in India' to the world.

In 1958, he had joined an official trade mission to suss out the US market and decide a strategy to captivate this Consumer No. 1. The homework had already been done when the influential American textile importer William Jacobson visited Bombay the same year and called on the textiles commissioner, T. Swaminathan, ICS. The commissioner directed him to Krishnan Nair. Weighing the options, our man selected and showed the buyer a lightweight cotton fabric with bright, tartan-like checks, worn by the Kalahasti women of Tamil Nadu.

Expertly fingering the fabric, Jacobson asked what was special about it. Krishnan suavely rolled out its USPs. It was woven using 60-count yarn for the warp and 40-count yarn for the weft. Its vegetable dyes used laterite stone, indigo blue, turmeric and local sesame seed oil, all of which made the fabric exude a distinctive scent. He added that it was already a hit in West Africa where it was being used for making flamboyant gowns for weddings and other celebratory occasions.

Krishnan then produced his weakness-as-strength trump card. The fabric had to be washed gently and separately in fresh cold water; with each wash the colour would 'bleed'– thus creating a different kind of check. The possibility of a 'new' garment with each wash excited Jacobson, and the two struck a dollar-a-yard deal. An immediate shipment of 10,000 yards was ordered. Brooks Brothers scooped up the entire lot, and tailored it into sporty jackets, shirts and shorts under its iconic menswear label. The shelves were stripped within a week. Laidback post–World War II baby boomers couldn't have enough of 'Bleeding Madras'.

But this did not happen before a crucial omission left many faces red with anger and embarrassment. In the 'excitement' over his discovery, Jacobson had 'forgotten' to mention the all-important 'care' instructions to Brooks Brothers, who therefore didn't mention them on the tags of the finished products. All hell broke loose because customers found that their colours would 'bleed' not only into the fabric's own checks, but also run into the other clothes which were unwittingly washed along with them.

Legal notices flew thick and fast, suing against the non-fast colours. Krishnan's expensive lawyers washed him clean of the whole caboodle because the fault was clearly Jacobson's, who admitted as such. The matter ended with the American importer paying damages to Brooks Brothers and a stroke of adroit marketing. That 'weakness into strength' formula was flaunted by Madison Avenue maven David Ogilvy, who came up with the tag line 'Guaranteed to Bleed'.

A 1966 Brooks Brothers catalogue stated:

> Authentic Indian Madras is completely handwoven from yarns dyed with native vegetable colorings. Home-spun by native weavers, no two plaids are exactly the same. When washed with mild soap in warm water, they are guaranteed to bleed and blend together into distinctively muted and subdued colorings.

Naturally, all the other *prêt* labels cottoned on, and made it part of their summer collections. *Seventeen* magazine provided the ultimate endorsement with an eight-page spread on 'Bleeding Madras – the miracle handwoven fabric from India'. Clever Krishnan would extol the qualities of this textile but never let on the details of its production. He knew the dangers, even in the times when GI stood for 'government issue' or 'general issue' and not for the complexities of the 'geographical indication' tag or, for that matter, the 'glycemic index' of food.

Here's a prescript. Nair, Jacobson and Brooks Brothers may have created this American fashion sensation of the 1960s, but the lowercase use of 'madras' as a generic name for a light, cotton fabric had a much older provenance. Though less storied than the Spice Route, Europe's maritime nations had also coveted India's fabled textiles. Not just the 'woven air' Dacca muslin, but the hardier calico.

The Dutch came for it first, but like for everything else, the East India Company bested the rest. The firm had been set up in 1599 on London's Leadenhall Street, and from an office just 'five windows wide' would command an empire as political as it was mercantile. As William Dalrymple chronicles in *The Anarchy*:[8]

> It accomplished a work such as in the whole history of the human race no other trading Company ever attempted, and such as none, surely, is likely to attempt in the years to come.

John Company, as the East India Company was nicknamed, established itself in southern India in 1611. In 1639, it moved to the area near the fishing village of Madraspatnam, known in history and legend for its weaver communities whose goods had, over the centuries, been sought after in Central Asia, Persia and the East Indies. With the practice that also led to the growth of Bombay and Calcutta, the Company wooed weavers, dyers and merchants from the region with the promise of a

---

[8] William Dalrymple, *The Anarchy: The East India Company, Corporate Violence, and the Pillage of an Empire* (London: Bloomsbury, 2019).

thirty-year exemption from duties. Soon, nearly 400 new weaver families from the region had settled in the area called 'Washerman's Peth' at the fortified trading post of Fort St George, Madras. This was how the material that rolled off its looms got its name.

Being lightweight and breathable, undyed madras cotton became popular in Europe. In time, a sample of cotton plaid madras arrived in the New World in 1718, as a donation to Yale University in its earlier avatar as the Collegiate School of Connecticut. The Average Joe got his first madras shirt from the Sears catalogue of 1897. But the real sensation of the bleeding variety would be created sixty years later.

And here's a postscript.

Krishnan and Jacobson had struck a dollar-a-yard deal, but several years after its amazing results, Bill Axelrod (no relation to Bob, the protagonist of the TV series *Billions*) offered to take over the entire production of Bleeding Madras 'at any price'. He had walked into the Indian pavilion at the 1959 Chicago International Trade Fair, made the staggering offer and invited our textile man to New York to finalize the deal. When Krishnan asked where they should meet, the business baron had replied, 'The Waldorf Astoria,' adding grandly, 'That's where I live.'

So, the village lad from Kannur arrived in New York and audaciously checked into the same mythic Park Avenue address. More audaciously, having learnt that Axelrod lived on the twenty-second floor, he booked himself a suite on the twenty-ninth. Then, when he called Axelrod to say that he was in New York, and Axelrod asked where he was staying, he had replied with practised cool, 'I'm at the Waldorf, Room 2908. Would you care to come up?' Axelrod did so, with not a little shock and awe. Captain Nair had a bottle of Chivas ready. As Axelrod sank into the plush settee, mine host surprised him further with, 'Let's not talk shop today. I want to know more about New York and about you.' It was two hours before Krishnan walked his guest back to the elevator. They met the next day at the Peacock Alley restaurant off the Waldorf lobby. This time they did talk business – much more than the seller expected. They struck a deal for a million yards.

The choice of hotel suite wasn't just literal one-upmanship, or rather seven-upmanship. It was a well-thought-out strategy. Captain Nair would later spell it out: 'In going into a big venture one has to display one's own strength. One has to go in with total self-confidence.'

The choice of conversation supported another of his biz mantras, 'When one goes to make a deal, big or small, keep the eagerness in low key. Don't rush the negotiation. Give the impression that it doesn't matter to you if it goes through or not. But the result aimed at must be clear in your own mind. You must go with your homework fully done.' He would add, 'You must make no promise that cannot be kept.'

This is a leaf out of the Mahabharat where Bhishma Pitamaha states his first principle, 'A king must honour his contract.'

On that trip, Captain Nair struck deals with some of the biggest clothing brands. He had a hundred yards of Bleeding Madras left over from the samples he had carried, which he gave to the owner of the clothing store Chips and Twigs. The store fashioned it into stylish garments and displayed them at a fashion show. This unspooled a request for another 1,00,000 yards. Net, net, he returned home with more orders than the current production line could handle. He stayed for a while in Madras to expand the supply lines.

The best, however, was yet to be, even if it took its own time in coming. His new best friend forever (BFF in today's lingo) Axelrod introduced Captain Nair to Conrad Hilton, who asked when they could meet. The legendary hotelier had seen our man in his hotel, and had noticed him getting enthusiastic salutes from the doorman, elevator boy and bell-hops – all of whom Captain Nair had presciently tipped generously to show his would-be American customers that he was a man worth doing business with. Which brings this story closer to the door at which we have been mysteriously hinting.

20

Lace to the Top

Arsenic and Old Lace, the 1944 American murder–comedy directed by Frank Capra and starring Cary Grant. Queen Victoria, who began the trend of the white lace wedding dress. The white lace sari that is de rigueur for her Parsi cultural heirs.

With such a worldwide array of cultural timestamps, it's strange that the first person to manufacture lace in India was a one-time Kannur village lad. Stranger still, what's the lofty Lord Mountbatten doing in the frame?

It all began with Mrs Leela Nair chancing upon this beautiful fabric during a visit to England in the early 1960s. Leela being Leela, it didn't end with her falling in love with lace. 'We must make this in India,' she declared. Her nonplussed husband asked, 'How?' How indeed, because lace is made on huge Nottingham looms which take seven years of apprenticeship to operate. 'You can do it,' said Leela. Thus began the quest. But, as what's now a given, Uncle VP had already started the ball rolling.

The still powerful Mr Menon had been encouraging his worthy protégé to loosen his father-in-law's textile strings, stop taking other people's fabrics to global acclaim, and instead become a manufacturer himself. So when Leela suggested lace, Uncle VP pointed out that the only place to go was Britain, where he still had the necessary clout. Without a reliable introduction, no supplier would give the time of day – let alone expensive machinery – to an unknown Indian.

Krishnan identified a manufacturer in Nottingham in the hope of beginning a joint venture: the UK company would supply the know-how and looms while he would pitch in with the premises, labour and working capital. He mentioned this to his patron, who contacted no less a personage than Lord Mountbatten, requesting him to please put in a word should it become necessary. He had already introduced young Nair to him during his last months as viceroy.

Captain and Mrs Nair betook themselves to Johnson Shields Company Limited and got an appointment with its MD, Lawrence Mitchell.

Mitchell usually exported to Europe and the US. He looked quizzically at these unlikely buyers of lace machinery and said politely but firmly, 'Sorry, I know nothing about you.' Trying not to look smug, the visitor politely asked if he could use a telephone. Fishing out his pocket directory, he put a call through, had a brief conversation, and, handing back the receiver to the bemused MD, said, 'Sir, perhaps this gentleman's word will suffice.' You can imagine Mitchell's shock and awe on hearing who was at the other end of the line. He shot out of his chair and snapped to attention as Mountbatten spoke. Needless to say, it was a done deal.

The Scottish partners visited India, were charmed by the Nairs' Bombay property and even more by their hosts' hospitality. A 25,000 sq. ft structure was raised next to their bungalow Leela Baug. The ground floor was of double height to accommodate the four giant looms. A mezzanine walkway enabled the technicians to monitor the complex manufacturing process.

Leela Scottish Lace Private Limited was inaugurated on 13 March 1964 by Cooverji Hormusji Bhabha, then vice chairman of the Central Bank of India. A Parsi businessman, his even more illustrious charge had been the commerce portfolio in independent India's first cabinet.

Uncle VP, the great facilitator, acceded to Captain Nair's request to be the chairman of the pioneering lace company.

Leela Nair took a hands-on interest in the new venture. The looms purred out bolts of delicate lace, table linen and curtains. Innovative designers fashioned the yardage into satin-lined dresses and skirts. The man who had stormed the US with Bleeding Madras garments and his father-in-law's furnishings now applied his marketing genius to his own product. He placed cutting-edge ads in Indian newspapers and glossies.

The lace creations were showstoppers at Bombay's fashion extravaganzas, which had begun to wow audiences thanks to the Spencer sisters, Sylla and Nergish, and then Jeannie Naoroji. They were modelled by Miss Indias Meher Mistry (1964) and Persis Khambatta (1965), who also represented India at the Miss Universe pageant in 1967. Persis is best remembered as the bald Deltan navigator Lieutenant Ilia in *Star Trek*, a role for which she famously shaved her head. The PR-conscious Captain Nair garnered great photo ops at the glitzy annual Femina Miss India contests which Leela Lace shrewdly co-sponsored for several years.

Even Bollywood's first superstar, Rajesh Khanna, wore his famous Leela Lace kurta at his birthday party in the days when he was dating Anju Mahendroo. He would go on to create a sensation when he married Dimple Kapadia, the teen star of the romantic blockbuster *Bobby*.

The unstoppable Captain Nair was constantly seeking and cementing business opportunities in India and abroad, especially at export fairs. His lace was so coveted that dealers and distributors vied with each other to wrest exclusive rights in their territory.

This was the time when he and his wife wove a special relationship with Jagdish Khandelwal of Delhi's famous Jagdish Stores. This bond would embrace the next generation of Nairs, at both a personal and business level. When Captain Nair eventually embarked on his hotel ventures, he asked Madhu, his younger daughter-in-law, who executed all the interiors, to buy as much as possible from 'Jagdishji'.

Then came a spanner in the works. A literal one. The Scottish machines were high-maintenance, and India's precarious forex situation made import licences for spare parts difficult. There was a constant requirement for these parts, and their lack invariably resulted in one or the other of the four monsters breaking down. There came a stage when two stopped functioning alltogether. At full pelt, there had been three shifts. Now some workers had to be laid off, resulting in unrest across the shop floor: labour could not understand what was so difficult about getting a few problem parts replaced. They struck work 9 September 1979. It was the proverbial entire war being lost 'for want of a nail'.

The Leela Lace strike was of a piece with the industrial unrest that was crippling Bombay, instigated by Datta Samant, the doctor-turned-union-leader who had made the city's booming textile mills sick. Tikamdas Kukreja, who had worked closely with Captain Nair to form the Apparel Exports Promotion Council (AEPC), had earlier cautioned him against the folly of a 1000-strong workforce in such close proximity to his residence. Not only he and Leela, Vivek and Dinesh with their wives and young kids all lived in the bungalow.

When his workers went on strike, the astute boss had his own ace ready. He had begun repaying all the credit loans normally given to exporters and brought himself to a zero-debt level. So much so that the worried chief general manager of the Central Bank of India actually called on him to ask if they had erred in some way. Captain Nair reassured the banker and confided in him that he did not want the burden of debt repayment coming in the way of giving the (non) workers a fitting reply.

The strike stretched on. The factory hands erected shelters just beyond the Leela Baug gate, shouted slogans and obstructed every car. In disgust and for safety, the whole family moved back to their old residence at Vatcha Gandhi Road, which by then had become Modi Lodge. It was still theirs for the asking.

After two and a half years of related court cases, the strike was declared illegal. By then a number of workers had left, and the remainder followed suit after taking their dues. Captain Nair shut down Leela Scottish Lace

Private Limited in 1981, vowing never to run a garment factory again. It would be resurrected in a new avatar by his son Dinesh in the mid-1980s, this time as the gold-spinning ready-mades for export business.

After the shutdown, Jagdishji proved to be the friend indeed, providing the finances needed to pay the workers' dues and even buying up the Leela Lace stocks. But there was still the business of settling with the Scottish partners, who had a 50 per cent stake – a near-intractable situation considering that the company was deeply in debt to financial institutions. The ever-resourceful Uncle VP had passed away in 1966, but Captain Nair was never without a trump 'Uncle' up his silk shirtsleeve.

This time it was N. Sundaresan, deputy governor of the Reserve Bank of India (1950–54), fondly known as Uncle Sandy. He was a larger-than-life man of the world who loved hosting parties at his home in the exclusive sea-facing, old-money Breach Candy Gardens. Captain Nair, a fellow bon vivant, was a regular guest, as was Dhirubhai Ambani, with whom too he would share a lifelong friendship. Uncle Sandy offered to mediate with the Nottingham partners.

Captain Nair sent the two gentleman first class tickets and put them up in style in Bombay. Uncle Sandy invited them to dinner, which he cooked himself with a flourish. The preceding Scotch was the smoothest, the accompanying wines were perfectly paired, the flatware was Wedgewood, the crystal Waterford, the silver monogrammed.

By the end of the very successful evening, it was mutually agreed that the UK partners would ship back their four Nottingham lace machines and be absolved of all liabilities. Captain Nair was still left with a pile of bank loans. But the company had the textile export business. With this, he hoped to cover the financial nakedness that had resulted from being stripped of lace.

Captain Nair would buy his peace with Dr Datta Samant. Indeed, he subsequently shared a cordial relationship till the militant trade unionist met his violent end in 1997. He was struck down in a hail of bullets outside his own home by four motorcycle-borne contract killers. The

Dr Samant–led 1982 textile mills strike had slain Mumbai's signature industry. The workers fell into debt, despair, even depression that often led to suicide. The mill owners, however, went laughing all the way to the bank. They made a killing on their huge real estate holdings in the heart of the city, when they were finally allowed to redevelop them in 1991.

21

Curtains for Gregory Peck

At a meeting called by the Indian consul general in New York to build on the success of Bleeding Madras, there was a sole Indian textile trader, Sham Sani. Try as he might, he couldn't get a word in edgewise. He sought out Captain Nair at the end of it and grumbled, 'Is it a crime to be Indian among all these Whites?' The staunch patriot at once countered to the contrary. When the fellow followed up that reassurance with, 'Then I too want Bleeding Madras,' the feted supplier said, 'Of course. And I'll give it to you at a discount.'

The next day, he went over with samples to Sani's Indian House Loom on Fifth Avenue. The owner seemed very busy, and he requested Krishnan to wait and disappeared to the back of the store. Our man stood around patiently, philosophically thinking, 'Waiting is a necessary part of doing business and there's no point fretting about it.' He would continue to underline the pointlessness of impatience, as we will see.

Sani finally emerged and ushered Krishnan towards the rear of the shop, where, to his astonishment, Krishnan discovered that this successful distributor had been packing a large order by himself. Impressed, he too rolled up his sleeves and pitched in. Indian House Loom finally placed an order for 2.5 million yards of Bleeding Madras. By then it was 9 p.m., so

Sani treated his guest to a Chinese dinner. They had lots to talk about. It was 1 a.m. by the time the Sindhi trader dropped him back to his hotel.

Sham Sani and his team, namely his nephew Lal Sani and ace salesperson Al Sandler, developed a huge market for the distinctive fabric. So much so that the Sindhi importer would soon be chartering flights from Madras to the US. Years later, Al would serendipitously reappear, and launch Captain Nair into an even bigger success story.

An entire generation had genuflected to Bleeding Madras, but fashion is programmed to be fickle. Well aware of this 'swept off today, shelved tomorrow' theme, Captain Nair widened his swatch pack, his Rolodex and his beat, exporting furnishing fabrics woven in Kannur, especially at his father-in-law's Rajarajeshwari Mills. Their exotic colours and patterns wowed the West Coast too. Thanks to his California importers, notably Rajendra 'Jindi' Singh, he also furnished Gregory Peck's new Beverly Hills mansion. He was invited to the housewarming party, which he characteristically used to home in on more Hollywood contacts.

22

The Path to 'Nirvana'

Krishnan had sorted out the problem with the UK partners. But his loans loomed larger than those giant Scottish lace-making machines. He didn't want to lose the beautiful 2 acre bungalow on the now-booming Andheri–Kurla Road, or the 25,000 sq. ft factory alongside. Facing his first financial crisis, he thought long and hard. And eventually decided to return to the hand- and power-loom textile import business which had created the Bleeding Madras sensation and even furnished Hollywood homes.

Picking up the threads was not going to be easy. He would have to untangle knotty in-law issues, and then start weaving new relationships in the US, the earlier ones having frayed.

He needed a great collection of samples, but the main source was nowhere as rich as it had been. His father-in-law, the illustrious A.K. Nair, had passed away on 14 December 1969. The management of Rajarajeshwari Mills had passed on to his children and a couple of nephews. Kerala's matriarchal system ensured that his daughter Leela was among the five new owners, but a son-in-law wasn't on the same footing.

Not only that. In the eight years he'd been away from the family business, Krishnan was given no commission whatsoever, not even a delayed one. This had forced him to appeal to R.K. Seth at the time of his wife's third pregnancy – a patently unfair situation considering the mill continued to ship huge consignments to his original client, Axelrod's company. The determined entrepreneur had to source other weavers in Kannur and Madras.

Then came the search for American buyers. His old friends weren't of much use because the entire nature of the business had changed. Instead of merely importing fabric, brands were outsourcing complete garments from sweatshops in Thailand, Hong Kong and China, which was fast whirring towards becoming the world's factory. Krishnan despondently booked a flight back home. And found Lady Luck seated next to him – in the rather hirsute avatar of Rajinder 'Jindi' Singh.

He hadn't contacted Jindi on this trip because the importer had gone bankrupt twice during their previous dealings. In fact, the no-nonsense Leela had even made an overseas call and minced no words berating him for reneging on his payments to her father's mill, which was the supplier. Krishnan was only the export agent.

The old friends were thrilled by this promising coincidence. Call it a ready-made opportunity. Krishnan was returning disappointed that the Americans now wanted only finished garments, and here was Jindi coming to India to set up a local supply chain of that very product. As was the practice, he would only play importer and financier. The rest would be looked after by the American salesperson and designer whom he had hired.

Jindi told Krishnan that this duo, J. Gerber and Elisa, would be joining him in Bombay in two weeks' time, adding the sweet-music words, 'If you can put together a unit which can tailor sample garments in trendy fabrics for American brands, I can prevail upon these two to deal only with you.' Reining in his racing pulse, Krishnan replied, 'Of course I can, Jindi.' He sent up a silent thanksgiving for this literally 'out of the blue' boon.

As they were about to land at Santacruz airport, which was then for both international and domestic flights, Krishnan said to Jindi, 'It will be lovely for you to meet Leela and my two boys. They will be here to receive me.' Hearing this, Jindi paled, remembering the tongue-lashing he had received years earlier from Mrs Nair. He shared his anxiety with his lost-and-found friend, who roared with laughter and assured him that all this was in the past, and his beloved Leela was not one to harbour grudges.

He was right. Leela welcomed Jindi with genuine warmth. Young Vivek and Dinesh too looked forward to meeting Jindi Uncle during his stay at the Taj Mahal Hotel. This would be pleasanter than their usual trips to this Bombay landmark: the monthly barber shop visit, a reluctant experience sweetened by the promise of sundaes at nearby Green's Hotel – where the new Taj Intercontinental would rise.

On landing, Krishnan hit the ground running. A fortnight was all he had to turn the wheel of fortune. After recruiting a sampling manager, he scouted for quality heavy-duty sewing machines. Through his contacts he learnt that Mrs Pramila Wagle of Paville Fashions was disposing of her imported ones. Reminding her that he had known Mr Wagle in his handloom days, he got a good deal on a dozen machines which together could do all the stitching and fine finishing needed for an export grade garment.

He set it all up in the section of his home which had previously been occupied by the Scottish lace technician. He added furniture and air-conditioning to make it a comfortable workspace for Jindi's designer and salesperson. His south Indian connections gave him the edge in sourcing great and little-known sample yardage for the designer Elisa to work with.

Among these was a crepe fabric he had discovered and developed for his trip to the US. Called 'cheesecloth', it could be used in its natural off-white form or dyed. It could also be yarn-dyed and woven into stripes and checks. When Jindi's team arrived at the ready-to-use unit, both pairs of eyes and hands fell on this unusual crepe. Elisa, especially, could not contain her excitement. It was as if this was precisely what she had set out to India in search of – like an adventurer from the days of yore chancing upon a spice, or a botanist sighting a rare orchid.

After Elisa had created a sheaf of designs for the cutting master and tailoring unit to work on, Krishnan and Vivek took her to the inspirational source: Kannur. Between them, father and son had identified some truly special weaves, and the ecstatic designer came back to Mumbai with a suitcase stuffed with new fabrics. The machines whirred into the night; within a fortnight, an entire spring collection was ready for Jindi's new label. He called it 'Nirvana'.

The samples were flown to New York. By the end of the week, the verdict was loud and clear. The market was blissed out. Orders poured in. Captain Nair was back in business. So was Leela Scottish Lace Limited, ready-made garments for export replacing the product which had given the company its name.

Jindi asked his old-new supplier to commandeer a bunch of garment factories which would work exclusively on Nirvana's growing avalanche of orders; this would ensure no defaulting on commitments. Krishnan too concentrated solely on this business, though having to depend on third-party manufacturers, it was often a challenge to maintain quality and timelines. But why would he complain? The money was rolling in – this being the US, volumes were humongous. He managed to clear his debts in twelve months.

Remember the business mantra about not putting all your eggs in one basket? As far as womenswear was concerned, Krishnan stayed exclusively with Nirvana, refusing the overtures of other American buyers. But with Vivek's sharp assistance, he did explore the European market, again via his old route of trade fairs and expos.

Krishnan had experienced problems arising from depending entirely on outsiders, so he set up his own quality production house. He bought a European-owned unit and installed its 300 sophisticated machines in the 25,000 sq. ft of the defunct Leela Scottish Lace factory building. The orders were so huge that he also retained the earlier job contractors.

The supply side was now ironed out. But creases began to appear at the demand end, caused by the vast distance between manufacturer and market. Add to that the notoriously short shelf life of fashion. Despite Jindi being an experienced importer, his calculations on what lines would sell occasionally went awry, and Krishnan would be left saddled with bolts of fabric for skirts, tops or dresses that were no longer needed. Krishnan and Vivek found this unfair, but it wasn't easy to replace as lucrative a label as Nirvana.

Jindi, on the other hand, blithely absolved himself of the wastage he had created. Worse, he saw nothing unethical in switching to one of the many Indian garment exporters eyeing this golden goose. Soon, this became a recurring pattern. But his miscalculations meant Nirvana would have a similar situation with the new exporter, and have to return to Leela Scottish Lace, which couldn't afford to lose its golden eggs.

Fortunately, a new glowing one was laid by Gul Samtani, agent of a major American store, Atherton Industries. He and Krishnan got on like a house on fire, or should we say like a 'honking farmyard', since we mentioned Aesop's salutary tale of the goose. Undoubtedly, our protagonist had a superior product, but he also had the panache to present it persuasively enough to get a hard-boiled Sindhi to bite. Samtani's bounty not only helped Leela Scottish Lace turn a corner, it also led our impatient entrepreneur into the higher-end women's ready-to-wear market, one on which he would build a fabled fortune – and lay the foundation of another venture altogether.

But that would happen in due course. This was 1979, and Jindi had made a killing on Krishnan's line of yarn-dyed handloom voile from Coimbatore. Fickle fashion lived up to its adjective in the coming seasons, and Nirvana was back to its old game of not picking up the growing piles of orders. However, thanks to son Dinesh, such an erratic customer would be more than made up for later.

23

Hoteliers to the World

Krishnan had gone to America to promote humble homespun fabric – but the trip would actually blast him into the league of luxe.

Booking himself into the storied Waldorf Astoria when he went to meet with Bill Axelrod wasn't a lapse into satined self-indulgence; it was a no-frills strategic decision. He wanted Axelrod to see him as an equal, not a supplicant. In fact, he had gone one step, actually seven floors, higher. But the discreet pampering at the Astoria had got him thinking. What does the classy traveller want? Certainly not just clean towels, a comfy bed and a halfway decent cup of coffee. And not merely to be treated as a guest rather than a customer. Not even a home away from home. The ideal scenario would have to be plush-plus-plus.

A traveller's expectations varied depending on the purpose of the trip. If it was for business, you could throw in every luxury, but the guest wouldn't return if the service wasn't as sharp as the finest sashimi knife. If it was a leisure trip, the must-must takeaway would have to be memories – but leisure must never be mistaken for laxity. Millions of dollars went into exceeding expectations, triggering surprise, creating the perfect photo-album-worthy moment. In short, distilling that amorphous essential: the 'wow' factor.

Not just the best hotels in the West, but even those in Asia (or especially Asia with their traditions of gracious hospitality) had aced the game. What of India, with its ancient mantra of '*atithi devo bhava*', the guest being considered equal to god? The Taj and the Oberoi had kept gilding their act, strutting away with global awards. But the best in business can never rest on laurels, either they bettered it or someone else would. On the long flight home from that US trip, Krishnan decided that he would be that someone. 'Of course you will,' said Leela .

Once again, he hit the ground running, as he had after his airborne meeting with Jindi, the textile importer. In the Bible, Jesus says, 'Ask, and it shall be given you; seek, and ye shall find; knock, and it shall be opened unto you.' He began doing the asking and seeking, knocking on those doors where he was sure results would be found.

Net worth is enhanced by networks. These had propelled Krishnan right from the time his mother used her connections, first with Sanku, the son of the local heavie Thunoli Sankaran Nair, to get him into Raja High School. Then, more momentously, the prawn pickle password used to get him into the ambit of his biggest door opener, Uncle VP. Now, Krishnan used his textile-trade Rolodex to help weave his luxuriant dream. The environment was also propitious – the government was helping with seed capital for private industry. An entrepreneur needed shareholder support. Krishnan recalled the earthy axiom, 'If more hands push, the cart gets quicker on the track.'

He made a list of 200 friends, cherry-picking them on the basis of their business acumen and financial strength, and also for their amiable disposition. He picked up the phone and pen, telling them about his grand scheme for a chain of luxury hotels. Not only would these exceed international standards, their USP would be the showcasing of India's culture and heritage. Each of his friends responded with a cheque for $5000, to which he added his own savings. However, it would be several years before he opened the first Leela hotel, in Bombay, in 1986.

The roots of that extravaganza set in luxuriant gardens would begin in a line of dusty Bombay taxis.

24

An Airport, NRIs and Designer Jeans

It was easy to see why Captain Nair took to Bombay like a prawn to Malabar curry. Like him, the city thrived on its chutzpah. It didn't wait for opportunity to knock; instead, its door was always open. Like his native Kannur home, it was a city on the sea, looking outwards, catching the wind in its sails so one could adventurously set forth. It scorned the power elites worshipped by Calcutta and Delhi, bowing instead to the animal spirit of enterprise. It didn't worry about the caste, creed or colour of those who came to its altar, as long as they knew how to make money with passion and use it with compassion. Captain Nair too had a hard head and a soft heart.

He had valued Bombay's ease of exit and access when he was promoting south India's textiles across the world. Calcutta had once held the reins of commercial power, but for the past few decades every Indian business worth its equity had to be stabled in this western city. Krishnan too wanted a base here. When he did find a place, the man from the Malabar coast didn't settle on south Bombay's posh hill of the same name. Instead, he was at the opposite unfashionable end, in Sahar village, one of the oldest habitations of East Indians, the first settlers of Mumbai after the native Kolis.

In 1961, Krishnan placed an advertisement asking for 'land for industrial use in the Andheri area' to set up his own home and the Leela Scottish Lace factory. What he got in response wasn't anything like the soulless space you'd associate with the words 'industrial use'. It was a bungalow on 2 acres of land flush with gorgeous trees and flowering plants.

The estate belonged to Kekoo Gandhy, whose previous tenants included the Belgian consul general. Gandhy had pioneered the promotion of modern art in the 1940s, displaying the works of artists from the Progressive Artists Group, M.F. Husain, F.N. Souza, S.H. Raza, etc., in the show window of his framing shop, Chemould.

The Parsi and the Malayali met to arrive at a compromise figure. Actually, it was a done deal even before the two sat down to negotiate. Invited over to see the property, Leela had fallen in love with it at first sight of its groves of mango, chikoo and jackfruit. An auspicious occurrence seemed to bless her decision. She had gazed longingly at a low-hanging green orb, and not one but two mangoes fell at her feet. 'We have to buy it,' she said. To her husband's pointless protest that it would be well beyond their budget, she had firmly responded, 'We will find a way.' Leela's will usually did. The agreement was signed.

Now the 'way' had to be dealt with. Mustering the funds was going to be a tricky high-wire act; fittingly, a circus man came up with the first tranche. Their close friend Gemini Sankaran, who had remained modest despite the global success of his eponymous extravaganza, agreed to buy the Nairs' shares in what had been their first industrial venture, Mangalore Mysore Timber Mills. It wasn't enough. No prizes for guessing who would again come to the rescue. Uncle VP stood guarantee for a loan from the Canara Bank.

One day, several years later, Leela looked out of the window of their bungalow, Leela Baug, and spied the long line of cabs on the broad Andheri–Kurla road. It was being developed for the new international airport at Sahar, just an arrivals announcement away. She turned to her husband with The Look which he had come to know could not be brooked. 'Er,' she said, 'why don't we start a hotel here? It would have captive custom.' It was indeed an inspired idea for the first luxury hotel built on the area which the new international airport had primed for development. But of course, it didn't fly in ready-made on a magic carpet, though ready-mades did help power that flight.

~

Mrs Leela Nair had given voice to an idea sparked in Captain Nair's hyperactive brain by his stay at the Waldorf Astoria years ago. In fact, he had even made his elder son, Vivek, and daughter-in-law, Lakshmi, who were then running a small garment business in New York, sign up at the School of Hotel Administration at Cornell University, Ithaca.

Air India had opened the Centaur Hotel at the existing airport at Santacruz. It was built by German architects, and its buzzy restaurants matched the high level of décor and service in its rooms. But no matter – the fabled Malayali network once again kicked in for Krishnan. He had a family connection with K.K. Unni, who had led the creation of Centaur. Although – or because – he had retired, Unni put his ambitious friend through the paces of building a world-class hotel. The two were quite close – Krishnan had accompanied Unni to Houston when his deteriorating heart condition needed the expertise of the pioneering cardiothoracic surgeon Dr Denton Cooley.

Krishnan knew that although he had closed down his garment factory, he could spin gold from the plot on which it had stood. The dreamcatcher area would have not only the international airport, but also the commerce of the upcoming Maharashtra Industrial Development Corporation (MIDC) and the exclusive export zone, Santacruz Electronic Export Processing Zone (SEEPZ).

He commissioned Bombay architect Pheroze Kudianavala – and then rejected his blueprint on two counts: one practical, the other emotional. The first because he realized that his 2 acres wouldn't do for a luxury hotel. The second because the design would entail cutting down a 100-year-old banyan tree. He had thundered, 'I would rather not have a hotel than destroy this magnificent, ancient, sacred tree.'

He made a presentation to the Airports Authority of India (AAI) asking for more land, arguing that the world over, a luxury hotel was an essential part of the infrastructure of any airport presuming to call itself international. His persuasive pitch worked. Thus began a private–public partnership with AAI.

He had enough funds to sign the lease and take possession of the additional 11 granted acres. But he would need institutional financing to give shape to the new blueprint prepared by Rajendra Kumar Associates (or RK Associates), which had recently built ITC's stunning Maurya Hotel in New Delhi, in 1978. Since the stomach is as much a way to a man's purse as to his heart, Mrs Leela Nair displayed her famed culinary skills and laid out a sumptuous lunch for the lenders with whom her husband hoped to curry favour. They agreed to raise equity – in the future.

Krishnan wasn't the type to remain in any soup he landed in. His old friend and financial adviser Alex Picardo told him to go it alone via a fundraising exercise rather than tap a single investor who would want a say as well as a share. Such an arrangement would never work with a man as independent – and, yes, as egotistic – as Captain Nair.

The hotelier-in-waiting said to himself, 'Let me go back to the US which has brought me so much success.' He did, but it was Europe which eased the passage. His older son, Vivek, approached Penta Hotels, the group owned by Lufthansa, British Overseas Airways Corporation (BOAC), British European Airways (BEA), Alitalia and SwissAir – they signed a franchise agreement.

So, global brand and adjacent land in place, Krishnan set off with Vivek to mop up funds from America. At the same time, he told the younger one, Dinesh, to pump up his languishing garment export business. Both horses were needed to pull the gilded carriage which the father was hell-bent on charioting. The obedient son would more than meet his father's diktat, beginning with the Gloria Vanderbilt–Mohan Murjani collaboration which famously created the 'First Jeans Exclusively

Designed to Fit a Woman'. The following chapter will show how that venture spun out to make the Nairs the biggest Indian exporters of ready-made garments to the US.

~

Captain Nair decided to convince wealthy non-resident Indians (NRIs) in the US to subscribe to a promoters' quota, offering a maximum of 5000 shares at a dollar apiece to each individual. He started his tour from his 'lucky playground', New York, hosting a lavish party at Gaylord, owned by his friend Jati Hoon. The evening sparkled. The response did not.

However, it was here that he met Vijay Amritraj, then at the peak of his professional tennis-playing days, and who would 'become like a third son'. Invited to join the Leela board, the Los Angeles–based Amritraj would introduce him to the who's who of not only Hollywood, but also Washington. The two men – separated by thirty-one years but joined by a common passion to win the highest stakes – would remain very close ever after.

New York had proved disappointing. So what? His NRI cousin Usha and her husband Manoharan were both successful gynaecologist-obstetricians; they suggested he tap the wealthy India-born medical fraternity. So Krishnan and Vivek both travelled from coast to coast with a presentation to encourage promoters to come on board. It appealed to the doctors' business heads and pulled at their patriotic heartstrings. The purse strings opened. Individual contributions ranging from $10,000 to $20,000 added up to a cool $1.5 million.

Next, the Nairs targeted the wealthy NRIs in the Gulf. Here, Krishnan's nephew C.K. Kutty was such a dedicated facilitator that Dinesh would later describe him as 'a Hanuman to Lord Ram'. He planned the whole trip. Once again, substantial funds were raised. Krishnan would continue to depend on Kutty, especially on matters relating to the civil works of his hotels. The nephew helped at all the construction sites – refusing to even accept a fee.

With this funding and the bounty from Dinesh's garment exports, the new company, Hotel Leela Ventures Limited (HLVL), under the umbrella of its major promoter, Leela Scottish Lace Limited, was primed for take-off on the Sahar property.

At sixty-five, an age when most people are ready to hang up their boots, the unstoppable Captain C.P. Krishnan Nair was cobbling together an all-new enterprise.

25

Portering Prêt

Krishnan had ordered his son to beef up the garment exports business so as to help bankroll his ultimate dream. Dinesh was expected to carry out this ambitious task when he did not have even a factory to his name.

Starting small but thinking big, he went on to snag some of the biggest labels in ready-to-wear fashion. It would be a hard day's fight. But, as the Beatles sang, he managed to 'get by with a little help from my friends'.

In 1976, one fashion legend joined seams with a young label that had already become an object of desire. 'Gloria Vanderbilt by Murjani' was pitched as the 'First Jeans Exclusively Designed to Fit a Woman'. The Italian-sounding partner was in fact a New York–based Sindhi. The talented Mohan Murjani had used the community's globally proven genes to launch a product that sounded Italian too.

Soon, he was big enough to get equal billing. His 'swan' embellished the front-coin pocket, and Gloria Vanderbilt's signature was embroidered on the back pocket. With this collaboration, denim jumped from cool casual to hot sexy. No ifs about it. Only butts.

Shrewdly deciding to corner the whole ensemble, Mohan Murjani set out to buy yarn-dyed blouses from India to match those jeans. Unsurprisingly, he asked a fellow Sindhi, Raj Melwani, to outsource them.

Melwani used an even closer connection, entrusting the execution and quality control to his sister Meenu Thadani. Dinesh was already doing business with Raj, and when the grapevine sizzled with the news that Meenu was farming out large orders, he knew he had to grab a share. But how? Krishnan had shut down Leela Scottish Lace on account of the harrowing strike in 1979, vowing never to own a factory again. His son had no option other than to set one up by himself.

Dinesh's resources were limited but he had his genetic resourcefulness, to say nothing of his father's diktat to corral the money needed for the dream hotel. He found a unit which had just forty machines, but very good technical masters and supervisors who had worked with him earlier. With this confidence, he pleaded with Meenu Thadani for a share of the Murjani pie. Aware of the Nairs' reputation for quality, she gave Dinesh an order for 7200 pieces in two patterns of 3600 each. This was a crumb compared to the lakhs bagged by others, but it was all that his unit could handle satisfactorily. More importantly, he got a foot in the door of Gloria Vanderbilt.

In fact, it led to bigger doors. Landing in Kannur to get supplies, he discovered that other looms were rolling out orders for the fast-moving Liz Claiborne prêt label. He called his father to make time in his busy fund-mopping schedule in the US to go over to the American designer's office and try to get on this brand-wagon. Now he could also 'drop' the Gloria Vanderbilt name. He knew his father could sell sand to the Bedouins, let alone a garment business proposal without having any samples to show.

Krishnan, never one to let go of an opportunity, landed up ten minutes early for his appointment with Liz Claiborne's manager and was asked to wait. Just then, a large man breezed in like he owned the place and, turning around, hollered, 'Hey, aren't you Krishnan? Don't you recognize me, old man? I'm Al. Al Sandler. Watcha doin' here?' It took a minute to connect this tycoon-type guy with the lanky young salesman of Sham Sani. The two hugged each other, and when Al learnt why Krishnan was there, he boomed, 'You don't need to meet anyone. Gimme five minutes to finish my meeting with Liz. I'll take you over to my showroom a few blocks away.' He added, 'Liz and her hubby Art don't deal with nobody but me.'

The two ambled over to Al's impressive studio, packed with fabrics, drawings and showpieces not only for Liz Claiborne but several of the big prêt labels, including Calvin Klein, Happy Legs and Jordache. Al told Krishnan that he worked with two Indian exporters, in Delhi and Madras, respectively, and if 'your Din-esh can set up a top-notch production house, he can have all my business. I'll be in India on my annual visit in three months. I'll see the factory, and if it's up to scratch, I can place orders right away.'

Krishnan rushed back to his hotel and called his son to find larger premises. Dinesh did so, promptly locating a 200-machine unit at an industrial estate in suburban Powai. With the assistance of his two dependable managers, Das and Bharathan, he got back the best of his earlier technical hands, and put up a well-lit, well-spaced-out factory. It fully met with Al's approval, and he gave the resurrected Leela Scottish Lace Limited tons of business from some of the best names in US ready-to-wear at undreamt-of prices.

With these names on his résumé, the multiplier effect kicked in. When Macy's set up a buying office in Delhi, it gave Leela Scottish Lace a trial order of 300 men's shirts. They made the grade, and another prestigious and profitable company was added to the trophy shelf.

Despite these classy names, Dinesh missed the mass customer base of Nirvana. His elder brother, Vivek, introduced him to his friend Sarfaraz Khan, working with Company One. Sarfaraz asked him to come to the US, and with his past experience in the voluminous volume segment, check out the fastest-moving lines. Dinesh put together his own collection. Another deal was struck.

The snowball kept rolling. One day, Dinesh caught up with his father's old protégé, Sammy Nanwani. Though they had a great conversation, the New York–based importer showed no signs of giving him any business. But everything changed when his curiosity got the better of him and he peered into the goody bag of samples. As it happened, when Dinesh had walked in, Sammy was yelling at one of his biggest Indian suppliers for not having the right product. It was the perfect conjunction of the stars. Sammy switched to Dinesh. It was the start of another business – and personal – relationship.

At this point, Dinesh got the enviable feeling of being in a fairy tale where one door led to another, and each one opened on to a roomful of opportunities. Many of these came about from his old networks falling in place; others from former partners falling out. What helped in both cases were his genes. He had inherited his father's unbending insistence on quality and, as important, Krishnan's hospitable affability. He was equally fortunate that his associates were Sindhis, who were known the world over for their sharp eyes for a main chance and their equally persuasive tongues.

A year after he started doing business with Sammy, Dinesh learnt that his Gloria Vanderbilt contact Raj Melwani had begun a separate division with a guy reputed to be the hottest salesman in the India–US rag trade: Andrew Kirpalani of Andrew Sports. Soon enough, this Sindhi duo arrived in Bombay and interviewed the dozen exporters on Meenu's roster. When Dinesh's turn came, Andrew was impressed enough to say they should meet again, this time on Dinesh's turf.

In a few days, he went over to the showroom on the ground floor of Leela Baug. Two factors made this an even more successful meeting. First, unlike Meenu's other exporters who also dealt with several countries in Europe, Dinesh concentrated on the US market. Secondly, Andrew's comfort level deepened on learning that Dinesh and he shared several business and personal friends – his new partner Raj Melwani, Gul Samtani and Sammy Nanwani.

For the rest of his Bombay trip, Andrew made it a point to keep the last meeting of the day with Dinesh, so that they could sit as late as needed. Working on his collection for Andrew Sports led to a great rapport. Dinesh would invite him upstairs to his home, and over convivial cocktails they would continue to discuss the US garment business threadbare.

Some nights, Dinesh would ask Andrew to stay on for dinner, an invitation readily accepted because his guest loved the Kerala curries which he found akin to those of Malaysia where Andrew had spent his early years. Of course, the Nair table would have hooked even the totally uninitiated. Krishnan would also join them sometimes for a drink and regale Andrew with stories of his Bleeding Madras days. These evenings paved the way for a concrete and continuing friendship.

After a successful year together, Raj Melwani and Andrew Kirpalani parted ways. Their closed door opened one more for Dinesh. Needing a new partner to deal with the large volumes he generated, Andrew asked Sammy Nanwani if he would come on board. Of course he would. The rag-trade vine shimmered with tales of Andrew being not only the smoothest of salesmen, but also someone with a keen sense of fashion and accessories. Mr and Mrs Nanwani took the next flight to Los Angeles to meet Mr and Mrs Kirpalani. A lucrative new partnership was forged. Wholly endorsed by Sammy, Andrew requested Meenu to begin dealing exclusively with Dinesh and Leela Scottish Lace.

Now, it was party time several times over. The takings from the rocking Andrew–Sammy partnership combined with the huge orders from Al Sandler and Gul Samtani swelled Leela Scottish Lace's coffers. While this was great per se, it also accelerated the thrust towards Krishnan's hotel dream. Remember, this had been the original imperative for his younger son revving up his idling garment business. Dinesh's personal equation with both Sammy and Andrew lubricated this engine of phenomenal growth.

The Nairs did not forget old friends either, or their indebtedness to them. One day, Dinesh was called to his father's office and he was introduced to an elderly gent chatting familiarly with him: 'My helpful old pal, R.K. Seth.' The son recalled the story of how the Mulji Jaitha market trader had helped out when his dad didn't have the money to admit his mother to hospital during her third pregnancy.

Seth was the one now strapped for cash, and too proud to ask for a handout.

Dinesh offered him the job of collecting the 'cash drawback' – duties paid at various stages of production of goods for export for which the government refunded 6 per cent of the turnover. This had added up to some Rs 10 crore. Seth did all the chasing for a more-than-worthwhile fee. At the end of the day, he would arrive at Dinesh's door and say, 'Chalo, let's go have soup.' It was invariably 'mushroom with garlic bread'.

Thanks to Andrew, Sammy, Gul and Al, et al., Dinesh now had the class plus mass market appeal – and with it the confidence that he could live up to his father's funding expectations. Leela Scottish Lace became the largest Indian exporter of ready-mades to the US. When the time came, Dinesh requested his father and Vivek to come on stage to receive the 1988 APEC Vendor of the Year award; they would keep receiving this accolade. The Nairs now knew they could generate the capital required to bankroll the proposed hotel business without having to depend on another – potentially undependable – partner.

Clothes don't only 'maketh the man'. Apparently, they also maketh a hotel.

26

A Tale of Two CMs

Back in Bombay with funds assured, Krishnan got down to raising his dream hotel. Since it was inspired by the likes of the Waldorf Astoria, it could not but be full of lavish luxury. Sahar may have been marsh, but Krishnan had known at the start that it would be a gold mine. Fortunately, a senior politician thought the same: Vasantdada Patil, Maharashtra's former chief minister twice over, knew that an adjacent luxury hotel would perfectly complement the international airport. It would catalyse growth, generate employment, create wealth. In short, help him in his own dream to infuse 'Maha' into Maharashtra.

At the time, in the early 1980s, Patil was general secretary of the All India Congress Committee (AICC); the incumbent chief minister was his fellow Congressman, A.R. Antulay. He kept sitting on the files on the grounds that the project would violate the Urban Land (Ceiling and Regulation) Act (ULCA), passed in 1976 to 'bring about an equitable distribution of land in urban agglomerations to subserve the common good'. The chief minister inexplicably chose to ignore the simple detail that hotels were exempt from the ULCA.

Or perhaps not so inexplicably. As always, whenever politicians and business are involved, there are whispers – in this case that the chief minister was weighing in for the established SoBo (south Bombay) biggies. Every time the Nairs approached him, he would fob them off with '*Dekha jayega*'. We'll see. Krishnan took every opportunity to press his case, even booking himself on the flight on which Antulay was travelling to Nair's home state of Kerala. Vasantdada was there when the hotelier-in-waiting called on his fellow Keralite A.K. Antony, who too was an AICC general secretary.

'Be patient,' Patil told Nair. 'I will soon be returning to Bombay.' He did, becoming chief minister again after Antulay was convicted for extortion and had to relinquish office in disgrace. On 13 January 1982, the Bombay High Court ruled that he had forced Bombay area builders to make donations to one of his many trust funds in exchange for allotting them cement in excess of their quota.

Krishnan was invited to Vasantdada's swearing-in at Raj Bhavan on 2 February 1983. When he approached with a garland, the new chief minister said, 'What's this? Where's your application?' He wanted it in Marathi, so they rushed back, got it translated by the architect's daughter, and took it to him at 7:30 the next morning. Vasantdada spoke to the municipal commissioner, Jamshed Kanga, and the secretary, housing and special assistance, D.M. Sukthankar, telling them, 'We must do this for Captain Nair. Antulay sent him on a runaround for months even though hotels are exempt from the ULCA.'

Turning to Krishnan, he said, 'I will lay the foundation stone before year end.' All the clearances followed in quick succession. The chief minister did indeed pick up the first ceremonious shovel – two months before his deadline. The ground-breaking ceremony or *bhoomi pujan* was performed on 16 October 1983. Also present was Khurshed Alam Khan, Union minister for tourism.

Captain Nair's first hotel would naturally also be the first showpiece of his passion for gardens, sown during his childhood in the verdant hamlets of Kannur. Remember how the maidans of the district headquarters were what had most impressed the boy on his first awestruck visit to a big town. His wife, Leela, had even greener fingers. Recall again how the orchards of the former Gandhy bungalow triggered her resolve to own what would remain her treasured home till her passing half a century later.

The couple set about greening the whole public area all the way up to the domestic airport at Santacruz, transforming the incongruous welcome of slum and marsh which had greeted those landing in India's swankiest city. The story goes that the Captain took up this magnanimous beautification after a VVIP guest, seeing the lines of people squatting for their morning excretions, had naively asked, 'What are they plucking?' To which a wag had quietly muttered, 'They aren't plucking, they're planting!'

Vasantdada Patil, chuffed at the faith he had reposed in Krishnan, would later say, '*Leela aya toh Sahar sudhar gaya.*' Leela ushered the development of Sahar.

27

Trouble at Take-Off

The hotel began with a franchise agreement with Penta Hotels, a company formed to billet crew and layover passengers in the cities serviced by Lufthansa, BOAC, BEA, SwissAir and Alitalia. RK Associates drew up a plan for 250 rooms set in large, lush grounds. The London-based luxury hotel interior designer Frank Solano gave it an international look and feel. The structural blueprint was imposing, with a double-height ceiling in the lobby and the presence of eight floors above the service level.

After the ground-breaking ceremony, civil construction had proceeded at a trot and reached thc fourth floor within a year. As Vivek would recall, 'Some fifty-five permissions were required to set up a hotel, involving constant trips to Delhi. One morning, while we were there, we were shaken awake by a banner headline in the *Indian Express* claiming that nineteen rules had been bent for our maiden Bombay hotel. There was an uproar in Parliament which, unfortunately for us, was in session.' The main allegation was that the Nairs were being allowed to build higher than the permitted height, which would therefore interfere with the flight path of planes at the adjacent Sahar and nearby Santacruz airports.

Vivek pointed out, 'This was absurd because there were already several structures taller than ours would be, including Air India's Centaur Hotel at the very entrance to the domestic terminal. Chairman and I camped at Kerala House where the state's MPs were staying, and they all volunteered to support us across party lines.'

Their earlier facilitator, Vasantdada Patil, who had understood the multiplier effect of a luxury hotel at Sahar, suggested they seek the intervention of Rajiv Gandhi, the former pilot who had become prime minister after his mother's assassination by her Sikh bodyguards in 1984. Oscar Fernandes was dispatched for an on-site study, and he reported back that the fears were unfounded. Construction resumed, but precious months were lost. When a project this size is grounded, bank interest and escalation costs mount. Had the opposition prevailed, the Leela would have had to limit itself to five floors. This would have sabotaged the idea of Captain Nair's dream of rewriting not only the definition of airport hotels, but of luxury itself.

~

A new hotel always rattles entrenched incumbents. The Taj Bengal, coming up across from the Calcutta Zoo in the 1980s, faced as baseless and prolonged a controversy. Here, the allegation centred on another flight path, that of the thousands of migratory birds which alighted every winter on the zoo's lake. The protest was fronted by the Chiriyakhana (Zoo) Workers Union, and was even taken up by the local reps of the World Wildlife Fund, but the hidden claw was believed to be the city's grandest hotel.

Variations on this theme play out across the industry, and not only in India. Realizing that their guests would prefer a hotel five minutes instead of fifty minutes away from the airport – especially since word was out that it was going to have all the style to which they were accustomed – SoBo's established hotels had allegedly whipped up the flight-path bogey.

On the advice of its merchant bankers State Bank of India (SBI), the fledgling firm HLVL floated an initial public offering (IPO) even before it began operations. With his customary flair, Captain Nair took out a full-page ad in all the major newspapers headlined 'Europe Comes to India'. The reference being to the airlines of Penta Hotels which had a sales and marketing contract with HLVL.

~

After a six-month soft opening, there was a gala launch on 12 October 1986. Mrs Anna Malhotra – a godsend for the Nairs twice over, as we shall discover in the next chapter – was invited to light the traditional lamp. At the lavish party which followed, the chairman of Penta, Guenter Berendt, who was also the chairman of Lufthansa, took the Captain aside to declare that the hotel looked way too luxurious for the limited needs of the Penta brand. 'Make it part of our Kempinski chain,' he said. This partnership continued happily till LHVL decided to tie up with Four Seasons in 1994. After that abortive attempt, it returned to the German chain for several years. The friendship between Captain Nair and Herr Berendt lasted a lifetime. Guenter passed away on 29 May 2017, three years and 12 days after his close friend.

The Leela Bombay's landing was spectacular, but it had been a bumpy flight. As its pilot would ruminate later, 'Big events are preceded by long periods of waiting. These have to be faced with equanimity, maturity and without self-doubt. With life dreams, so with dream projects, their fulfilment needs patience.'

~

Patience was a virtue Krishnan would carry to the end – and this held just as true in his personal life. Here's a story from much later.

Dr A.S. Shetty, the medical officer at Leela Bombay since 1990 – and a tennis friend of Dinesh since 1976 – had accompanied Krishnan to a 5 p.m. appointment with the noted cardiologist Dr Jamshed Dalal. They arrived early. The doctor was late. The clock turned to 6 and then to 7. Dr Shetty's agitation mounted in proportion to the delay. The busy chairman did not lose a milligram of cool, let alone his temper. Instead, the patient calmed his medico, saying, 'If Dr Dalal is late, it must be because he is caught up in an emergency, attending to someone whose need must be greater than mine.'

Then he added, 'Ashok, I will wait quietly because I'm the one who needs the specialist, not the other way round.' Chastened, Dr Shetty recalled the Hindi proverb about the thirsty man who must go to the well and not expect the well to come to him.

28

(M)anna from Heaven

Europe's Age of Enlightenment was posited on 'the social contract', the moral imperatives of governance. Social contacts form the bulwark of business ventures. As a Mumbai entrepreneur would drawl much later, 'If in the course of a party I haven't initiated at least two deals, I consider it an evening wasted.' Our protagonist never wasted an evening, or any time of day. His eye was always on the main chance, his hand always ready to grab it, and his clutch of qualities always there to optimize the opportunity.

A business network is a complex machine with many moving parts, and Krishnan lubricated them in all his dealings and travels. The friends he made in one US foray would continue to appear to help him out in another. They weren't all textile traders; he also won the trust of bankers and bureaucrats. Among the latter was a remarkable woman who also happened to be one more influential Malayali. She turned out to be a godsend not once, but twice.

Anna (nee George) was India's first woman Indian Administrative Service (IAS) officer, and she was married to the equally brilliant bureaucrat Ram Malhotra. Krishnan came into her ambit when she was revenue secretary. He made a case against the excise duty wrongly slapped on his lace products. Not only did she agree, she rectified the error with retrospective effect – refunding the large amount that the company had shelled out to the government. As it happened, this money saved him personal embarrassment as well.

Lack of funds had forced him to leave unfinished the house he had begun to build in Kannur's cantonment. His father-in-law had asked his son Ravi to assess the amount required to complete the bungalow. He would underwrite it, since the structure was sticking out like a sore thumb in such a prestigious area. Pride wounded, Leela requested her brother not to take this forward and said that her husband would soon do what was needed. With the excise windfall, Krishnan paid the contractors in advance to speed up the work. It was worth the wait. The bungalow was exactly what the couple had always wanted. They named it 'Krishnan Leela', and with its ethereal beauty it could well have been in the mythic groves of Vrindavan.

Anna would help out again, playing a major role as Dinesh added his assistance to his father's hotelier dreams during the booming garment years. The ground floor of his export ready-mades factory had been let out to the Union Bank of India (UBI). He wanted it back because his snowballing orders needed more space. However, evicting a Bombay tenant was almost as difficult as booting out COVID-19 would be decades later. Their family friend Ram Malhotra was now governor of the Reserve Bank of India, though that upright gentleman would never pull rank for a personal favour. Nor would the Nairs dream of asking him to.

The equally principled Mrs Anna Malhotra had just relinquished her post as chairperson of the Nhava Sheva port. She had chosen to resign rather than take an extension, which would mean having to deal with ministerial pressure to waive penalties for delays on the foreign contractors. When Krishnan casually mentioned his son's predicament, Anna took it upon herself to intervene. She spoke to the UBI chairman, telling him that an export house badly needed to get back its premises.

Her clinching argument was that 'a bank branch can easily find alternative space, but the country's forex earnings cannot be allowed to suffer'. In three months, UBI vacated the space.

Greatly indebted to Anna for helping him save face and then salvage his son's export orders, Krishnan invited her to light the inaugural lamp for Leela Penta at Sahar. She also became a regular visitor to the Nair home and was even godmother to Vivek and Dinesh. Krishnan and Anna would always bring in the New Year together at the Leela Goa, along with Malayali superstar Mohanlal and Kannur-born K. Madhavan, who would go on to head Disney+ Hotstar.

29

Ain't No Airport Hotel

Airport hotels are the bottom feeders of the industry. A no-frills place to crash in for the night before catching a flight at the red-eye hour that international airlines take off from India. But the equivalent of the 'Wham-bam-thank-you-ma'am' quickie was certainly not the blueprint stirred in Krishnan's mind by the Waldorf Astoria. He may have never owned a hotel, but he was an old hand at recognizing opportunity and seizing the market.

The northern suburbs were growing apace. The Centaur near the domestic airport of Santacruz and the Sun 'n' Sand and Juhu Hotel several kilometres away were the only five-stars around. Krishnan's home and Leela Scottish Lace's property, on the other hand, were next door to the biggest force multiplier, the new international airport at Sahar. The man with the wide-bodied vision filled the gap and covered it with a red carpet.

An airport hotel has captive business twice over. The checkout time is 12 noon, but incoming and outgoing international flights are usually around the ungodly hour of 12 a.m. While economy passengers are prepared to rough it out at the terminal, front-end travellers want to rest in style. So a departing passenger would check out of the Leela, and the arriving passenger on the same aircraft would check in during those early hours between landing and take-off. One aircraft seat yielded two room nights. A bonus for the new hotel!

Rajiv Kaul, a protégé of the legendary Rai Bahadur Oberoi, was poached in 2006 to turn all the subsequent Leela Hotels into a brand. He explained the uniqueness of that first sensuous foray. 'The Leela was an airport hotel only insofar as its zip code. Its jumped-up luxury quotient, club floors, suites, bar, spa and nightclub turned it into a tony watering hole. Eighty per cent of its business was airport-centric, but this was the platinum level of frequent flyer – those who had to use Sahar because international flights were yet to favour their own emerging cities: Hyderabad, Bangalore, Ahmedabad. Captains of industry such as Wipro's Azim Premji checked into the Leela before checking in to their flight. It wasn't crew; it was the front-end passengers.' And they gilded the lily that was the Leela.

~

The Chaos theory applies in a unique way to the tourism industry. Wars, market crashes – and pandemics – are far more vigorous than the flapping of butterfly wings. So such cataclysmic events in one part of the world create a devastating tsunami even at the furthest point of the globe. Travellers get paranoid about going for business or a leisurely getaway and getting stuck in a foreign land thanks to closed airports and airlines stymied by no-fly zones.

Geopolitics doesn't care a wasp's ass for a hotelier's dreams. The long-drawn-out Iran–Iraq conflict turned Krishnan's into a nightmare, hotting up as the first Leela readied to receive a flourish of guests. Rai Bahadur Oberoi had stared at a similar catastrophe two decades earlier, the India–Pakistan war of 1965 coinciding with the opening of the Oberoi Intercontinental in Delhi.

Then came the West Asian conflagration of 1991. It was the first 'TV war'. Leela made the most of a bad deal by quickly installing a dish antenna to broadcast CNN's coverage in all its rooms. Remember Peter

Arnett? He became a household name worldwide as the only reporter to telecast live from Baghdad – especially during the first sixteen hours of 17 January – complete with the background cacophony of bombs and blasts. The foreign press corps stationed in Bombay huddled together to watch.

But if wars in another compass point of the continent emptied its rooms, an eruption closer home filled them two years later. The Bombay riots, triggered by the demolition of the Babri Masjid on 6 December 1992, had the city burning for months. Climaxing in the serial revenge blasts of 12 March 1993, which ripped through thirteen of the city's most iconic towers in almost as many minutes. This prompted all major international airlines to stop billeting their crew at the Taj and Oberoi in SoBo, and make them stay at the Leela, just minutes away from Sahar airport.

Business picked up more dramatically due to a less dramatic development. Emerging a short drive away were the commercial hubs of the MIDC and the export-oriented zone, SEEPZ. So, combined with the international airport, Conrad Hilton's 'Location, location, location' factor now applied to the Leela, literally on three counts. The occupancy here was often higher than in the top SoBo duo; so was the ARR or average room rate.

This boom wasn't confined to its room business. The Leela at Sahar was far closer to Bollywood, while SoBo hotels were at the other end of a town with notorious traffic. The stars now had a far more convenient – and luxurious – hangout spot. The Leela had the largest banqueting space, and the Cyclone became the grooviest disco thanks to its celeb swingers. It became THE destination hotel.

But all this high-flying was followed by a drop in altitude. During 1998–2002, international chains woke up to this gold mine. Economic liberalization and the IT boom had global business rushing to India, where Mumbai was the financial centre. There was an influx of hotels. The Leela could name its price when it was in a seller's market. Now, in place of its monopolistic 400 rooms, there were a total of 1500 brought in by the ITC Grand Maratha, the Lalit, Hyatt Regency and

Le Meridien – all within a 1 kilometre radius of the airport. They were newer and swankier. The Leela had to be refurbished, but its coffers had been depleted by, among other major works, the Leela Palace Bangalore, which had risen in 2000 – with an inventory bigger than the entrenched Taj and Oberoi combined.

30

Winter at Four Seasons

After the opening of the Leela in Bombay in 1986, Kempinski began pushing for a hotel in Goa because Lufthansa's charter wing, Condor, had started direct flights to this holiday destination from Frankfurt, Dusseldorf and Munich. The only luxury hotel in Goa was the Taj Group's Fort Aguada in north Goa. So, Captain Nair went south and created a 75 acre paradise on Mobor beach.

However, to divert the big spenders who flocked to the $500-a-night resorts of, say, Bali, Captain Nair knew he needed the cachet of a global brand. Moreover, such a tie-up would facilitate his bigger pan-India vision. He had toyed with the likes of the storied Ritz-Carlton and Mandarin Oriental, but finally chose Four Seasons. The relationship would end up wintry in sunny Goa without ever a taste of spring. The chain's Canadian founder, Isadore 'Issy' Sharp, would give his version of the fallout in a bare-knuckled chapter titled 'A Few Bad Apples' in his book *Four Seasons: The Story of a Business Philosophy*.[9]

We need to pause a bit to understand how such an operational marriage was even possible. The Indian hotel majors were territorial. Socialist India

[9] Isadore Sharp, *Four Seasons: The Story of a Business Philosophy* (Penguin US, 2012).

was itself protectionist and risk-averse. Moreover, the tight forex situation discouraged any adventurism. No foreign chain was allowed to come in as a full-scale operator. The only options for them were as a franchisee, a tie-up for reservations through its distribution network in the pre-website days, or via a sales and marketing contract by which the foreign chain received commission, but had to take a minimum of 26 per cent equity.

Such a lopsided arrangement was of little interest to the global big players. In their initial years, it was the Oberoi Sheraton in Bombay, the Oberoi Intercontinental in Delhi and the Taj Intercontinental for the newer tower of Bombay's historic hotel. But neither of these American chains could set up on their own when these ties turned knotty.

In 2004–05, several international hotel chains relooked at their policies for investing in India because the rules had changed to allow them to operate hotels The person who helped set this ball rolling was Captain Nair's elder son, Vivek, who handled the acquisition and deal-making part of Hotel Leela Ventures Ltd (HLVL). He achieved this far-reaching change during his first term as president of the Federation of Hotel and Restaurant Associations of India (FHRAI) in 2003–04.

The Four Seasons partnership was meant to extend across the group: Bombay, Goa, the upcoming hotel at Bangalore, to be followed by those planned for Udaipur and New Delhi. But the Canadian chain refused to play ball unless it was given complete 'operator' status. Vivek took the case to the source of the problem, the Government of India, not just for HLVL but on behalf of the entire tourism industry. He pointed out that allowing foreign chains to come in as operators would be win-win for the national economy, not just for the hospitality sector.

How? With operator status, global chains would be more engaged, because now their take-home would be approximately thrice as high as it would be through a limited sales and marketing contract. The exchequer would benefit because these chains would promote India as a destination in their lavish campaigns, plus their global customers would respond because of their existing comfort level with the brand. Ergo! More foreign exchange for the coffers. And, yes of course, more business for

India's hospitality sector, which, by the way, was also among the topmost employment generators. The partnership would upgrade the standards of Indian hotels as well. What was not to like?

After six months of to-ing and fro-ing, convincing and cajoling, the Indian government was finally convinced to lift the 'operator' barrier. Vivek also managed to get a waiver on the 26 per cent minimum equity. His efforts resulted in the way matters stand today. The Indian owner builds the hotel and hands over operations to the foreign chain, which brings in systems, design and brand value. Thus, the Rahejas became heavily invested in JW Marriott and the Chauhans in Le Meridien. The Grand Hyatt Regency was co-owned by the Shubh Karan Jatia business family till they parted ways precisely on this co-ownership issue.

The sticking point unstuck, Captain Nair invited the Four Seasons chairman to Bombay, and then took him to the real item on his agenda, the Leela Goa. The not-easily-impressed Isadore Sharp was floored by the Eden that had been so caringly created. But he said he would have to 'gut and rebuild the structure', adding, 'Are you sure you want to do that? The hotel is doing reasonable business.' The Captain replied, 'Yes, I want to do it. I want it to be a true Four Seasons.'

As Sharp continued in his book, 'We brought in our designers and consultants and made many changes, taking off the lobby roof, raising it to make a grand entrance, creating for him an outstanding five-star resort.' The remodelling had included breaking down walls to double the size of the rooms and making the Hampi elements in the lobby 'more dazzling'. Captain Nair had created the architecture and décor as a throwback to the glorious workmanship of the World Heritage Site in the neighbouring state of Karnataka .

Apart from the huge costs incurred in this endeavour, the property had to be shut for two years to bring it up to the chain's standards. Ten months before the targeted opening, an experienced team of fourteen expats, including the general-manager (GM)-to-be, Dieter Janssen, arrived to instate the standard operating procedures (SOPs) and train the entire staff to offer each guest the full experience of a Four Seasons stay.

The foreign chain promised higher revenues since its brand association would justify the higher ARR.

However, when the operator presented its first-year budget, it was far below Captain Nair's expectations. Another issue was the ongoing West Asian crisis which deterred Western travellers. Besides, the northern beaches had been the conventional Goa destination; you couldn't make tourists switch to south Goa in twelve months. Mohammed Khan's advertising agency, Enterprise, created an audacious campaign to re-engineer perceptions; it deserves its own chapter.

There was another flashpoint, more blinding because it involved egos. Big ones. The Captain wasn't prepared to be a faceless investor, and insisted on his Goa resort bearing the Leela name. Sharp bluntly said that this was in contravention of the Four Seasons' SOPs, and would lead to other partner hotels asking for similar co-branding. In fact, this was also a major reason why his later two-year-long, off-and-on negotiations with Biki Oberoi – as Prithvi Raj Singh Oberoi is known – finally came unstuck. The name issue itself would have been the deal-breaker for HLVL. But there was a decisive 'last straw' in 1998.

Captain and Mrs Leela Nair had wanted to spend a weekend at the Goan paradise they had created. When his secretary called the hotel to convey their arrival time, she was told that the Four Seasons 'GM would have to give his consent to any bookings'. 'What nonsense!' fumed the resort's owner, and landed up anyway. He then told his firstborn son, 'Pack them off', referring to the fourteen expat-experts who were being paid a huge sum in dollars net of taxes.

Vivek recalled it was a Friday, and though he resisted telling them to 'pack' their bags, he did politely and firmly ask them to book the next flight home. They did. Four Seasons finally came to India only in 2003, in Mumbai, with Shubh Karan Jatia who, at the time, still had a tie-up with the Hyatt in Delhi.

So, as we can see, the Four Seasons knot was untied even before bride and groom reached the altar. Ironically, this happened in the honeymoon destination of Goa.

Captain Nair returned to the chain of his original partner and dear friend, Guenter Berendt. The hotel was branded the Leela Kempinski, Goa.

At its reopening, Captain Nair charmingly escorted Mrs Anna Berendt to the floor – not for a sedate waltz, but a shimmying disco dance. The moves must have been something. As the understated Anna put it, 'I believe we performed very nicely, receiving Leela's support and praise.'

31

A Taste of Madhu

The Four Seasons non-starter had created a churn, but from that *manthan* emerged an elixir for all of HLVL's future extravaganzas. It was Madhu Nair's deep dive into hotel interior design and systems.

Coming as she did from Kerala aristocracy, her marriage at twenty to Captain Nair's younger son, Dinesh, a 'low-caste' Vaniya, stunned a society ordered by rigid hierarchies. That it was arranged by both sets of parents – who were the best of friends – speaks volumes about their progressiveness. More importantly, their example helped facilitate future alliances across the caste divide.

Madhu was a happy-go-lucky bride, quite content to let her strong-minded mother-in-law run the sprawling family bungalow, while 'I played house-house with my little baby', Samyukta, born four years later in 1985. 'I was comfortable with who I was. I wasn't looking for a career in which to make my mark.' The career came looking for her in 1988, when she was twenty-seven. Her father-in-law knocked on her door one morning, and nonchalantly asked the total novice to iron out the problem of replacement furnishings for the Leela Bombay, then his sole hotel.

Madhu picked up the gauntlet and the intricacies. She made the pattern cards for forty or fifty of those Italian fabrics for repeats, and got them woven on the high-tech shuttle-less jacquard looms of the family textile business. Her initiative saved them the 300 per cent import duty.

After that there was no going back to 'playing house-house'. She began taking baby steps into the hotel business. The Great Leap Forward came with Captain Nair deputing her to the Four Seasons' renovation of the Leela Goa. He told her to learn from the team of expats who had come to train the staff in providing the full global deluxe experience.

This one move provided an upskilling and exposure which would put Madhu at the nerve centre of all the future Leela properties planned as 'Palaces'. Her innate aesthetic sense did the rest. She was, after all, a diplomat's daughter, well travelled and educated abroad.

She was made understudy to HLVL's own project manager, S.R. Krishnan, and had to start with the ABC of how to read a blueprint or give form to an elevation drawing. It was a daunting stage for a young woman with no training in design – to say nothing of the patronizing 'Go play with your dolls, little rich girl' attitude of some of those know-all GMs of that time. Regardless, she quickly found her groove.

Working elbow-deep with the Four Seasons team gave Madhu hands-on experience. It taught her in ten months what no school could have. She learnt about big-picture planning and attention to niggling detail; satin-smooth service and brigade-ground discipline; and the SOPs which must be in place before the opening of a top-end hotel.

In this initiation period, she was also called upon to teach. On a subsequent visit, Isadore Sharp, the Four Seasons owner, told his vice president of development, 'Take all Madhu's inputs. She knows local conditions perfectly. That's going to benefit us immensely in this project.'

In the early years, Madhu travelled extensively with Dinesh to the best hotels in the world. Better than any formal school, this was the best training for her. She quickly grasped the various dimensions of design and luxury along with the highest quality operating standards. For her part, she infused warmth and caring, giving form to her father-in-law's mantra of not merely building luxuriant rooms, but handing guests the key to a second home.

Having been thrown into the deep end at Goa, Madhu got on swimmingly. Well, on her admission, 'after slowly getting brave'. After she got the lumbering Bangalore project off the ground along with Dinesh, Captain Nair was confident that she could flesh out his dream hotels on her own.

With Bangalore, Madhu fine-tuned the Four Seasons 'experience' with her natural aesthetic and unbending precision. It gave her a template for future projects, garnering new learnings for additional layers of luxury as she moved from one Leela hotel to the next.

Madhu had put together her almost all-women team, 'bringing in the men only for the electrical and mechanical work. The guys got totally bullied by us.' The girl gang developed 'a great camaraderie, travelling from project to project, and having a lot of fun too. They are still with me,' said Madhu with pride.

With each project, after poring over books and manuscripts to get every detail right, Madhu would scour the state for artisans and artefacts to make each hotel resonate with its local vibe. She commissioned the big names of contemporary Indian art, and thanks to her, the Leela hotels boast some stunning and valuable pieces.

Madhu's belief 'that everything must have a touch of India because people come here for the Indian dream' perfectly dovetailed into her father-in-law's impetus for building hotels: showcasing the country. She equally grasped that displays of past richness had to be complemented with cutting-edge service and systems. Only then would emerge the total picture which they wanted to present.

She took charge of architectural analysis, space planning and interior construction. Of the FFE: furniture, fixtures and embellishment. Of the pre-opening processes and training of staff. All that it took to create the synergies which made the whole greater than the sum of its parts. Her role was formalized in the designation of director, design and operations.

Like the hoary pioneer Rai Bahadur Oberoi mandating the length of the exposed stem in a bud vase, Madhu created a manual of Leela standards. The height of the differently purposed chairs, the depth of the sofas, even the way housekeeping staff had to pat the cushions on the sofas so that they looked luxuriantly ready to be used by another guest – all had to be uniform.

'Everything has to be bound to measurements. For example, the tea console, the tray and the kettle which sit atop it, must fit perfectly into one another.' At every Leela Palace Hotel, the GMs were told that they should not alter the layout of any public area without Mrs Dinesh Nair's express permission. You could be forgiven for thinking that she played bad cop to the benign chairman's good cop.

In course of time, the old Four Seasons 'student' became a source of lessons. Many in the industry would learn from her contributions to the Leela chain: sharp grooming, beautiful flowers, warm candles adorning beautifully complemented spaces, and the warmer smiles on the faces of staff members who knew they were loved and cared for. These details were often conjured up when Madhu and Dinesh travelled or at the family dining table where the couple and their little daughter Samyukta sat to eat with Captain and Leela Nair.

In her journey into the centre of this universe, she 'realized that you are not creating a room for yourself, but must project yourself into that of everyone staying here, even for just a night. The opulence has to be balanced by functionality. I wanted old-fashioned switches because a guest doesn't want to stand in a dark, unfamiliar room figuring out buttons on a panel, however hi-tech that may be.'

And ultimately: 'Each of our hotels had to have its identity, but with a fine thread that stitches them together.' She added, 'Even more important than all the tangible hardware is something that doesn't get itemized on the bill: the memory of being cared for.'

32

More Bangalore for Your Buck

There's no better example of 'metromorphosis' than Bangalore. It certainly was the first of its kind. Old-world Hyderabad, laid-back Pune, Rashtriya Swayamsevak Sangh–associated Nagpur – they were all sleeping beauties who would rise with the charmed kiss of IT. But Bangalore had first-mover advantage, changing almost overnight from a placid pensioners' paradise to silicon plateau. It was where suited legacy met its nemesis in the form of nerdy twenty-somethings in cargo shorts. Brick and mortar demolished with a click.

This made Bangalore a fitting arena for the one-hotel wonder to challenge the industry old guard. Those already famous founders too may have come from hamlets as modest as Captain Nair's Alavil Kunnavil in Kerala – Jamshedji Tata from Navsari in Gujarat, Mohan Singh Oberoi from undivided Punjab's Bhaun. However, well before Y2K, Taj was already royalty and Oberoi was aristocracy. Enter the arriviste with a cocky air to cock a snook at both.

The Taj West End, with fireflies in its mystic glades and bullfrogs revving up in lily pools, had 106 'keys' – hotel parlance for rooms. The Oberoi, 'composed around a centenarian rain tree' had 120. Both had been thinking of upping their game with ten or twenty more, when along came Captain Nair. He didn't so much shift the goalposts as run away with them by envisioning a 256-key extravaganza. Kunal Chauhan, who became the GM of the Leela Palace Bangalore (but was then at the Oberoi), recalled the incredulous buzz circulating: 'There's a guy going crazy down the road.'

As a boy of seven, Krishnan had been taken by his uncle to see Mysore's fabled Dussehra celebration. The spectacle had stunned the child, who till then hadn't ventured beyond modest Kannur. Here was a scene straight out of the tales he had raptly listened to by flickering village lamps; it was as if he was right there in Ayodhya, all aglitter to welcome Prince Rama after his fourteen-year exile. The epic proportions of the seat of the Wodiyars were made even more other-worldly by burning torches and decorative lights. Let alone this phantasmagoria, the lad had never even seen such crowds, all as wonderstruck as himself.

At that time, uncle and nephew couldn't hope to get inside the palace. Sixty-five years and incredible leaps of faith later, Captain Nair would be ushered into the maharaja's durbar hall itself on the invitation of Karnataka's chief minister, Ramakrishna Hegde, who, halfway through the evening, had leaned towards him and said, 'Captain Nair, why don't you open a hotel in our Bangalore?'

If the seven-year-old could ever have imagined this double whammy of a durbar darshan, would he ever have believed that, at age seventy, he would evoke those royal contours himself? In his words, he created the Leela Palace Bangalore as 'neither a city hotel nor a resort, but an experience of ancient grandeur in modern times'.

He once again commissioned the American firm WATG (Wimberly, Allison, Tong and Goo). Their chief architect, Donald Fairweather, would supervise the ambitious project; he was already in India to renovate the Leela Goa.

But dreams have a nasty way of turning into nightmares. The Leela Palace Bangalore, modelled on the Mysore Palace, threatened to turn into a white elephant quite unlike the richly caparisoned beasts of the dazzling Dussehra procession. The party pooper was a four-letter word which would continue to haunt Captain Nair's vocabulary: debt.

The renovations at the Goa venture ordered by the abortive Four Seasons tie-up had loaded HLVL with almost Rs 100 crore of debt, not all of which could be covered by its major promoter, Leela Scottish Lace. Neither was the initial revenue stream anywhere near what had been expected because many new hotels, especially multinational chains, had arrived, like Raj-time adventurers, to 'shake the pagoda tree'. This had led to extreme competition. Its gargantuan Bangalore project was haemorrhaging the company.

Bank loans had been taken on a too-short repayment schedule. The money stopped, so construction followed suit. Mr Venkatachalam was hired to help pull HLVL out of this grave financial trauma. The new chief financial officer (CFO) impressed upon the family that all non-productive assets had to generate income to service the quarterly interest, and ultimately the loans themselves. It was a Catch-22. How could the 256-room Bangalore hotel start earning if the lack of funds had forced it to remain an empty shell?

Once again, a coincidence daylighted the dark tunnel. Like 'Jindi' on the way back from an unsuccessful US mission, Captain Nair had a chance airborne meeting with Deepak Parekh. Exuding his usual confidence, he impressed upon the HDFC chairman how profitable his Bangalore hotel could be if only he had the funds to complete it.

Hard-headed bank chairmen aren't a soft touch; they don't part with crores because they like the colour of your eyes or the cut of your suit. They do so on the basis of long and sharply honed belief. At the end of the ninety-minute flight, Parekh came to believe in C.P. Krishnan Nair. He asked the ambitious hotelier to meet him at his office.

The captain went with his son and deputy chairman, Vivek, and his CFO, Venkatachalam, who had detailed the wherewithal needed. A senior HDFC official was asked to prepare the loan release. Parekh added in no uncertain terms that he wanted to see results. On the double.

Work on the Bangalore venture restarted, but it didn't have the luxury of lapping up all the HDFC largesse. The CFO had to perform his own version of Christ's miracle of feeding 5000 with just five loaves and three fishes. He had to keep paying interest and paying off loans to prevent the venture from sinking ignominiously into a non-performing asset. A large chunk of every HDFC infusion was diverted in that direction. It impeded the pace of the Bangalore hotel's completion, jeopardizing the faith the visionary banker had placed in his flight companion.

Rudi Greiner, who had been closely involved with Captain Nair's friend, Bob Burns, in building the Regent brand's luxury properties, was brought in as senior vice president, HLVL. He upped the game. Madhu Nair contributed her learnings from the Four Seasons team at Goa. Together, they had all the talent to clothe that naked shell in the finery needed to make it the belle of the ball. If only they had the necessary money to do it all at one go.

The deputy MD, Dinesh, and his wife realized that they had to fall back on the old strategy of 'eat the elephant one bit at a time'. The west wing was the best place to take on first – the lobby; the Library Bar; Citrus, the all-day restaurant; ninety rooms and all the alluring gardens. These they completely furbished down to the lowliest detail and the highest standards.

It could not have been done without him, so Deepak Parekh was the no-brainer choice to inaugurate the Leela Palace Bangalore on 13 August 2001. 'Well begun is half done' goes the saying, but ninety rooms were less than half of the envisaged 256.

A larger amount was needed to complete the remainder. The CFO had to perform his juggling act, again. This time, the promoter company, Leela Scottish Lace, decided to pitch in almost all the funds needed for the hotel. Since they were both paymaster and piper, they could doubly call the tune in terms of design and execution. Captain Nair and Vivek were happy to stay out of it as long as the job got done. Madhu meticulously proceeded area by area: the Indian restaurant, Jamavar; the pan-Asian dining space Zen; the ballroom; the pampering spa. And, of course, the remaining 166 luxurious guest rooms, for which she handpicked everything down to the – well – goose down for the pillows and duvets.

By the time it was complete, Leela Scottish Lace had pumped in roughly Rs 210 crore of inter-corporate deposits into HLVL. No interest asked. The sweat and the equity paid off. Bangalore would rake in enough to make the company debt-free again.

~

The white elephant turned into a cash cow. The Leela Palace Bangalore was in the right place with the right product at the right time. By 2001, the city had caught its second wind. Captain Nair had sensed this in advance and flown in. The new kid on the block outstripped the competition. It averaged 90 per cent occupancy, its tariff soared to as much as $400 a night, its ARR was far higher than anyone else's. From Rs 8000 it went up to Rs 20,000. In the words of HLVL president Rajiv Kaul, 'Emerging India was expressing itself through Bangalore, and, boy, did we milk it.'

How do you tangibilize luxury, or to put it more bluntly, how do you justify the fat bill? You could put in Swiss Evian instead of domestic mineral water as a doff to VFM. The more pertinent point is that Value for Money has an intangible definition in this champagned bubble. You create the right ambience, and you make associating with it aspirational. Then no one's going to tote up the actual price of milk, sugar and beans in your Rs 500 cup of coffee. The Bangalore Leela's success, said Kaul, 'also made the world's luxury chains wonder what the hell was happening'.

33

Life Is a Beach

The Coastal Regulation Zone (CRZ) is the bane of all waterfront wannabes. Of course, safeguarding sensitive coastal zones from the clutches of rapacious builders is a legitimate environmental concern, more so in a country with a 6000-kilometre shoreline. The protective 'Lakshman *rekha*' within which no construction was allowed had always been 50 metres from the high-tide line (HTL). This is why early resorts such as the Ashoka at Kovalam, Kerala; the Oberoi Palm Beach, Gopalpur on Sea, in Odisha; the Taj in Goa; and the Fisherman's Cove in Mahabalipuram were all within lapping distance of the sea.

Then came a death blow. The CRZ Act, 1986, multiplied the original 50 metres to 500. This was not prompted by any ecological study, but reportedly on account of bureaucratic overreach.

Here's insider information on the genesis of the new CRZ. In 1982, Prime Minister Indira Gandhi had gone on an aerial survey of cyclone-affected Odisha accompanied by her personal secretary, P.C. Alexander. Seeing some buildings, she had wondered aloud why state administrations permitted construction so close to the sea. This random statement prompted Alexander to start the process of changing the long-held status quo. For rivers and lakes, the ban was now 100 metres from the bank.

After his mother's assassination in 1984, Rajiv Gandhi became prime minister. He also held the tourism and civil aviation portfolio.

Vivek Nair played a key role in the serial attempts to make the CRZ revert to the original 50 metres. Indeed, as an executive committee member of FHRAI since 1988, and its president in 2003–04 and 2012–13, Vivek helped win several advantages for the whole hospitality sector, even if, on occasion these victories came too late for his own hotels.

Remember, he had already worked towards getting operator status for foreign chains, making them more willing to enter into partnerships with Indian hoteliers. Thanks to this, most of the global giants have a footprint here, and Indian-owned ones are now in the minority.

Let's return to the CRZ battle.

In 1988, Vivek and other hoteliers made a presentation to Rajiv Gandhi. They pointed out how most beach resort countries such as Indonesia, Sri Lanka, Thailand, Mauritius and the Maldives mandated a distance of only 50–100 metres, some far less. They argued that the new CRZ would be disastrous for tourism and dash the huge potential that came from India's stunning length of coastline. 'How can we compete with the world?' they asked.

Rajiv Gandhi said he couldn't make as drastic a reversal as to the original 50 metres, but, after deputing M.S. Swaminathan to study the issue, he reduced the statutory CRZ from 500 metres to 200 metres. When the hoteliers cried that this was still too much of a setback, the prime/tourism minister agreed to reconsider it 'in due course'. That didn't happen because in 1991 Rajiv Gandhi too was assassinated. But the beach hoteliers didn't give up their fight to get the CRZ back to the original 50 metres from the HTL.

Twenty-one years later, on 18 May 2012, when Dr Manmohan Singh was the Prime Minister, the Union Minister for Tourism, Subodh Kant Sahai, constituted a high-level committee to rationalize CRZ rules for the development of beaches, rivers and backwater tourism. It was chaired by Vivek Nair, then in his second term as FHRAI president.

Again, the main members were Karnataka, Maharashtra, Gujarat and, of course, Kerala, which had the considerable clout of Amitabh Kant – the dynamic bureaucrat who had so successfully packaged this southern state as 'God's Own Country'.

The hoteliers hadn't demanded a reduced CRZ for the entire 6000-kilometre coastline. As Vivek explained, 'We had requested reverting to the original 50 metres from the HTL for a mere 20 kilometres, and that too not continuously. It was for 7 kilometres in Kerala, 6 kilometres in Karnataka, 4 kilometres in Maharashtra plus other bits and pieces. Moreover, we were talking only of stretches suitable for beach development, not rocky terrain or ecologically sensitive zones harbouring corals and sea turtle nesting sands.'

The Ministry of Environment and Forests agreed to revert to the original 50 metres for hotel construction in these limited zones. It added a proviso: the population density in the involved villages or talukas should not exceed 2161 per kilometre. Why such an odd figure? That was the 2011 Census's determining factor.

However, for the notification to be approved and put into practice, the Chennai office of the ministry had to review the recommendations from each state. Then it would finalize which areas of each could have a reduced CRZ of 50 metres. By the end of September 2021, Maharashtra had received its approved plan. Till that time, proposals from Kerala, Karnataka and the rest still awaited the Chennai office's green light.

The east coast is frequently battered by cyclones, so it was largely the hoteliers of the west coast who had wanted a more reasonable CRZ. Gujarat didn't figure because prohibition was a perennial (not merely seasonal) deterrent to tourism. While Narendra Modi was chief minister, he had agreed to a 'visitor permit'. You got a stamp on your boarding pass which allowed you to buy a limited amount of alcohol at a designated kiosk, which you had to drink only in the confines of your hotel room. The hoteliers petitioned him to at least allow guests to drink in their club lounge, which would be more sociable and less morose. Vivek added,

'Then Mr Modi went off to Delhi, and that was that.' They didn't even try to pursue the matter with his less visionary successors.

Vivek also let on that there was one exception made by Chief Minister Modi as he was keen to boost tourism in Gujarat, along with everything else. Some 350 travel agents had attended a conference to this end, and liquor had flowed in Ahmedabad's Grand Bhagwati hotel. It was the first and last time. Mr Modi reportedly told the hospitality industry representatives who tried to convert the concession into a rule: 'If I make exceptions on prohibition, Congress will make it an election issue, and I could well lose.' That was then.

~

Vivek Nair's petition to Prime Minister Gandhi would benefit the whole beach resort sector, even if it was prompted by the family's own new hotel in south Goa. The chief town planner is the official who demarcates the CRZ limit. However, more than officialdom, NGOs are guardians of the coastal zone. These CRZealots struck soon after the Leela Kempinski was up and swinging.

This ecologically rich state quite rightly has a robust environmental lobby. But crusading can be misplaced. Soon after the resort opened, Claude Alvares's vocal Goa Foundation claimed that its health club violated what was still the 200-metre CRZ; the structure was in fact a metre away from the demarcated line of control.

The hotel was sent a notice under the Environment Protection Act (EPA). The stringent EPA obliges the violator to rectify the transgression within a week, failing which power supply to the entire property could be cut off. It was peak Christmas season. The Leela Goa was at capacity and in full festive mode.

The hotel's firefighting team dashed off to Panjim. It petitioned the vacation judge to give two weeks' grace, after which they would demolish the structure 'even though it was well outside the limit', said

Vivek, recalling the trauma. Permission was granted. The health club was demolished after two weeks as promised. The official survey later proved that it had broken no rules. It was rebuilt at a cost of Rs 80 lakh – cheaper than paying lawyers to fight for damages.

34

The South Soars North

If the first Leela hotel in Bombay took business away from the south of the city to the north, the second one in Goa did the reverse. The flower children of the Serendipitous Sixties had tripped to Calangute and Anjuna in north Goa. Though the ganja gang soon moved on to Kathmandu, the sybaritic beaches of the tiny state remained imprinted on the global subconscious. North Goa became the tourist hub, dominated by the Taj Aguada at Candolim. In his six decades, Captain Nair had always taken the unexpected path. This time was no exception. He went south, discovered a more pristine location, and then set about upgrading nature.

On a recce, he had been shown Cavelossim's Mobor beach. When the path he and his associates were exploring came to an end, the chairman said, 'Let's keep walking,' as if drawn by an inner lodestar. The party ploughed its way through the dunes and shrubs, and just when the rest were ready to turn back, lo and behold, a vista opened before their incredulous eyes: the sun-sheened Sal river gliding towards the Arabian Sea. It was a eureka moment. Captain Nair had found the perfect place, embracing beach and delta. By the time he had finalized the expanse – it would be absurd to call it a mere 'site' – he had acquired 75 acres.

He would proceed to enhance it with his two passions, greenery and waterbodies. Before that, however, the god-given sea – the property's very raison d'être – rocked the Captain's ship even before the keel had been laid. Not the sea per se, but the CRZ created to protect it. This regulation had prompted his son and the HLVL vice chairman Vivek Nair to campaign for a reversal of the arbitrarily extended limit.

The Leela Goa landscaped its way round the reduced restriction. A nine-hole golf course was laid on the 200 metres where no construction was permitted. Six of the villas looked out on to the sea from that designated distance; the rest had an equally spectacular view. The strawberry-pink units lined two lagoons 20 kilometres long, their meandering course festooned with brilliant bougainvillea and lush creepers. They were formed by digging a channel from the river – locks adjusted the flow, and a specially treated base ensured crystal clear water year round.

The child of 'liquid' Kerala, Captain Nair instinctively understood the palliative qualities of water. All his properties would be replete with the murmur of streams, the splash of fountains, the drama of waterfalls. For the resort guest, these features were a given. But our nature upgrader knew that at the end of an exhausting day, even the business traveller needed a watering hole that was not the bar.

Villa-ringed lagoons were the USP of the landscaping genius Tom Pugliaso. He had been recommended by Bob Burns, a prodigious hotelier whose Regent brand had been constructing properties in Hong Kong, Bali, Milan and New York. Giving shape to Captain Nair's dream of weaving past Indian glory into ultramodern luxe, the architectural brief to the California firm of Wimberly, Allison, Tong and Goo was to evoke Hampi, capital of the fourteenth-century Vijayanagar empire.

The site had originally been scrub-covered sand. Captain Nair loved telling of how he 'brought in 80,000 tonnes of Goa's evocative red soil' to enable the planting of hundreds of thousands of shrubs, bushes and trees, including his favourite plumeria. An orchidarium would flaunt 7000–8000 exotic beauties as well as erotic anthuriums. Birds flitted and flashed, chirped, chirruped, even chortled.

Here's how the Leela Goa became a sky-clad aviary. During its Four

Seasons makeover, Captain Nair found migratory birds struggling to survive in and around the waterbodies. That prompted him to create islands in the lagoons where they could nest and roost. Fish were bred and fruit-producing trees consciously planted so that the birds could be fed as lavishly as the guests.

Rajeev Kumar Mangalad, son of an old Kannur acquaintance, had joined Captain Nair at the start of his hotel project in 1984. He was handling the engineering part of the Goa landscaping in 1987 when the chief horticulturist left and 'Captain asked me to take over. He knew I shared his passion'. For thirty-seven years, Mangalad helped create the signature sylvan spectacle of all Leela properties, walking with Captain and Mrs Leela Nair as they showered their tender loving care on every leaf and bloom.

While the Goa Eden was being created, Captain Nair would camp in a mock-up room from Monday to Friday, surveying and enhancing every inch of those 75 acres. He would go every day to the soul-stirring spot where the river merged with the sea. Woe betide the team if the entire stretch of the beach, including what wasn't his property, hadn't been scrupulously cleaned.

As much as this metamorphosis, the promoter of south Goa found deep satisfaction in something quite unrelated. *Leela, My Life*, the English translation of Captain Nair's Malayalam autobiography, would quote him saying:

> The hotel was built after those displaced from that area had been provided with new residences. We were able to provide employment for some of them. I understand that my picture hangs on the walls of many of their houses. I have the prayers of these people protecting me. My personal philosophy is that my projects should move forward without a single tear shed by anyone. As we rejoice, others should also be given an opportunity to do the same.

~

nnavil Elementary School which Captain Nair attended as a boy

Chirakkal Valiya Raja of the Kolathiri dynasty

Captain Nair with his mother, Madhavi Amma, and son Dinesh

As a wireless officer at Abbottabad, Pakistan

Group image of Captain Nair with Field Marshall K.M. Cariappa and other officers in Pune

Rajmata Vijayaraje Scindia of Gwalior at the opening of the Leela Fibre Foam factory at Baliapattam, Kannur

Captain Nair with Princess Usha Raje Scindia of Gwalior, Laura Eihleen and Robert Eihleen, Chairman of Schlitz Beer, at a reception in New York

With Prime Minister Jawaharlal Nehru and others to discuss the levy of 1 paisa tax on textile yardage

aptain Nair with an Indian trade delegation in Germany

Captain Nair at the opening of Leela Scottish Lace Limited in 1964. Seated from left are Lawrence Mitchell, MD of Johnson Shields, C.H. Bhabha, Vice Chairman of the Central Bank of India, Leela N and V.P. Menon, Indian politician and author of The Integration of the Indian States

Garments made by Leela Lace Limited for export

Rajesh Khanna, dubbed the 'First Superstar' of Indian cinema, wears a shirt made by Leela Lace Limited at his birthday party

Captain and Mrs Leela Nair with sons Vivek and Dinesh in the gardens of their Mumbai bungalow, Leela Baug

Captain Nair with Swami Chinmayananda Saraswati

Captain Nair welcomes His Holiness the 14th Dalai Lama to the Leela Mumbai

Muchilot Bhagavathi temple, Chirakkal, Kannur, restored by Captain Nair

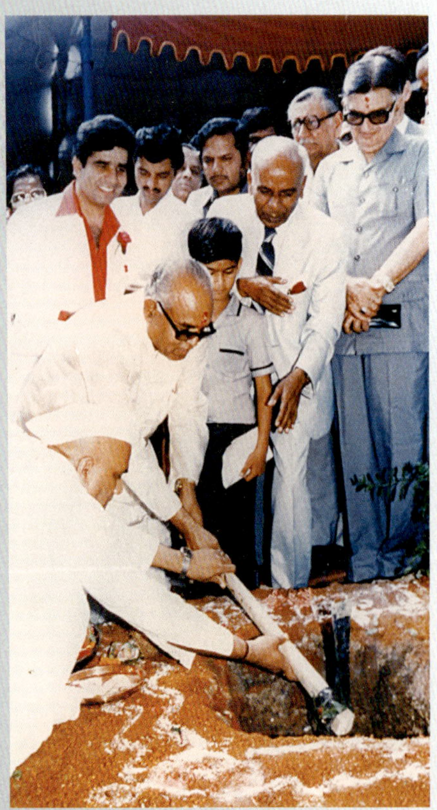

Vasantdada Patil, Chief Minister of Maharashtra, at the ground-breaking ceremony of the first hotel, Leela Penta, Mumbai, in 1983

Anna Malhotra, first woman IAS officer, does the hon at the opening of the Leela Penta in 1987

Captain Nair and his wife Leela in the gardens of the Leela Penta hotel in Mumbai

ptain Nair, Vivek Nair and staff during the 10th anniversary celebrations of the Leela Group in 1997

Lamp-lighting ceremony at the ening of the Leela alace New Delhi. Seen from left to ght: Madhu Nair, vek Nair, Deepak ekh, Praful Patel, Sheila Dikshit, odh Kant Sahay, Captain Nair, rappa Moily and alman Khurshid.

Deepak Parekh, Chairman of HDFC, ceremonially inaugurates the Leela Pala Bangalore, in 2001

Captain Nair with his wife Leela in their Mumbai bungalow

Captain Nair with his key management team at th Leela Mumbai standing-lotus pond. Seen from left right: Rajiv Kaul, Vivek Nair and Dinesh Nair

Captain Nair with his Rolls Royce Silver Ghost

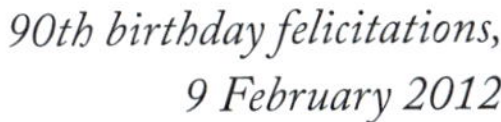

90th birthday felicitations, 9 February 2012

Walking in the gardens of the Leela Mumbai

Captain and Mrs Leela Nair with their family. Standing from left to right: Aishwarya, Aushim, Lakshmi, Amruda, Vivek, Dinesh, Samyukta and Madhu

The Leela Palace Udaipur photographed by Hardev Singh

Grand porte cochere of the Leela Palace Bangalore photographed by Atul Pratap Chauhan

Amrut Mahal, private dining room at the Leela Palace Udaipur

The grand dome with 24 carat gold leaf in the lobby of the Leela Mumbai

The Lobby Lounge at the Leela Palace New Delhi

Spa tent with a pool at the Leela Palace Udaipu

Captain Nair and his wife Leela with US President Bill Clinton at the Leela Goa

The Nair family welcoming British Prime Minister Margaret Thatcher a the Leela Mumbai

Captain Nair greeting US President Barack Obama and First Lady Michelle bama at a formal reception in their honour in Delhi

With Balasaheb Thackeray, Founder President of the Shiv Sena, and Farooq Abdullah, Former Chief Minister of Jammu and Kashmir

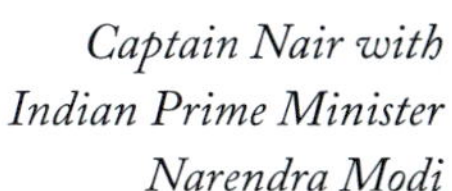

Captain Nair with Indian Prime Minister Narendra Modi

With close friend Mohanlal, prominent actor of Malayalam cinema and winner of five National Awards

With Vijay Amritraj, tennis champion and UN Messenger of Peace

His Excellency Yukio Hatoyama, Prime Minister of Japan being welcomed to the Leela Mumbai

President Pratibha Patil honouring Captain Nair with the Padma Bhushan, India's third-highest civilian award, in 2010, for his contribution to the hospitality industry

Kenji Manabe, anese Environment Minister, elects Captain Nair to the lobal 500 Laureate Roll of Honour of the United Nations Environment rogramme (UNEP) in 1999

Captain Nair receiving the 'Hotelier of the Century' award from Dr Ghassan Aidi, President of the International Hotel and Restaurant Association, in 2010

Print advertisement from a successful campaign titled 'Friends at The Leela'

Print advertisement for the launch of the Leela Palace Bangalore
Writer: Mohammed Khan
Art Director: Bhupal Ramnathkar

Print advertisement for Fiorella, the Italian restaurant at the Leela Mumbai
Writer: Freddy Birdy
Art Director: Bhupal Ramnathkar

Captain Nair knew that Goa could be as desirable as Bali or Hawaii. He was determined to re-chart its 'charter' destiny. Luxury had been his agenda right from the time he made his final and flashiest career shift. He also conceded that he would need to link up with a chain which would bring in the high-end traveller. As we saw, the Leela Goa partnered with Four Seasons, becoming the first beneficiary of Vivek's successful persuasion of the government to allow foreign chains to operate hotels. Ironically, as we also saw, while his success may have helped the entire hotel industry, the Nairs' own joint venture crashed before it even took off.

After parting ways with Four Seasons, Leela Hotels had reverted to partnering with Kempinski. But Captain Nair knew he still needed a specialized magnet to attract the big-spending sun-worshippers.

This time, he turned to Dubai-based General Hotel Management (GHM).

'Veni, Vidi, Vici': To evoke Julius Caesar's famous 47 BC victory in the Battle of Zela, GHM came, saw and were conquered by the Leela Goa. The Gulf company offered an attractive deal: pay us only on the additional business we bring. That turned out to be just 15–20 per cent more guests than what the hotel had attracted on its own.

Moreover, while the new custom was undoubtedly crème, it wasn't the crème de la crème that the Captain had sought right from the start. Since the majority of the guests were driven by the Leela brand, not GHM, it was easy to let the new partner go. But unlike the earlier fiasco, they parted as friends.

However, just as daughter-in-law Madhu's invaluable learnings sprang from the abortive Four Seasons venture, Leela Jack Horner pulled out a plum after sticking out its thumb at GHM. Even after Captain Nair decided finally to go it alone, GHM helped HLVL create The Club, a resort within a resort. It brought in a fantastic designer who conjured up sixteen breath-stopper units. It was a decade ahead of today's boutique hotels.

Then a new wave swept over Goa's beaches, carrying more custom from the northern plains. By 2006, domestic low-cost carriers filled the skies, improving connectivity with Delhi and upper India. There was no beguiling sea there; the long vacation was in summer. Goa offered a new getaway quite different from hill stations such as Shimla, which had been ruined by cavalier over-construction and overrun by raucous holidaymakers.

There was another reason for the Leela Goa getting a large share of the new influx. Delhiites, long familiar with the Taj and Oberoi brands, had begun to sit up and look at the challenger. How come? Around the same time, 2007 to be precise, HLVL had started managing the larger-than-life property of the Ambience Group in Gurgaon, showing north Indians its mojo as a hospitality czar.

The Goa high season had traditionally been only the five months of the European winter; its tourism dependents had to extract their year's revenues from this limited engagement. Now May turned into a must-go, with all the *masti* that sun, sea, sand and free-spirited Goans offered like no other.

The windfall continued. Goa's new summer bonanza got extended by an unlikely accomplice: rain. For this, Captain Nair had his own state of Kerala to thank. The visionary bureaucrat Amitabh Kant had made 'God's Own Country' the verdant jewel of his 'Incredible India!' tourism campaign. By pitching Kerala's rain-soaked splendour, he had also converted the tourist-dry monsoon into a lush new holiday season. It was all about marketing. Goa followed suit.

In the past, hotel guests actually demanded part of their money back if premature showers ruined their summer holiday. But suddenly, no sweat. SWOT turned around the months that beachside hoteliers had traditionally spent swatting flies. Turning weakness into strength, advertising's Goan whizkids made 'Goa in the rains' the most romantic time to visit.

It wasn't only in Kerala and Goa that the sun had found an unlikely rival. Rain had come to the rescue of hoteliers much earlier, and via a less salubrious route. The Beirut war of the late 1970s had bombed out the traditional playground of the Gulf Arabs. They turned to as-close-at-hand Bombay, and never more excitedly than during its lashing monsoon. The desert people couldn't get enough of the sheets pouring down. They flocked to Marine Drive to marvel at the 60 foot waves roaring, rising and crashing on the promenade's parapet.

Advantageously located at its Nariman Point end, the Oberoi Towers made hay while the rain poured. This serendipitous new tourist season actually saved the Oberoi Group's skin. Rai Bahadur Mohan Singh had bid an astronomical price for this prime plot. Additional caissons had to be embedded in the foundations to prevent the sea from reclaiming what had always been its own. Doubly reinforced glass was needed to withstand the monsoon's 120 kmph winds tearing at what Rai Bahadur wanted to be the tallest building of Nariman Point's Legoland.

All these had created huge cost overruns, depleting the World War II fortune he had made from Calcutta's Grand Hotel, and threatening to take the whole company down with it. Then, thanks to the Beirut war and the Bombay monsoon, this white elephant turned into a cash cow.

~

To meet the double-dose demand, the Leela Kempinski Goa reconfigured the Four Seasons-GHM-ordained suites to get back a larger number of rooms. It became the market leader for all seasons. At 30 per cent higher than the competition, it had always been a rate leader. Across the luxury sector, there is a direct correlation between ARR and demand – revved up by that amorphous but vital AQ factor: the aspiration quotient.

35

The Dowager and the Challenger

As the saying goes, 'You can lead a horse to water, but you cannot make it drink.' Captain Nair had bucked the trend like a bronco and built his sylvan getaway in south Goa. Now he had to make tourists drink from this beauteous pool. How was he to prise them away from north Goa, which – thanks largely to the historic glamour of the Taj Group – was considered the only place to be?

That's where the 'silent persuaders' came in. Mohammed Khan of the advertising agency Enterprise would become friend, son, sounding board (and even the sound itself) in the years that they worked together. He proudly said, 'Captain Nair always introduced me as "This is the man who put Leela on the map". And only then mention my name.'

Selling the Leela Goa became the agency's biggest challenge. The only way to meet it was to stand accepted wisdom on its head. Khan recalled, 'It was a very cheeky, almost preposterous idea for a Johnny-come-lately to take on the Taj. I told the Captain, "You haven't yet built any great reputation, so we have to reposition the competition." "How?" he demanded. I said, "By putting it into people's heads that staying at the Taj Aguada isn't any big deal." Captain Nair was nothing if not a risk-taker. He had the balls. "Go for it!" he had roared in glee.'

Khan shared their two-pronged strategy. 'One, price it above the Taj because for many in this country price equals quality. [Outpricing was Captain Nair's chosen path anyway.] We put the Leela at the top of the Goa pyramid; the product already lived up to that position. Two, don't sell just the Leela, sell south Goa, making that the better destination than the conventional north.'

It wasn't an empty boast. The beaches of the south were unspoilt and out of this world. Importantly, they had the logistical advantage. Till the first Russian-designed bridge on the Mandovi was built in 1971, you had to get to the north from Dabolim airport by making the circuitous, eating-into-precious-holiday-time journey by car and ferry. The southern beaches could be approached directly by road. Leela co-opted the two smaller hotels of the area, the Cidade de Goa and the Hyatt, who put their bit into the budget to reset Goa tourism's compass points.

Khan added impishly, 'Then the most unbelievable thing happened. However great your ammunition, to win advertising wars the gods have to be on your side. They were. That Mandovi bridge collapsed in 1986. Which meant the north Goa guests were back to the cumbersome ferry. We exploited this unabashedly, with an ad showing tourists sitting sullenly atop their bags waiting at the jetty.' Another bridge would be built, but not till 1998, seven years after the Leela Kempinski Goa opened.

Khan found Captain Nair a great client. 'I can't think of any other in that newbie position who would have taken on the formidable Taj. He worked like a gangbuster to get the Goa hotel going. On my initial trip, I expected the usual senior executive to take me around. But he was there waiting himself. We had walked together some 30 yards, when he stopped short, called out to one of his guys close by and said, "There was a pot with such-and-such plant here. Who moved it? Who took it away? Get it back." In a property of 75 acres, the chairman knew that one small pot was missing.'

The boss's passion was so infectious that Khan found himself getting involved with much more than advertising campaigns. 'He was always pushing you, prodding you for ideas. One morning as we were having breakfast at that evocative riverside coffee shop, an idea struck me. When my wife and I had stayed at the Taj Lake Palace, we loved the royal barge that took us to the hotel. So I told Captain Nair, "You have this river, why don't you get a fancy boat too? Your guests can take joyrides, maybe have lunch on it."

'As it happened, there was a boat moored on the other side of the Sal which had probably triggered my memory of Udaipur. Captain Nair straightaway summoned the GM and said, "See that boat? Buy it." Someone else would have mulled over it, but he grabbed an idea and ran with it. You know what? The next morning, he asked the manager, "What about the boat?" And the man replied, "We've bought it, Sir." It was operational in a month.'

That became one of the many 'Wow' experiences of the Leela Goa. At sunset you could take a cruise on it and experience the sensuousness of the limpid Sal river slipping into the tumultuous embrace of the Arabian Sea. Captain Nair would informally refer to the stretch of the Mobor beach that led up to this magical spot as 'Aparanta', meaning 'western border'.

Formally, he gave that name to the hotel's ballroom. Aparanta was an actual geographical region of ancient India, corresponding to the northern part of the Konkan region on India's west coast.

36

Return of the Native

Captain Nair was a proud Kerala boy, but he had burnt his fingers thrice trying to do business there, and worse, had disappointed his patron Uncle VP. At one point, he even said in exasperation, 'I think creating disputes is the most thriving industry in my home state.' Still, Conrad Hilton's 'Location, location, location' remains the failsafe mantra of hoteliers the world over. And you would be hard put to find a site as alluring as the three crescent-shaped, pristine, white beaches that go to make Kovalam. The name itself sounds like the sea murmuring endearments to the shore. So, taking a deep breath, Captain Nair plunged into a hotel venture already neck-deep in controversy.

In 1967, Karan Singh, part of Kashmiri royalty, had been appointed India's youngest minister for tourism. He had cast his eye on the beach property owned by a princely clan at the other end of India, the heirs to Travancore's Ivory Throne. It included the granite Halcyon Castle built in 1930 by the regent Sethu Parvathi Lakshmi Bayi, and which her eldest son, Raja Sree Chithira Thirunal Bala Rama Varma appropriated as his summer retreat. The entire Kovalam property was, by agreement, transferred to the state government in 1964, a move which embroiled this stunning mansion in Byzantine-grade intrigue.

That was during India's socialist era when Prime Minister Nehru had elevated the public sector to the commanding heights of the economy. A few years later, the Kovalam beach property was sold to the India Tourism Development Corporation (ITDC), whose portfolio included transport units and duty-free shops as well as hotels at the best destinations.

Naturally, the Kovalam Beach Resort became the jewel in its crown. The hotel was designed like an Aztec temple by the globally feted architect Charles Correa, with the lobby on the topmost tier. Its other claim to fame was that Vikram Sarabhai, architect of India's space programme, suddenly died here in 1971 at age fifty-two.

However, like all those once-grand ITDC hotels across India, it fell to corruption, cockroaches and the fact that it catered more to political masters than paying guests. This public sector behemoth had run the Kovalam resort for twenty-five years, and then run it into the ground. The precipitous decline can be gauged from the fact that it sank to a loss of Rs 172.32 lakh in 1999–2000 from a profit of Rs 79.93 lakh just a year earlier.

By then, Dr Manmohan Singh's economic liberalization policies had ended the public sector's self-indulgences. The ITDC was finally carved up into one-property companies, and each was put up for auction.

In 2002, the 195-room hotel on this 64 acre palm-fringed paradise went for Rs 44 crore to the Kerala-born Mohamed Ali, owner of the Oman-based Galfar Group. He renovated it extensively, including a Rs 100 crore refurbishment of Halcyon Castle, and handed over operations to the Le Meridien Group.

Soon enough, a controversy which had been bubbling from the start boiled over. V.S. Achuthanandan's CPI(M) supported the Congress at the Centre, but piquantly, he led the opposition in Congress-ruled Kerala. The Marxist leader claimed that Halcyon Castle had not been part of the original maharaja–state government deal, let alone its subsequent transfer to ITDC.

The district's chief land revenue officer backed this, saying it was in 'adverse possession', meaning the title was not clearly settled. The heritage activists joined the clamour, pointing out that in any event, a 1930s structure could not be sold.

A red rag to the Marxist's bull was the new owner's proximity to members of the Congress chief minister A.K. Antony's cabinet. Achuthanandan's cadres would shout slogans and stage lie-downs, obstructing movement into and out of the hotel. This was hardly the serene sun, sea and sand 'experience' for which guests had paid top dollar.

As it happened, Vivek Nair's youngest child, Aushim, was a classmate and football buddy of the son of Habil Khorakiwala who, apart from owning the pharma major Wockhardt, had partnered with Mohamed Ali. Mrs Khorakiwala confided in Mrs Lakshmi Nair that 'our investments in Kovalam are causing my husband sleepless nights' and 'can your husband step in?' Vivek met Mohamed Ali, who reiterated, 'Only you can handle this ordeal – and that grumpy old man.' Achuthanandan was then seventy-nine.

This arc of heaven in 'God's Own Country' was worth the headache. Besides, not only was Captain Nair's umbilical cord tied to Kerala, he had emotional links with Kovalam itself. He had been there several times with the late Lt Col P.R. Godavarma Raja, Kerala royal and eminent tourism (and sports) promoter. He had sunk his toes in its white sands and crested its foaming waves.

More to the prevalent point, he had enough friends and admirers in high places to find a way out of the controversies. He bought it over, lock, stock and nuisance, in 2004. In 2005, the Leela Kovalam had a signature grand opening.

The original resort had been built well before the 200 metre constraints of the CRZ; in fact, it was within 10 metres of the HTL. Its crowning glory was a forty-two-room clifftop annexe, The Club. Staying there was like being on a cruise liner, and it rewarded the guest with a surreal view. As you stood on the balcony watching the roiling ocean, a fleck of surf would soar from a crashing wave and plonk into your luxurious coffee cup.

Captain Nair himself had waxed poetic about that annexe. 'Those cliffside rooms offer something rare. You stay up at night to watch the ever-awake waves lashing the shore, or the moonlight playing on the surface, turning it into a silver screen. In Kovalam, one can see the sea in its various forms, gentle and calm or roaring and fearsome.'

Leela's name remained exclusively on this other-worldly beach resort for eleven years, but ownership had to be sacrificed on the altar of a fiasco called HUDCO, the Housing and Urban Development Corporation. In 2011, HLVL regretfully sold this jewel for Rs 500 crore to another Keralite, Dr Ravi Pillai, the NRI tycoon who was reportedly the largest employer of Indians in the Gulf.

The Leela Group had bought the Kovalam property off Mohamed Ali for Rs 118 crore, and spent another Rs 200 crore on luxe-ing it up to their standards. They didn't lose it completely, signing a management contract for Rs 6 crore a year. Renamed the Raviz Leela, they ran it right till crushing debt forced them in 2019 to part with all their hotel holdings, bar the flagship Leela Mumbai.

~

Captain Nair had departed five years before the final sale of the Leela hotels and brand to the Canada-based private equity firm Brookfield Asset Management. Surprisingly, or perhaps not, it was he who had taken the original initiative of transferring the maharaja of Travancore's property to the Kerala Tourism Development Corporation (KTDC). Here's a condensed version of that process in Captain Nair's Malayalam memoir:

> Making a case to the state's tourism minister, V.R. Krishnan Iyer, I had said: 'Kerala is the equivalent of Hawaii for tourism, and can be developed on those lines. We have the natural and manpower resources. We can showcase the culture of our tribal communities. Their dances, music and art will all be of interest to tourists. This will also help soften the communal divide.'
>
> Iyer had listened carefully, but done little. He was replaced by T.K. Divakaran. Showing greater interest in my proposal, which

was already on the ministry's files, he had asked, 'But Captain Nair, where is the land?' I offered to buy the 75 acres of the maharaja's Kovalam estate, including the castle. The minister and I went over to meet him.

I could not help telling the maharaja that we had met decades ago when he was a seventeen-year-old attending a religious event conducted by the Chirakkal Raja. I had been introduced to him, his mother and the Diwan [prime minister] Sir C.P. Ramaswami Iyer. Pleased, the maharaja told Divakaran, 'If Captain Nair suggests this, we shall agree to transfer the Kovalam property to the state government.' KTDC, however, could not move this project forward in an economically feasible way. When a private entrepreneur offers to do what the government could not, it is only to be expected that objections and obstructions would be placed in his way. The experience was no different in this case.

The memoir continued to detail his disappointment.

One of the opposition planks was that the Kovalam palace should be protected as a national heritage. We were planning to do that in any case, but nobody wanted to listen. It was our aim to protect the entire property, be it beach or palace, yet make it global in quality. In fact, we would later transform a stretch overrun by scrub into a resort which matches world standards.

Captain Nair then recalled how insult was added to injury when the property did come into his hands.

I had to face an allegation that I had stolen two coconut trees from the property. In fact, these palms had been blown down by strong winds, and I had arranged to restore them. The report on my 'theft' was carried prominently in *Mathrubhoomi*. This had been cooked up to defame me, a man who had planted hundreds of thousands of trees

> in Goa, Bangalore, Udaipur and Sahar to green the environment! The readers of the newspaper looked upon the report as a laughable story. Even my enemies know that Krishnan Nair's circumstances do not exactly compel him to steal two coconut palms!

Captain Nair concluded this chapter on a less miffed, more optimistic and characteristically proud Indian note:

> Large business groups and corporates have already accepted India as an important centre. There will also be a large-scale influx of leisure tourists. There is such natural beauty and areas like Silent Valley are unequalled anywhere else. We can build fancy tower blocks, but we cannot match nature's bounty of seas, lakes, rivers, forests, and magnificent mountain ranges. This wealth is an invaluable and eternal asset. Tourists will come here to get away from surging crowds and clouds of pollution. We should ensure that they are not disappointed. Good food, good relaxation and an environment in which body and mind find peace are what everybody yearns for.

37

The Hurdle Called HUDCO

The Captain always had several irons in the fire. His deal with Four Seasons was for the same number of hotels at Mumbai, Goa, Bangalore and Delhi. The garment exports business was a money-spinner, as we have seen, so the financials were a sound enough foundation on which to build this dream quartet. But along came a spoiler that blotted the balance sheet.

The Housing and Urban Development Corporation Limited (HUDCO) was set up in 1970 as a wholly owned Government of India company under the administrative control of the Ministry of Housing and Urban Affairs. The 1960s had shown the first signs of a serious shortage of affordable housing. The new entity had been formed to play a role in financing residential projects as well as in the larger issue of urban infrastructure development. As part of its business, it very occasionally auctioned public land for hotels and state guest houses in New Delhi.

At one such auction held in 1994, Pavan Sachdeva's MS Shoes East Limited, hoping to enter the hospitality trade, had won the bid for a 4 acre plot. The location was near the swanky Friends Colony, worth every paise of the over Rs 117 crore which MS Shoes paid to HUDCO.

However, the bidder company got into legal troubles over the rights issue it had floated for this planned diversification.

The Central Bureau of Investigation (CBI) began its enquiries in 1995, and in 1997, Sachdeva was charged with violating the Companies Act and the Prevention of Corruption Act. The CBI net also dragged in senior officials of the Securities and Exchange Board of India (SEBI) as well as SBI Capital Markets Limited (a subsidiary of the State Bank of India) for allegedly manipulating share prices. The public issue was devolved. All these murky developments prompted HUDCO to cancel the bid. Left bereft of both the money it had paid and the auctioned land, MS Shoes filed a suit against the housing corporation.

HUDCO did not wait for what would certainly be a much delayed legal outcome. It reauctioned the plot. HLVL made a successful bid and paid the due Rs 200 crore. Despite being a crippling amount, its financial advisers said it was worth it. The contract was a convoluted one in which the hotel would have to be built in three years, but HUDCO would obtain all the approvals since it was a government body. For that same reason, there were major delays. HUDCO decided to cancel the contract on flimsy grounds. HLVL filed a case and won. During the ten years that the litigation dragged on, the Rs 200 crore remained inaccessible, and, like MS Shoes, HLVL did not get possession of the land.

This had put great pressure on the balance sheet since the fund-guzzling Bangalore hotel was still under construction. Plus, HLVL had already spent another Rs 100 crore on the Goa hotel's renovations, which hadn't resulted in the expected return on investment. It gave up the idea of building on the Friends Colony plot, which, by the way, remained in limbo till 2021.

Leela Hotels would have to wait till 2018 to obtain its long-desired foothold in New Delhi – again, an auctioned 4 acres in the Diplomatic Enclave of Chanakyapuri. Despite its past experience with HUDCO, Dinesh Nair persuaded the rest of the board to bid aggressively because another such opportunity would not arise in the foreseeable future. They secured the plot for a whopping Rs 611 crore in a nail-biting two-track process which we will describe along with the building of that hotel.

There was a sense of déjà vu about this belligerent bidding. Hadn't Conrad Hilton said: 'Never risk what you can't afford to lose'? Hadn't Rai Bahadur Mohan Singh Oberoi offered Rs 100 per sq. metre more than the next bid for the Nariman Point plot, telling his son Biki, 'Never let money come in the way of getting something you badly want'? That outrageous offer had prompted Sir Dorab Tata to exclaim, 'Rai Bahadur, have you gone mad?'

38

The Palace on the Lake

You can't be a major hotelier and not have a presence in Udaipur. Moreover, you can't be in maharana-land without a royal resort. But there already existed here the Taj Group's 'Lake Palace', and the 'Fake Palace', which is what rivals had dubbed the Oberoi's architectural extravaganza till Udaivilas began sweeping the top travel and leisure awards. The competition was enough to daunt the most undaunted of them all, namely Captain Krishnan Nair. Would he give in, give up and shift his Rajasthani dream elsewhere? Hadn't Maharana Uday Singh himself surrendered Chittor to Sher Shah Suri in 1544, and begun work on a less vulnerable new capital in 1559?

Udaipur's founder had been compelled to do so because his resources were exhausted from quelling the Mewar civil war. Captain Nair's finances too were overstretched – by his own vaulting ambitions and the drain called HUDCO. He would have to ward off his old adversaries, the CRZealots and other NGO armies which would rise to defend the fabled Pichola Lake – built by a Banjara gypsy in 1362, and reinforced by Maharana Uday Singh exactly two centuries later. He would also need to deal with neighbours protesting the demolition of their ancestral homes.

So what?

By now we know that Captain Nair was like the mythic King Arthur who, when confronted by Saxon hordes, had said, 'The thicker the hay, the easier it is to be mowed.' Or like Churchill, whose finest hour was snatched from the jaws of ignominious defeat. Or we could stretch the maharana comparison itself to cite Pratap Singh's indomitable warhorse, Chetak.

However, let us put aside the myths and get down to prosaic facts. Udaipur had been part of Captain Nair's dream quartet very early in his hotel game. No way would he have abandoned it. It was Vivek who found the way – and location. Serendipitously.

As a member of the exclusive Young Presidents Organization Forum Group since 1987, Vivek was in Udaipur in 1993 attending one of its two annual retreats. The high-powered group stayed at the Palace Hotel and hired the Taj's luxury boat, Gangaur, for the evening. During the cruise on Pichola Lake, Anand Mahindra had pointed to a garish pink structure on the shore, saying that he wanted to build a simple three-star hotel there as part of his time-share network. Then, changing his mind he sold the half-constructed property to Mumbai's real estate baron Niranjan Hiranandani around 1994.

What would be anointed the World's Best Hotel in 2019, in Vivek's words, 'looked little better than a slum redevelopment housing colony'. But it was a eureka moment. He could barely wait to return home and tell his father about his find.

Alas, finders don't automatically become keepers.

Vivek bought the lakeshore property – and fell into hot water. There hadn't been a squeak while the Mahindras and Hiranandanis were building their modest hotel, but as soon as the Nairs stepped into the picture, they were met with a flurry of PILs filed by two NGOs. Their charge that the Leela hotel in Udaipur would pollute the lake was ironic: in the midst of this litigation, Captain Nair was a guest of the maharana, invited to receive the Uday Singh Award for his stellar efforts at enhancing the environment. Udaipur was becoming Goa redux.

The cases dragged on for thirteen years. The NGOs lost in the civil court and appealed against the order in the division bench of the Ajmer High Court, and lost again.

Through all this, the doughty warrior refused to budge. It was just like in Bangalore, where he dug in his heels despite everyone begging him to scale down his gargantuan hotel when the HUDCO fiasco plunged the company into debt.

In Udaipur, instead of letting go, he more than doubled his stake, extending the original 2.5 acres to 6. HLVL was a listed company, and mopped up additional funds with a rights issue. However, the delay of fourteen years and the problems with the New Delhi hotel, also in the pipeline, pushed up the interest costs – and pressed hard on the company's financial jugular.

The case finally reached the Supreme Court – and was dismissed in minutes. The law was on their side; so was the brilliant lawyer, Arun Jaitley. However, it was only then that they could start construction.

Or try to. The CRZ equivalent for lakeshores is 100 metres, but the Pichola's historic status extended this to 150. The Taj could be the 'palace *in* the lake' because it had been converted from a royal indulgence built on one of the lake's seven islands. The Oberoi's spectacular Udaivilas, which came much later, was forced to stay outside the CRZ limit, and was thus the 'palace *away from* the lake'. Leela could be the 'palace *on* the lake', because the Nairs slipped through the loophole that existing structures were exempt from the CRZ stricture.

The original shabby plot on the Pichola's banks which they had bought from the Hiranandanis housed a tumbledown haveli, a portion of which actually abutted into the water. The Nairs built the terrace restaurant, Sheesh Mahal, atop its sunken column.

The next problem came with the trucks carrying construction material having to negotiate narrow lanes with old bastis and bustling bazars, that too only at permitted hours. The restive locals had to be pacified with the promise that the hotel wouldn't harm their generational way of life; instead, it would increase livelihood thanks to guests in search of local colour and crafts.

Then came the final, totally unexpected blow. The heritage lake clearly couldn't be used as a transportation thoroughfare for building materials. However, it was to be the main access and grand entrance for the hotel's guests. But when the Leela Palace Udaipur was ready to open, fate threw down a mocking card – the Pichola Lake had dried up. It was like the punishment of Tantalus in Greek legend, the succulent bunch of grapes cruelly just out of reach.

High-voltage drama followed. So now we must cite Hannibal, the historical character, not Hollywood's cannibal Mr Lecter. Warned that he could never cross the Alps in his 218 BC battle against Rome, the Carthaginian general had quotably declared, 'We'll find a way or make it.' Captain Nair had been echoing Hannibal for much of his multiple careers. The hotelier hadn't come this far to be denied what development-wallas call 'last-mile connectivity'. In this case, it was 1.5 acres.

That's how much he required to build a motorable road to his latest palace. And he had to acquire it stealthily. It was a seller's market – the buyer was desperate, plus he presumably had a fat purse. So the Nairs resorted to the old Indian ploy of hiding behind a third, oft-times fictitious party. It was much like the young Mohan Singh mopping up the shares of the fabled subcontinental chain, Associated Hotels of India, by proxy and then presenting the all-Brit board with a fait accompli in 1923.

Three houses had stood in the way of access to the almost complete Leela Palace Udaipur, and the negotiations got progressively tougher. It was a replay of the kind when the last Goan landlady of Candolim had held out against the inducements of the Taj when it wanted to extend its Fort Aguada hotel. Captain Nair finally got his road. So did all of Udaipur. Anyone could use it.

The exquisite Taj Lake Palace was 100 years of living history. Biki Oberoi's Udaivilas stunned with its 7 acre scale. How was the newbie to compete in design? Enter the American architect Bill Bensley. His eponymous atelier had 200 hospitality projects in fifty countries, and his creations had run away with the Best Hotel in the World Award three years in a row.

Bensley had worked on the landscaping of Udaivilas, and chafed for more. The Nairs offered him the whole enchilada, caviar-stuffed, of course. In the tradition of all Leela hotels, inspired by the palaces of their location, the brief here was to 'invoke royal Mewar'.

Bensley was a master of drama, and a drama queen himself. The hospitality grapevine had buzzed with his 'creative tensions' with Biki, who had masterful (and very firm) ideas of his own. Captain Nair was no pushover either. There were histrionics mainly on two points. The Leela boss wanted more colour (we will come later to his rainbow wardrobe). And he wanted more softscaping (he was the consummate gardener).

Along with softscaping and hardscaping, the third element of landscaping is nightscaping. The Captain had sussed out its importance. He told Bill, 'The best view of the Leela is from the Taj Lake Palace, most so at night. Show it off.' The architect brought in a lighting whiz from Bangkok, who managed to 'drape the hotel in jewels'. Guests of the dowager saw it from their windows and came over for coffee to check it out. And decided to check in on their next visit to Udaipur. As soon as possible.

Hardev Singh, the Leela's go-to lensman, delivered what he had promised Captain Nair: 'One photograph that will sell your hotel.' He spent several evenings over his night shot, getting the Bangkok lighting expert to engineer the correct subtlety of sparkle.

He waited for Cartier-Bresson's 'decisive moment' when the sky deepened to velvet and the Aravalli range faded into a phantom silhouette in the background. He tried out different angles from the lake, from a boat and from the Jag Mandir – summer palace of the maharanas and now the coveted and colossally expensive venue of destination weddings.

Hardev Singh's stunner was worth a million dollars – and almost as many guests. It aroused a deep emotion called 'I want to be there'.

The Leela Palace Udaipur had rooms far larger than those of its two storied rivals, and the most sensual of bathrooms. Right-loaded corridors ensured that every guest had an equally great view of the lake. None of these indulgences made economical use of space, but who cared. The idea was to optimize luxury to the nth degree and offer a sensuous s experience that bordered on the sinful. Unapologetically so.

Complementing Bensley's architecture, the equally celebrated Canadian Jeffrey Wilkes was hired for the interiors. Asked in an interview with the Design Society how he'd describe his design style, he had replied, 'Eclectic . . . I am a big fan of mid-century modern but also appreciate the intricacy of a carved Dutch colonial cabinet from Sri Lanka. I love to mix styles, love using colour and pattern. Antiques in a contemporary setting and vice versa make for an interesting layered experience.' You can see exactly why he was Captain Nair's 'kinda guy'.

More important perhaps was the contribution of Madhu Nair. Udaipur would be both her greatest challenge and her greatest triumph. Together with Wilkes, she breathed life into what was Captain Nair's mantra when he embarked on his hotel journey: Indian traditions set in world-class systems.

Everything was uncompromisingly authentic. All Rajasthani royal abodes had *chhatri*s and *chabutra*s, a raised-dome-topped cenotaph and a space to feed pigeons, respectively. But each Rajput fiefdom had its own distinctive variations. It was the same with turbans. The team spent long nights getting the Mewar shape right.

Rajasthan has among the world's richest oeuvre of handicrafts and artisanal excellence. Madhu showcased them all – with an OMG twist. She commissioned a stunning Tree of Life in Udaipur's signature glass-mosaic *thikri* work. The ubiquitous Rajasthani puppets appeared not in conventional cloth, but as works of art. What was traditionally in metal or papier mâché she got made in glass or leather. Brass stopped being brassy under her subtle touch.

The brass tacks of service were her domain too. Once again, she polished these to the Four Seasons standards she had learned and augmented. So, on their first day, guests went around this jewel box of a hotel, gasping at and photographing its treasures. On the second, they sank into its beauty. But on the third and last day, the feedback cards invariably appreciated the experience, the warm attention that they received. As every hotelier knows, the greatest wow is not the solid silver of the antique tureens, it's the gossamer of memories.

~

Only the grit of Captain Nair could have stayed the turbulent course. It wasn't only long-drawn-out lawsuits, or finances and lakes drying up with equal viciousness. The positioning in a formidable field was equally daunting. But the stakes were high not just for a daring hotel, but at the brand level itself. Both flourished.

Captain Nair had won over the maharana of Udaipur with his charm as much as his determination. A great chemistry developed between the two, which extended to his suave son, Vivek. The chief minister of Rajasthan was Vasundhara Raje, whose parents, the Scindia royals of Gwalior, were old friends via Uncle VP. Her mother, Rajmata Vijayaraje Scindia, along with her other daughter Usha, had accompanied Captain Nair to the US for the Cassava project. After all the serial hurdles, the Nairs finally had with them the two people who mattered most in Udaipur.

~

Maharana Arvind Singh Mewar performed the inaugural puja on 12 April 2009. The grand opening a month later was fit for royalty. In the dazzling line-up were two ersatz maharajas: a beaming Bill Bensley and Jeffrey Wilkes rigged out in the brocade sherwanis that Captain Nair had got custom tailored for them. And why not? Hadn't they so spectacularly dressed up his latest palace hotel?

39

Landing on Another Planet

Udaipur vs Gurugram. Wealth vs money. Courtly vs corporate. Low-rise vs Legoland. Leisurely vs frenetic. Historical vs millennial. You get the drift? Hotel Leela Ventures Limited arrived in the Gotham of Gurugram three months after the opening at Udaipur. Just an hour's flight away, it could well have been 2009: A Space Odyssey.

The project was different any which way you looked at it. The socio-cultural chasm apart, even the operating mode was another ball game. And a totally new one at that. For the first time, they weren't building their own hotel, they were managing someone else's, Raj Singh Gehlot's Ambience.

Considering the monumental construction-stage challenges the Nairs had faced every single time, it was a relief to be spared that hassle. The Gehlots were professional builders, and knew how to negotiate the speed-breakers. On the debit side, Captain Nair wasn't the 100 per cent boss. However, his know-how and, no less, his celebrated charm minimized the clash points.

Gehlot developed an admiration for the father – and affection for the son. Vivek Nair, as always, had wrapped up the management contract. The Leela Ambience Hotel and Residences Gurugram opened on 12

July 2009. Present at the launch were tourism minister Kumari Selja and Delhi chief minister Sheila Dikshit. In what was now a habit, it became a market leader straightaway.

The original plan for a hotel in New Delhi had been HUDCO-ed; the Nairs would not get to build one there till 2011. This Ambience deal gave them a footprint at least in the National Capital Region (NCR), and it was also an evolutionary leap. Moving beyond ultra-luxury resorts stretched HLVL's bandwidth twice over. One, winning a management contract was evidence of third-party belief in their domain expertise. Two, it provided brand synergy. Gurugram was a buzzing business hub. The corporate bosses who used Leela Bangalore weren't using the Mumbai hotel, and vice versa, but both chose Leela Gurugram.

It was a big-box project. The Gulliver-grade, mixed-use property included a mall with 2 kilometre corridors on each level plus ninety 1/2/3 BHK flats for long-stay guests. The view carried a lifelong guarantee. Adjacent was the protected Rajokri Greens, an urban forest on the state border: 'The tree is in Delhi and the fruit falls in Haryana.' Thus, it also satisfied the Conrad Hilton imperative – you could not find a more strategic location.

The original Ambience Hotel had an almost ready restaurant, but Gehlot agreed to nix it on the advice of his new partners. Leela brought in Spin Associates, Japan's avant garde design house, to create Spectrum – you walked in under a canopy of chandeliers, and seven live kitchen-sized counters added to the drama. It was a celebration of bling, which is what Gurugram is all about, as opposed to the understated old money of 'Deh-li'.

Still, this was a business hotel, so gravitas was needed. Since the hotel was already built, the Leela couldn't do it with architecture. Instead, it co-opted art and commissioned the impresario Rajeev Sethi, mastermind equally of the national cultural festival Apna Utsav, New Delhi, in 1986, and the riveting art corridor of Terminal 2, Mumbai's international airport, 2014. At Leela Ambience, he celebrated the new millennium with digital masterpieces.

A management contract is an owner–operator relationship which can easily go awry. It is a delicate balance, with each party legitimately entitled to ego assertion. The former says, 'This is my property so it has to be my way', but it is the operator who has to deliver results. Walking this tightrope with aplomb gave HLVL the confidence – and the credentials – to go in for other management contracts, and even technical services agreements where the owner agreed to build to their specs.

Examples of this are the 170-room Leela Hyderabad at Banjara Hills, Leela Ambience Convention Hotel in East Delhi, and Bangalore's 280-room Leela Bhartiya City and Leela Residences where they managed the clubhouse, public spaces and services. There is also the Leela Gandhinagar, a convention hotel attached to the 6000-seater Mahatma Gandhi Convention Centre. Together with the Mahatma Gandhi Museum, the eye-popping complex stretches atop a gargantuan railway station, the terminus for the prestigious bullet train. After all, Gandhinagar, Ahmedabad, is Mr Narendra Modi's pocket borough; it was here, not in New Delhi, that he hosted Japan's Abe Shinzo and Israel's Benjamin Netanyahu when they were prime ministers.

With Gurugram in the NCR secured, Captain Nair was ready to seize the capital itself. But Delhi had buried seven dynasties. Would a hotel empire also meet its nemesis here?

40

A Capital Idea Killed by Interest

'We are already a market leader in Gurugram, so why do we need to be in New Delhi? Especially since we went so out-of-pocket in Udaipur. Especially since we were almost sunk in Bangalore. We are now on an even keel, why rock the boat?' asked everyone who mattered at HLVL as well as at the promoter company, Leela Scottish Lace. Everyone except the man who mattered most.

Captain Nair scoffed, 'The National Capital Region is NOT the same as being in the capital itself. How can we say we are India's leading hotel company and not be in New Delhi?'

He was echoing Mohan Singh Oberoi's sentiment from half a century earlier. That pioneer always measured himself against J.R.D. Tata, so he simply had to have a hotel in Bombay, the city of the flagship Taj. Which is why he didn't care how much he spent as long as he got it. Once again, we see the déjà vu that flits through the luxe hospitality industry – worldwide.

All land worth its name in the city is owned by the Delhi Development Authority (DDA), and the only chance to lay hands on it is when a coveted chunk is auctioned. In 2008, the DDA decided to have one of these. The Commonwealth Games were to be held two years later, and there was a woeful shortage of hotel rooms. Up for grabs was a 3 acre plot, prime thrice over. It was in the Diplomatic Enclave, just outside the heritage Lutyens zone where you could not build at all – and it was freehold land.

The last DDA auction was about thirty years earlier, the impetus again being a major sporting event: the Asian Games of 1982. This had given rise to eight hotels, including the Taj Palace, the Hyatt Regency and the ITC Maurya. So, like the Presley number, it was 'now or never'. Captain Nair held on 'tight', he wanted it to 'be mine tonight'. He went for broke.

It was a two-track process – sealed bids followed by a live auction, the winner being whichever amount was higher. In the open auction, the faint-hearted kept dropping out till, at Rs 375 crore, only two players were left. Mystery heightened the nail-biting drama because it was held online and was therefore anonymous. The bidding war continued frenetically, and finally ground to a halt at Rs 610 crore. In the sealed bid, the Nairs had taken a deep breath and put in a staggering Rs 611 crore. They won the endgame.

The rival party turned out to be the Emaar Group, owned by the Emirati global entrepreneur Mohamed Alabbar. One of the twelve children of a traditional dhow captain, his empire would include such iconic properties as the Burj Khalifa and the Dubai Mall. It had a joint venture in India, and its CEO proposed a deal by which Emaar would buy over the plot, and HLVL would design and operate the hotel. It was tempting considering the company's precarious finances, but having fought so hard, the winner decided to take all.

With stamp duty, the land cost spiralled further to Rs 850 crore. Paying up was fraught because the auction condition was that the whole amount had to be deposited upfront within three months of the date of the award. This was a crushing departure from the usual method which allowed you to put down a percentage, and pay the rest over the years as lease.

Their old friend Deepak Parekh of HDFC came to the rescue. But – and it was a killer but – the interest on the loan totalled Rs 550 crore. The construction cost weighed in at nearly Rs 600 crore. The standard ratios between costs of land, construction and interest went cripplingly askew.

With such a location coming your way just once in a lifetime, it was a Big Boys game, and Captain Nair played it with a heart that matched his vision. It was the one-word mantra common to every top-of-the-league entrepreneur: passion.

But how was HLVL to shell out these colossal sums when two problems made it next to impossible? The first was Captain Nair's unbending demand, 'I want better than the best.' Two, Delhi's floor area ratio (FAR) of 1.5 (built-up area in proportion to plot size) was the lowest of all metros. In Mumbai, the equivalent floor space index had been raised from 2 to 3.5 thanks to the notorious builder–politician nexus which had replaced the underworld in calling the city's shots. It had also pumped up the hotel boom.

Problem No. 1 stemmed from Captain Nair wanting his hotel to be grander than any existing No. 1. The architect chosen was John Gerondelis of the Atlanta-based firm Smallwood, Reynolds, Stewart, Stewart (SRSS), reputed across the US and Asia for his high-end hospitality projects and convention centres. Since Delhi had none of the palaces on which earlier Leela hotels had been modelled, inspiration was to be taken from the sandstone majesty of Rashtrapati Bhavan.

While the tourism ministry's minimum standard for five-star rooms was 250 sq. ft, Captain Nair insisted on no less than 500 sq. ft. Which also meant fewer rooms from which to earn. The bathroom design, a barometer of luxury, had to be equally mind-blowing. All of them had to feature a range of showerheads releasing an optimal pressure of water and luxuriant bathtubs, even if barely any guest would use them in a predominantly business hotel. The thread count of the bedsheets had to be 300; the pillows had to pass the 'Goldilocks test'.

Every deluxe hotel tom-toms these features, right? HLVL president Rajiv Kaul riposted archly, 'There's 18 carat gold, and there's 24 carat gold. The Leela New Delhi was a generation ahead, forcing the competition to break down and rebuild to catch up.'

If it is difficult to verify this claim, what is on record is the smitten crown prince of Abu Dhabi telling Vivek Nair, 'Can't you transport this entire hotel to my emirate?' Unfortunately, neither had the services of Aladdin's genie or the Ramayan's Hanuman who had transported an entire mountain with the magical herb *sanjeevani*.

As for the statutory Problem No. 2, the hotel could never break even at that measly FAR of 1.5. So, in one more of his unrelenting efforts which would benefit the whole sector, Vivek managed to get it raised to 2.5. Remember his efforts towards getting operator status for foreign chains partnering with Indian groups, and getting the 500 metre CRZ restored to 50 metres for beach hotels in non-eco-sensitive sections of the coastline? During his second term as FHRAI president (2012–13), he would fight for industry and infrastructure status for the hospitality sector.

Here's how Vivek Nair pulled the Delhi ratio FAR-ther. During his first stint as FHRAI president way back in 2003–04, he had initiated a move in this direction when Delhi's master plan was being revised. Now, he appealed to Jaipal Reddy, union minister for urban development under Prime Minister Dr Manmohan Singh.

Pointing out that Delhi would need 7000 more rooms for the Commonwealth Games, and that this would create greater direct and indirect employment, he made a case for raising the 1.5 FAR to 2.5. for hotels, albeit outside the protected Lutyens zone.

The minister saw the point. The hotel industry team went through all the bureaucratic procedures – and hit a roadblock at the lieutenant governor's office. The luminary had nothing against Vivek Nair. Ironically, it was quite the opposite. In Vivek's words, 'He had known my father for thirty years, and acceding to the proposal would have seemed like a personal favour to facilitate the upcoming Leela Palace in New Delhi.'

The father, suffering from no such qualms, told the son to try another 'personal' connection. Sonia Gandhi had been holidaying at the Leela Goa with her children every year after Rajiv's assassination. Vivek would pay a courtesy call at 10 Janpath every time he was in Delhi, and each time Mrs Gandhi, the powerful Congress president, would graciously tell him to ask if he needed any help. Captain Nair told his son, 'Ask.

After all, it's for the good of the whole hotel industry.' Vivek duly left a note at her office, detailing the case and the problem.

He was driving back on the highway to the Gurugram hotel when Jaipal Reddy called, saying, 'Where are you? Come back to the ministry. I've just received a message from Madam asking me to clear the file. The DDA has been told to approve the increased FAR.' It had already been cleared by the board and was awaiting the lieutenant governor's okay.

The extra FAR came through in two months, enabling the Leela Palace New Delhi to build 259 rooms instead of only 180, which the old 1.5 would have permitted. This was a huge windfall for the whole hospitality sector. Each additional square foot yielded more profit. On the same amount of land, hotels could increase their room inventory, and in the process their asset value itself.

Alas, HLVL itself couldn't pop the champagne. The additional FAR turned out to be a Catch-22. Considering the huge amount they had paid for the land, it would be a formidable task finding the finances to build the extra rooms allowed by the increased FAR (and to the level of opulence demanded by the chairman).

The total cost of land, stamp duty and the premium which had to be paid for the extra FAR pushed the land-related cost plus interest to 45 per cent of the total project cost instead of the normal 15 per cent.

The company was making Rs 100 crore a year, but didn't have that kind of handy cash. The bottom line was haemorrhaging on account of the Leela Palace Udaipur which was still under construction and the renovations which deluxe hotels must keep at. As Biki Oberoi is quoted saying in his father's biography, 'It's like showbiz. You have to come up with a new act all the time.'[10]

The Nairs decided to resort to the flavour of the times: foreign currency convertible bonds (FCCBs). Mopping up the additional amount this way would be as easy as ordering room service. In 2008, the company was

---

[10] Bachi Karkaria, *Dare to Dream: A Life of Rai Bahadur Mohan Singh Oberoi* (Viking Penguin, 1992).

at the pinnacle – its shares were rocketing; it was among the industry's highest taxpayers.

Then came a bigger BUT. On 15 September, Lehman Brothers tanked, climaxing the subprime mortgage crisis and taking the worldwide money market with it. A later chapter will deal with the juddering details. For now, let us point to the much later COVID-19 pandemic. That underlined more virulently how the hospitality industry is among the fastest to get infected by global upheavals. The luxury sector's health depends on that of the world's economy.

Before disaster struck, the Nairs had reasonably calculated that if Delhi's historic Imperial Hotel could rake in an ARR of Rs 15,000 per night, their newer and grander one could easily command Rs 20,000. When the Leela Palace Delhi opened in 2011, the former had to settle for Rs 10,000; the latter could manage Rs 15,000 at best. Interest spiralled north, income plummeted south. More than serving guests it was servicing loans. The Leela Palace New Delhi finally cost Rs 2,200 crore. Vivek Nair's third FAR push for the hotel industry couldn't really save his own.

~

The Leela Palace New Delhi boasts some of Madhu Nair's greatest art picks.

The central courtyard flaunts two massive masterpieces by Satish Gupta. 'Devi', a metal sculpture, towers majestically in the gardens. Inspired by the eleventh- to thirteenth-century Chola bronzes from southern India, this contemporary expression of the goddess represents the benign, beautiful and fierce in Hindu mythology. It is 18 feet in height and is made of 1.5 tonnes of gold, silver, bronze and copper.

'The Golden Lotus' is a stunning mural on gold-plated brass. It is a symbol of purity, knowledge, wisdom, growth and wealth. A lotus bud rests on a mandala – a spiritual and ritual symbol in Hinduism and Buddhism representing the universe. The bloom grows bigger and bursts into its full glory at the centre. This is meant to reflect how each living thing has its own unique destiny, and is important in the larger scheme of divinity. The lotus flower is the leitmotif of the Leela Palace Delhi. It appears in various expressions, including guest stationery and other art across the walls.

Then we come to 'Harnessing' by Satish Gujral. Deities, tribal motifs, geometrical projections, animals and humans, mechanical devices and entwined harnesses have been the recurring theme of this master artist, the subject of most of his paintings and sculptures. The painting which hangs in the club lounge uses the imagery of the horse to symbolize power harnessed by humans.

'Mood Series', also in the club lounge, depicts sculptor Dimpy Menon's engagement with the physical form, and manifests the resilience, joy, strength, wonder and freedom of the human spirit.

'Trinity', another of her bronze works, brings life to the ninth-floor corridor. Here the physical form is lyrical, balance and energy are frozen in movement. You feel that the icon will continue to dance even when your gaze tears itself away. Each figure is infused with inspiring qualities of joy, hope and creativity.

The painting 'Face of Life' by Paresh Maity in the business centre passage features some of the artist's recurrent motifs: birds, boats, waterbodies, dilapidated buildings, and the *nayak* and the *nayika* – the archetypal man and woman who re-enact the drama of life without which the world would cease. A strong undercurrent of eroticism pulsates through this canvas.

'Conversations' by Sanjay Bhattacharya, again in the business centre passage, is from a series executed with metal heads and figures in combination with architectural paintings. In the artist's own head, they are living figures talking to one another, confined within the heavy metal.

Also gracing the club lounge, 'Parampara' by Subhash Awchat is part of the eponymous series recalling India's past. It depicts the proverbial pilgrim's journey, capturing the spirit of the nameless monk. The vivid red and saffron bring alive India's continuous traditions.

'Goddess' by Jayasri Burman is a vibrant watercolour in the lobby lounge. The artist has used her signature rich hues and bold themes with a mythic element – strange hybrid animals with human heads, female figures depicting folk themes. 'Egg Dance' by Prodosh Das Gupta is an impressive, powerful and moving sculpture, one of the foremost works of a modern artist that captures energy through his unique emphasis, stresses and gestures.

41

The Ironies Which Rust

The most dangerous arrogance is the arrogance of success. If dizzied by it, you can crash. The chairman of HLVL kept borrowing to build one palace after another, the debts often running simultaneously. Comet Krishnan had arrived on the scene only in 1986, and he wanted to better the deluxe chains which had taken over a century to get to the glittering top. True, he saw his hotels as monuments not so much to his own ego, but to India – to its past splendour as well as its present ability to equal the world's best. India shone through his hotels, but he paid the price for the polish.

We will soon see how snowballing interest became the avalanche that forced a company at the pinnacle of financial success barely ten years earlier to sell all the hotels it owned or managed, barring the flagship Leela Mumbai, to the Canada-based equity fund Brookfield in 2019.

So, how cruel the irony that the largest advantage which Captain Nair's older son, Vivek, managed to wrest for the hotel industry came too late to save what the family had built with such pride and success.

That hard-fought battle was to gain infrastructure status for hotels. In as capital-intensive a sector, its denial meant that loans had to be repaid in just eight years, the permitted two-year grace period coming with penal interest. Yet, hotels were a key feature of tourism – to which successive governments have paid great lip service. There were three main reasons why government had to put its money where its lips were.

One, forex. The official goal was to increase foreign tourist arrivals (FTAs) from 10.56 million in pre-pandemic 2019 to 33 million in 2024, which would lead to increased earnings of $56 billion. Two, the tourism industry generates huge employment, directly and indirectly. According to the tourism ministry, it accounted for 90 million jobs in 2019. The multiplier effect has actually been calculated: Rs 10 lakh invested in the hotel industry nets eighty jobs compared to only twenty-two in other industrial sectors. The raised goal for FTAs would also bring an increased GDP contribution of Rs 8.5 lakh crore. Three, intangible, but certainly not insignificant, is the way luxury hotels burnish Brand India, with all its quantifiable spin-off benefits.

So, it was totally illogical that hotels should continue to be denied the infrastructure status given to tourism's other arms such as airports and ports.

It wasn't just a label. Infrastructure status would entitle hotels to several concessions. They could have a higher debt–equity ratio of up to 4:1; a longer tenure of term loans enabling repayments up to fifteen to twenty-five years; and lower interest rates. These concessions would make it easier for them to expand, and thus reduce the yawning gap between supply and demand. Infrastructure status would allow hotels to pay industrial, not commercial, tariffs on electricity and water. In addition, the electricity duty would be reduced from the existing commercial rate of 21 per cent to 7 per cent as applicable to industry.

During his second term as FHRAI president (2012–13), Vivek Nair petitioned the Manmohan Singh government to this end. Citing the report of the Planning Commission's Working Group on Tourism, he had pointed out that the sector would directly support about 63.79 lakh jobs by 2016–17.

Vivek had pressed this case a year earlier too. In 2011, he could put his foot in the door wearing his hat as chairman of the London-based World

Travel and Tourism Council, India Initiative (WTTCII). At the time, Turkey was being subjected to terror attacks resulting in travel advisories issued by different governments. Manmohan Singh happened to be in Istanbul then. He asked tourism minister Kumari Selja for India's foreign footfalls. Her reply was that they used to be 6 million, but had marginally increased to 6.5 million courtesy the warnings against travel to Turkey.

Kumari Selja asked the tourism secretary and the WTTCII chairman for suggestions. Vivek set up a committee and submitted a comprehensive report detailing fifteen points. Among the main ones was infrastructure status for the hotel industry, which would include the key point of low interest rates and a longer period for repayment of term loans and an initial moratorium of at least five years.

The prime minister as well as the finance minister, Pranab Mukherjee, saw the point in granting infrastructure status to the hospitality industry, and it was formalized by the Gazette Notification of 8 October 2013 issued by the finance ministry, followed up on 29 November by an RBI circular. But once again, the bubbly fell flat. The proverbial slip between the cup and the lip came from the misinterpretation of a crucial clause.

The disastrous clause said 'effective from the date of this notification' instead of 'interest on existing loans'. Several months had elapsed between the decision and its gazetting. This subverted the concessions, and ultimately resulted in almost Rs 22,000 crore of loans borrowed by about 250 hotels becoming Non Performing Asset (NPA) and insolvency and bankruptcy code cases. The industry was not asking for retrospective effect, only for easier terms on loans currently on the books. And in any event, the real agenda was the larger issue of infrastructure status.

As he did during the CRZ impasse, Vivek refused to give up. In 2014, the BJP swept to power, and Narendra Modi pronounced the importance of the 5Ts: tourism along with talent, tradition, trade, technology. Arun Jaitley, as finance minister (and also the lawyer for HLVL during its successful fight against the NGOs in Udaipur), saw the lack of logic in that earlier gazette notification. He asked the secretary, economic affairs, to rectify matters.

Just one phrase had to be changed, from 'date of notification' to 'existing loans'. Easy, right? Not if you factor in politics. RBI governor Raghuram Rajan refused to play ball even though the change had been approved by the Cabinet Committee on Economic Affairs.

As Vivek continued to recount, 'I met Arun at the wedding reception of Amit Shah's son. With tears in his eyes, he told me, "Rajan said no." Then Jaitley walked away, but not before saying, "You'll see the back of this man soon." As you know, Rajan's RBI governorship was not extended to a second term, and he returned to academia.'

Vivek rued, 'Hotels continue to get eight-year loan repayment tenures with high rates of interest. All the 250 hotels lost their assets. We had borrowings of Rs 5000 crore. We had the cash flow to see us through. Under the changed rule, we would have had fifteen years to repay and the provision to extend it by another five. A thirty-year bond period at just 3.5–4 per cent interest in US dollars is a standard across the world.'

He added, 'As of August 2021, Rs 51,000 crore credit had been given by banks to hotels, and these loans were in danger of being NPAs. Some hope lies in the setting up of the development finance institution for capital-intensive projects, including hotels.' As always, the questions are when will the government make it effective, and will hotels be included in it?

Infrastructure status apart, there is the equally important, and somewhat overlapping, issue of industry status for the forex- and employment-generating hospitality sector. Here, while the Centre was always supportive, the actual implementation lies with individual states. Some had put this into effect.

Way back in 1990, the Hotels and Restaurants Association of Western India had appealed to the Maharashtra chief minister, Vilasrao Deshmukh, who fortunately also held the tourism portfolio. He was agreeable to extending 'industry' advantages to hotels. The key ones related to reduced stamp duty rates and change of land-use charges, allotment of government land by way of auction and payments by way of annuity, and continued exemption from the ULCA. And again, industrial, not commercial, rates for power and gas; this would be a huge saving since a hotel's biggest outgoing cost, after payroll, is light and heat.

Once again, that old bureaucratic hurdle played spoiler. A Maharashtra government resolution granting industry status was issued as early as 7 April 1999 – it had remained ungazetted till 2019 when the pandemic threw everything into a coma. Finally, four chief ministers later, Vivek Nair approached the incumbent, Uddhav Thackeray. His cabinet approved the proposal in November 2020, and industry status for Maharashtra's hospitality sector came into effect from April 2021. By then the Leela hotel empire had passed on to Brookfield.

So, once again, Vivek's victory was of little use to the Nairs themselves. It was like the famous line from Maharashtra's own history: '*Gadh ala, pan sinh gela*' (The fort was won but the lion was lost) – a reference to the recapture of Sinhagadh fort in 1670 which came with the death of Shivaji's trusted general, Tanaji, in the battle.

42

Jumping on the Brandwagon

How far can you travel on a journey which began with a line of dusty Bombay taxis? Remember how this sight from her window prompted Leela Nair to connect the dots from international airport to international hotel? The synergy between the couple had prompted her to prod the dream her husband had nurtured ever since he had been wowed by the Waldorf Astoria, when he was little more than a travelling salesman for Indian textiles.

Some sixty years and nine take-your-breath-away properties later, the Leela Group outdid Captain Nair's early aspirations and outranked all his early inspirations. Leela Palaces, Hotels and Resorts was crowned the Best Brand in the World by *Travel+Leisure USA* magazine for two successive years, 2020 and 2021. This had topped the Leela Palace Udaipur being voted the Best Hotel in the World in 2019 by the same coveted forum. The only shortfall was that of the founder himself. Captain Nair, ever wanting to give his guests 'the best of the best', had passed away in 2014. Still, somewhere up there, he must have beamed his trademark beam.

The *Travel+Leisure USA* awards are the hospitality industry's Oscars. The winners are chosen by some 30,000–40,000 discerning voters from across the globe via a meticulous survey developed by the magazine in conjunction with the research firm M&RR. Wresting the Best in the World ranking is more than an ego agenda. It makes the hotel or group a global object of desire, and sends business rocketing skyward. For the Leela Group, it got something more basic: survival.

Debt had forced HLVL into the cold, calculating arms of its bankers. Being ranked the Best Brand in the World would be a hedge against them selling off individual pieces of the family silver. The temptation to do so was real; the world's greatest hotel chains were already eyeing the bejewelled Leela Palaces of New Delhi and Udaipur. Yes, a Mandarin Oriental and a Peninsula or, for that matter, an Oberoi or a Taj, could (and did) create astonishing individual hotels, but as all of these had themselves proved, the collective brand is in another higher league altogether.

A brand is greater than the sum of its parts. That is the je ne sais quoi but vital attribute which takes far longer to build than the most spectacular stone and mortar creations. The Best Brand awards helped to hold the vulnerable portfolio together – with threads of gold. The Nair family held that ace, and the brand is what Brookfield astutely paid top dollar for.

On a more mundane level, the *Travel+Leisure USA* awards also garner more management contracts for a group – which is now the asset-light way to grow in the industry. Most hotel groups aim at a portfolio where ownership comprises a scant 15–20 per cent. Management contracts are also a milestone marking the maturity of a brand, signalling third-party faith.

Four of the eight Leela properties that went to Brookfield were in this category: the ones at Goa, Gurugram and Kovalam we have spoken about, plus the Leela Ambience Convention Hotel East Delhi (which can seat 3000 for dinner in its 30,000 sq. ft pillarless banquet hall). Three more massive ones were to open shortly: Bhartiya City in Bangalore; the Leela Gandhinagar, above the bullet train station; and the Leela Hyderabad.

So how did the Leela Group go about (1) building this topnotch brand and (2) getting the world to acknowledge it as the best via the *Travel+Leisure* ranking? 'We did it the old-fashioned way, one guest at a time,' said Rajiv Kaul. This old Oberoi hand was poached in 2006 to create a corporate identity, a big jump from being a one-man show. Captain Nair, for all his cultivated larger-than-life presence, had understood this need. Just as he had understood in the late 1980s the need to bring in a foreign chain so as to lure the $500-a-night beach-resort tourist to his new Goa hotel.

Rajiv set about strengthening the five Ps which are the bedrock of operational excellence: product, people, procedures/policies, profit and passion. He had observed how the gold-standard *Travel+Leisure USA* awards had catapulted the Oberoi to the global stage after Udaivilas wrested the Best Hotel in the World crown in 2008, followed two years later by the Oberoi Group winning Best Brand in the World. Rajiv set those targets in his cross hairs. But his task was more difficult because, unlike the long footprint of its rivals, the Leela Group had fewer touchpoints, and all only in India.

'We did not have a massive marketing budget which would have allowed us to take out full-page ads in the world's media. The lender banks controlled our purse strings, remember? So we had to mainly depend on word of mouth, or digital in more recent times. The key was to offer a truly memorable guest experience.'

But every hotel in the world aims at this luscious plum, so what could be the crucial differentiator? The guest feedback cards asked two questions: (1) Did your stay exceed/meet/not meet expectations? (2) Will you come back/recommend us to others? Again, what's new? These are standard across the industry, right?

The difference lies in how management responds to the feedback. The Leela aimed at 95 per cent guests checking the 'exceed' expectations box and 97 per cent saying 'yes' to question two. To turn aim into actuality, a task force was set up. Its mandate was to learn from each less-than-exultant responder what had been lacking, and then spruce up their act on that score. Excellence had to become a habit if they wanted that breakthrough. A total commitment to that goal was imperative.

Next, the team set about engaging with those who hadn't actually stayed at a Leela Palace, but had heard about it. Or seen it from their own hotel – such as the Leela Udaipur nightscaped to look like a jewel on the Pichola Lake, beckoning to those staying at the Taj's jewel in the lake or the Oberoi's away from it. A guest who had come to check it out over coffee would get a Christmas card or a discreet 'what's new/special offer' notification. This was potential custom at the doorstep, so much easier to convince than through the most persuasive advertisement in distant glossies.

Of course, the task force continued to lubricate the already established relationships. Guests who had been immersed in the Leela experience would came back for more, and, more importantly, spread the word.

Leela pushed its USPs: the world-renowned spa ESPA and the globally acclaimed restaurants Le Cirque and Megu. But the biggest of them all was its standard of luxury. Unstinting. Unabashed. Rivals may have scoffed at it as OTT, but who cared as long as the guests didn't? They clearly revelled in it and voted with their feet – and with their fingers in those *Travel+Leisure* surveys.

In 2011, Captain Nair appointed Landor Associates to recast the Leela brand design and logo. The renowned Paris-based consultants added another layer to his hallmark. Like each of his showpieces, it was a marriage of Indian artistry and global excellence.

Landor used the award-winning font Kohinoor Latin, created by calligraphist Satya Rajpurohit, across all brand material, even stationery. The redesigned logo is the simple, lyrical initial 'L'. Its copper tone is borrowed from the tail fan of India's flamboyant national bird. Its single, continuous, flowing line evokes the thread which links not just all the hotels, but also the founder's past – as an indefatigable salesman of India's storied textile traditions.

A great hotel is one that makes you feel great, a place billed as a palace should make you believe you are royalty. It is not about cold architecture, but a warm, fuzzy sensory experience. 'Creating a successful hotel is about tangibilizing the intangible,' said Rajiv Kaul. The brandmaster orchestrated all that it took to go beyond this cutesy quote.

A sensory experience must involve all the five senses. A luxe hotel room has the opportunity to touch the guest in a way so intimate that anything less than refined would be crass. The customer demands all manner of fancy stuff, but at the end of the day wants only a good night's sleep. A dream hotel often narrows it down to just that.

So, the Leela hotels cosseted the guest in 300-count bedsheets. Pillows had the exact ratio of duck down to goose feathers so as to provide both softness and structure. The mattress did the same, making you not want to get out of bed as opposed to being unable to extract yourself from that sinking feeling. The duvet trod that fine line too, being both superlight and superwarm. Everything had to attain the Goldilocks measure of 'just right'.

More than the bedroom, the bathroom has to be the gold standard of luxury, one that goes beyond gold-plated faucets. So, the shower pressure was fine-tuned – 30 seconds in the stall and you knew it was just right. The supersize bath towels were more like bath sheets to swaddle yourself in like a baby. The toilet paper too wasn't merely super soft but also super wide.

Touchpoints catered for, next came the second sense, olfactory – it would be awful to refer to it as just 'smell'. The toiletries were Penhaligon's, which advertised itself as having 'entertained English nostrils since 1870'. A proud holder of Royal Warrants, it was also the brand of choice on Cunard luxury liners. Beyond the guest rooms, there was the potpourri exuded by Captain Nair's pampered gardens. Or if you were at the Leela Delhi, this sense would be aroused by the 2000 fresh roses arranged in the lobby's antique bowl (ever eco-conscious, the previous day's profusion of petals were sent to an NGO to be upcycled into floral products). Other public areas too were marked by the subtle signature Leela fragrance. Meanwhile, the auditory senses were beguiled by carefully chosen playlists, or the tinkle of fountains and the splash of waterfalls.

As for the most obvious sense of all, there was the surroundscape of opulence and art. Understanding the emotions that it evokes, beauty was everywhere in grandeur and detail. A stunning sculpture, the carving on a staircase, multi-shaded marble inlays on a ceiling panel – the list was long.

From palettes to palates – we will devote a whole chapter on the cuisines which had to pass the personal test of an owner family that took its food very seriously. The china was Bernardo in all the fine-dining restaurants. And, as mentioned before, even the banquet halls used imported bone china and crystal as well as the same superior quality of ingredients.

While Rajiv gushed over the sensuality of the experience, he was quick to admit that 'you can cover the ceiling in 24-carat gold leaf, but if the service was leaden no guest will return. There are no patents in our business, the only distinguishing factor is the degree of attentiveness – not easy to up when the competition has so impressively raised the bar.'

Old-fashioned manuals used to be full of minutiae on the angle of a cup's handle or the temperature of the coffee inside it. Today's luxury traveller takes all this as a given, and looks for something beyond it. Therefore, as important as the authenticity of artefacts is the genuineness of the caring. Starched body language counts for less than the concern expressed through small gestures or solicitous queries.

Trying to capture, bottle and then dispense spontaneity is a contradiction in terms. It is much like the nuns' dilemma in conveying the essence of Maria in *The Sound of Music*: 'How do you catch a wave upon the sand? How do you hold a moonbeam in your hand?' You can train a person to serve a lavish banquet, but how do you train them to smile? You have to do this by example.

In this, the Leela hotels had an innate advantage – a chairman who smiled all the time and cared genuinely for everyone down the line. If your staff didn't feel like they were part of the family, it was hardly possible to make the guest feel likewise. Arguably, the Leela's differentiator was that the top boss was proof that life is a celebration, not just a set of rules.

That said, you don't want anarchy. Service is both science and art. The former is about procedures, precision failsafe systems, even treading the fine line between friendliness and familiarity. The art lies in allowing staff to be a gracious host each in his or her own way. Leela encouraged its people to own sincerity.

Take the example cited by Madhu Nair. A guest staying at the Leela Palace Udaipur always travelled with her miniature Hindu idols. She had rushed out after checking in, casually leaving her mini-pantheon on the dressing table. On her return to the room, she was touched to find that someone in housekeeping had arranged the gods reverentially on a red square of silk, and even taken the trouble to find a ritual marigold to place at their feet.

To return to those feedback cards. The job was considered done – and the awards won – when, more than the priceless artworks, Sharmila of housekeeping or Shyam at the breakfast buffet or Sharan the gardener was mentioned by name on account of what she or he had done to make the guest's Leela experience memorable with, in Madhu Nair's phrase, 'the little gestures that aren't itemized or billable'.

Such acts became part of the DNA of the Leela chain. That's why, despite the change of hands, the brandwagon rolls on.

43

A Man in Full

It is easy to describe the man in physical terms. In his later years, he was a portly teddy bear who had lost his hair, with twinkling eyes which lit up his chubby face. He stood 5'8" tall in his designer socks, provided you could catch him standing still. It was less easy to tease out the skeins of his DNA, the nitty-gritty, itty-bitty, oft-times witty, sometimes shitty stuff that goes into creating 'A Man in Full'. However, more than this title of Tom Wolfe's novel, Rudyard Kipling's poem 'If' is a better fit when deconstructing Captain C.P. Krishnan Nair. Specifically, these lines:

> If you can dream, and not make dreams your master;
> If you can think, and not make thoughts your aim;
> If you can meet with Triumph and Disaster
> And treat those two impostors just the same . . .
> If you can make one heap of all your winnings
> And risk it on one turn of pitch-and-toss,
> And lose, and start again at your beginnings
> And never breathe a word about your loss . . .
> If you can talk with crowds and keep your virtue,
> Or walk with kings, nor lose the common touch . . .

If you can fill the unforgiving minute
With sixty seconds' worth of distance run,
Yours is the Earth and everything that's in it.
And – which is more – you'll be a Man, my son!

Dreaming big and building bigger; never overthinking; taking triumph in his stride and scoffing at disaster; walking with kings and being kind to ordinary people; risking it all to stick to his resolve; filling the 'unforgiving minute with sixty seconds' worth of distance run' even at age ninety; and, yes, being rewarded with the acclaim of all the world. These qualities are the common thread that runs through every description of Captain Nair by friends, family and employees. Here's a list of what made him what he was.

An unflagging sense of adventure that led him through so many careers and down so many paths, notably as a garment exporter and hotelier. For the bon vivant that he was, this exploration extended deep into food. It was so important to him, and therefore to his hotels, that it merits a chapter of its own.

Curiosity is the handmaiden of adventure. His eldest granddaughter Amruda spoke of his hunger to know of the 'next big thing'. Her sister Aishwarya as well as Vijay Amritraj in his velvet baritone marvelled at his 'childlike curiosity right till the end'. Aishwarya added that it was equally remarkable considering his stature. The tennis star illustrated this point with: 'If someone had a new phone, he would want to know all the ways it was better than the old one.'

Aishwarya traced his remarkable trajectory to a 'willingness to learn', which was prompted by this unbounded curiosity. 'He would casually extract details about my subject, art history, at Cambridge. His probing mind and his observations of the great hotels in which he stayed explained the amount he knew about the finer things of life. That is how he leapt over the circumstances of his birth. Curiosity facilitated his ambitions. The actor studying the part, and then becoming the movie star.'

Rajiv Kaul never stopped being amazed by 'his incredible inquisitiveness and eagerness to apply new knowledge'. The same unstoppered curiosity subjected his secretary Minal Srivastava to a barrage of questions as soon as she reached work. They ranged from the morning's breaking news and the previous night's mythological serial episode to the progress on GVK's redesigned international airport and that of the upcoming Mumbai Metro. 'I had to be prepared for whatever rabbit he pulled out of his many hats.'

Tie up all these with his other granddaughter Samyukta's assessment: 'He was always on the ball not because he had to be, but because he wanted to be.'

No success is possible without passion. Captain Nair had an extra-large helping of this too. All his associates exulted over his unrelenting drive that brooked no impediment. Adman Mohammed Khan said: 'He wasn't building hotels, he was chasing dreams. The company was sinking in debt, but he refused to downsize the gargantuan Bangalore property under construction. We'll find a way, he said, and he did.' It was the same tightrope with every new hotel project, and he walked it unwaveringly every time. Faced with an impasse, his standard response was, 'This too shall pass.'

Vijay Amritraj said, 'He was already at the top of his [garments] game at sixty-five, but he got behind the wheel of this hotel bus and drove it with passion, desire, determination – and delivered.' He added, 'Also with divine intervention because god gives the final blessing.' The tennis star was right, for we have seen time and again how a deus ex machina often arrived at the eleventh hour to save the day and the hotel.

And here's an example of the boss's non-hierarchical involvement. Amritraj was to feature in a photo shoot on the tennis court named after him at the Leela Goa. The tennis partner didn't show up, upon which Captain Nair said, 'Why postpone? I will fill in.' He promptly went to his villa, changed into his white shorts and played for the shot.

Just as curiosity is the mother of adventure, passion dies at birth without the sustenance of discipline. Captain Nair's morning routine was sacrosanct, whatever time he went to bed. Close buddies Madhavan and

Mohanlal happened to be in Bombay then, so all three naturally met up although it was close to midnight. They chatted till such an ungodly hour that the media magnate missed the morning meeting he had come for, and the movie star his flight. They bumped into each other at 11 a.m., and, worried about having kept their octogenarian friend up so late, phoned to find out how he was feeling. His response: 'Why? I got out of bed at my usual 5 a.m., went through my exercises, and I'm at work.'

Consider his day. After his early rising and exercise routine, Captain Nair walked around the Leela Bombay (along with the city renamed the Leela Mumbai in 1995) grounds chatting with the malis – and oft-times the trees – rounding this off by offering plumeria blooms to the small Buddha statue sitting serenely under a canopy. He would then move to his table by the poolside by 9 a.m., soak in the sun over a green tea or Madras coffee, and greet his secretary with an incandescent smile. She would read out the headlines from a selection of English papers, and he would peruse the Malayalam ones.

Next would come a procession of managers, horticulture, security, GMs and various heads of departments from whom he'd get a summary of the day. He would check, make decisions and advise on the way forward. The horticulturist was a must. He would have a long discussion with him, always reminding him to 'see the plants through my eyes'.

On the way to his office on the Mumbai hotel's eighth floor, he would continue bombarding people with questions. 'His mind never stopped ticking. He never seemed to tire, physically or mentally,' said Minal, who took over from the long-standing, much-travelled Asha.

Once at his desk, he would list out his priorities. He was totally approachable – not for him the barricaded corner office, with a Doberwoman of a personal assistant ferociously barring entry. He would dispense simple and practical solutions to the problems brought to him – or to those he astutely prised out.

The boss personified joie de vivre. His twinkling eyes would often light up his face before he burst into laughter. He was willing to overlook a task not completed to his liking provided you had given it more than your best shot. But integrity was non-negotiable. He would read the riot act to anyone who had been dishonest or compromised the hotel's reputation.

Part of the day was marked for the avalanche of mails he received. This busy man would read and reply to each letter, no matter how trivial. The drafts of what he dictated would be amended over and over till he was completely satisfied.

At 5.30 p.m., he'd get a call from his wife, and promptly go down to the hotel lounge to have tea at their earmarked table. Then they'd both go for a drive in his Rolls Royce. Before the airport got privatized and GVK had its own ideas about landscaping, that evening spin was also to check out his greening efforts. Dinner was always with the family at 8 p.m., and every member was at the table, sharp. That, however, was the rule of the castle's chatelaine.

Amruda said, 'He was shooting hoops at ninety, though not playing basketball. It was for his motor coordination, and he went through it willingly at the set early hour.' He would tell the Leela's medical officer Dr A.S. Shetty, who monitored him meticulously, that he should have started this exercise regimen much earlier in life. A physiotherapist came in daily in his later years. Arguably, however, the secret was Ayurveda. He loved his food and had a zillion matters on his plate, but without fail, since he turned fifty, he spent a whole month each year at the Arya Vaidya Sala at Kottakkal. He had the discipline to stay the course of the entire rigorous regimen. At ninety, they told him to stop coming. He passed away two years later.

And speaking of unflagging energy at ninety, here are some examples from the New York trip he made two months after crossing that milestone on 9 February 2012.

His close friend and neurologist at New York University (NYU) Hospital, Dr Gopinathan, had invited him for his daughter Manju's wedding. 'Dr Gopi' and the Captain had met fifteen years ago, and they would unfailingly spend enjoyable evenings along with their wives during Captain and Mrs Nair's annual trips to New York. Much of the conversation would be on how the medical infrastructure in India could be raised to US standards, and other ways to up the country's progress.

The now-nonagenarian Captain Nair insisted on making it to the April wedding. Dinesh, Madhu and Samyukta decided to travel with him so that he was in safe hands. As always, his adhesive Man Friday, Aneesh, went along. Although the Nair family had a large apartment at Trump Palace on the Upper East Side , both Dinesh and Madhu felt that 'Dad would love staying at the Four Seasons', so they booked a two-bedroom suite for him and his butler.

They took a non-stop Air India flight and landed in the early hours at JFK. While the limousine was turning on Park Avenue into 57th Street, he asked the chauffeur to stop for a while and admired the brilliant springtime tulips adorning the divider on Park Avenue. They reminded him of the numerous trips he had made to New York in the late 1950s.

The very first night, Andrew Kirpalani, Dinesh's friend from the garment export days, invited the family to a restaurant just two blocks away from the hotel. While they were walking to it, the ever-vigilant Madhu noticed that her father-in-law was stumbling uncharacteristically. The Captain, of course, insisted that he was fine. So, they had dinner, but alerted Dr Gopi, who promptly organized a check-up at the NYU hospital. The MRI revealed that he'd suffered a minor stroke. Treatment began immediately. Within forty-eight hours, the ninety-year-old had bounced back, ready to fling himself into all of Manju's nuptial festivities.

In the next ten days, and regardless of the minor detail of the stroke, Captain Nair was determined to extract Kipling's 'every sixty seconds' worth of distance run' in New York. This was where he had made a fortune – from the Bleeding Madras days to becoming the largest Indian exporter of ready-mades to the US with Dinesh's help. For all his gung-ho, he knew deep inside that this was the last time he could travel abroad.

He had the day mapped out. Immediately after breakfast, the family would join him, and he'd hit his favourite clothing stores, Stefano Ricci, Brioni and Zilli. While driving down Fifth Avenue, the nonagenarian still remembered the exact location of the stores.

After the morning shopping spree, it was lunch at one of his favourite restaurants, Nello at 696 Madison Avenue, where he was heartily welcomed as 'the Captain'; after all, he had patronized it for over fifteen years. On another afternoon, it was Milo's, where he loved the flown-in seafood, especially the sardines. They reminded him of their abundance in the waters off his Kannur home, though here they were grilled to perfection the Greek way. He relished them so much that the day before the family was to return to India, he asked Dinesh to make one last booking there.

Leisurely lunch over, he would return to his Four Seasons suite and Dinesh and Madhu to their Trump Palace apartment. It was not the ninety-year-old but his fifty-seven-year-old son who needed to rest and recharge his energies for whatever hectic plans his unstoppable father had for the evening. These would certainly include more shopping.

Incidentally, one morning, Captain Nair decided to invite an old textile friend for breakfast at the Four Seasons Lobby Lounge. It was none other than the designer Tommy Hilfiger. Dinesh, who had fronted most of that period of the 1980s, joined them. The shopping had to wait since it turned out to be a three-hour marathon of a catch-up. At the end of it, Hilfiger took the Captain's hand and kissed it, knowing that this would be their last meeting.

On that short trip, it was impossible to oblige all the friends who wanted to invite Captain Nair for dinner. So, instead, Dinesh organized an elegant lunch for twenty-five at the exclusive Le Cirque – which the Nairs had brought to their Mumbai and New Delhi hotels. The ninety-year-old gave an impromptu speech on where he saw India in the years to come, an insightful window for the NRIs present.

Remember his niece Usha and her successful gynaec-obstetrician husband who had helped immensely to mop up funds for his hotel dream from the medical diaspora in the US? The Manoharans refused to strain their uncle with yet another journey, and instead flew to New York. Along with Dr Ashok Shetty's son Mayur, the family met at the convivial brunch at the Peninsula which Samyukta always hosted during her grandfather's visits.

The day before their departure, one fixture was missing. Aneesh, the 24x7 old faithful, had been sent off on a guided tour of the Big Apple. Son No. 2 filled in with all the required personal help his father needed in the absence of the indispensable Man Friday. This had prompted the touched father to tell Rajiv Kaul later, 'I did not know Dinesh loved me so much.'

In any case, Dinesh, Madhu and Samyukta were Every Day Family. They had lived with Captain and Mrs Nair after white ants ate away the wooden foundations of the old Sahar bungalow. Two new homes were constructed in the Leela Baug compound. Madhu was the devoted 'daughter', ministering to every need of her in-laws right to their end. Tender loving care was buttressed by her equally important efficiency. In their last years especially, she arranged for and oversaw every detail of medical intervention.

But then, her redoubtable father-in-law was as famed for the caring relationships he nurtured. Indeed, his defining feature was being a 'people's person'. His eldest granddaughter Amruda went so far as to say that it 'was his real imperative for being in the hospitality business. Not the luxury space, but the people connect at multiple levels, one on one.'

Age no bar. His family all admired his age-neutral ease. Madhu spoke of his ability to reach out across generations, 'be eighteen with an eighteen-year-old; a man of the world with the high and mighty; simple and gentle with ordinary people. Part of the secret lay in his being a good listener.' This was prompted partly by that unwalled curiosity.

Her daughter, Samyukta, reiterated, 'He could talk comfortably to us grandchildren and our friends, showing genuine interest in our very different world. I mean, c'mon, he knew of the Chemical Brothers.' He had found out about this electronic duo while chatting with her cousin, Aushim.

With Aushim's elder sister, Aishwarya, the grandfather bonded over their similar interests in yoga, the outdoors and the benefits of early rising. Later, when she had trained as a sommelier, they 'would discuss issues such as why the legend of a label cannot outrank its ability to pair with a particular dish'. All three granddaughters have independent careers in hospitality; the grandson, who is the youngest, has broken free to work in music.

On one of his trips to Europe, Captain Nair readjusted his busy itinerary because he wanted to check out Samyukta's college, Ecole Hôtelière de Lausanne. 'He went around just as a grandfather, not some grand hotelier, because he felt that would embarrass me.' She added, 'He could connect with everyone without being judgmental. But if you were wasting his time, he'd make that quite clear.'

That age was no bar in his quality of closely nurturing relationships is evident when you realize how many young friends he had. His close buddy Madhavan was forty years younger, and he wasn't an exception.

Dr K.U. Mada, banker and independent director of HLVL, could not get over his long-time friend being 'like a boy always in enthusiastic mode. He was constantly telling youngsters about the importance of fitness, dance, and personal neatness. He used to see the future of the Leela through the eyes of his grandchildren. Indeed, at the last AGM over which he presided, his speech took a twenty-five-year perspective.'

Dr Mada's daughter, Lakshmi, shared a more personal example. 'My earliest memory of Krishnan Uncle was on a trip to Goa when I was fourteen. I stood on the dockside, twisting my hands nervously, debating whether to take the hotel boat ride. He noticed me from a distance, came over, and said reassuringly, "Jump aboard, Lakshmi. This will be fun. It doesn't matter, just give it a try." So I did. And it was. He had that ability to put people at ease.'

The point was reiterated for Lakshmi. 'I had stepped on the stage for my *arangetram*, my first public Bharatanatyam recital. This time I was far more anxious than on the Goa riverbank. Then I saw Uncle beaming supportively from the front row, and remembered his dockside advice. I found my confidence, and "jumped" into my performance. The applause at the end confirmed that I had danced perfectly.'

Captain Nair was a close friend of the legendary film stars Nargis and Sunil Dutt, a pillar of support through this family's many tragedies.

Their daughter Priya remembered him as 'such a jovial, unassuming man who didn't patronize us. Sanjay and I related to him even as children.' A couple of decades later, her own kids would feel the same. 'When I became MP, he invited all of us to the Leela for lunch, and, in a such a grandfatherly way, told my boys stories about my parents. Sumair and Siddharth listened transfixed because unfortunately they had never known their nana–nani.'

Hardev Singh and his son Harmeet had photographed the Kovalam hotel when it was still part of the Le Meridien Group. They had come to Bombay and were in the midst of an early morning shoot in the garden at the Leela when the chairman encountered them on his usual walk. He asked Harmeet several questions about the Kovalam property, and then said, 'Only if you tell me to, I will buy it.' He had already inked the deal, but his words made one young man feel important and chuffed all day.

Ashok Rajani was another person whose life Captain Nair similarly touched. This was before he became a famous hotelier but already a legend in the garments trade. Rajani treasures the recognition the successful exporter gave to his suggestions despite him being such small fry in those days. 'We were supposed to identify ourselves when each of us got up to speak. But before I could say my name, he boomed in a friendly voice, "I know you. You are my son Dinesh's friend." He went on to invite me to the core committee of the Small Apparel Exporters Forum. In fact, Captain Nair was a hero to all the small exporters whose interests were usually trampled upon by the big boys in the business. He always threw his weight behind us.'

Aishwarya spoke of the similar glow that must have suffused a pastry chef at her grandfather's favourite Berlin hotel, the Kempinski Adlon. 'There were like a hundred bakery items on the breakfast buffet, but Achacha was totally taken up by a perfect golden brioche. He asked if he could meet the chef, and so warmly expressed his appreciation.'

Yes, this was the same hotel made infamous by Michael Jackson dangling his baby from his suite's balcony in 2010. The late Kempinski chairman, Guenter Berendt, had a more humane memory.

'During our many trips together, Krishnan and I shared a number of emotional moments. Among the most overwhelming occurred at the official opening of our Adlon hotel in Berlin in 1997. Alongside the mayor, Krishnan and I stood at its front, facing the historic Brandenburg Gate. Since I grew up in East Berlin, I could not help but think about the awful, decades-long division of the city. This gate was a part of that Wall. I could not hold back my tears. Krishnan noticed this and comforted me with great feeling and understanding.'

If age was no bar, class was certainly no chasm for a man who never forgot his humble origins. 'His favourite people were his gardeners and the doormen. He'd tell stories to them, and tell stories about them,' recalled Amruda.

Ah, his stories! All of which the listener would find 'amazing'. He would regale everyone – guests, associates, friends, family. Mohammed Khan and Vijay Amritraj remembered the ones about his army days and being stirred by Netaji's speeches broadcast on Azad Hind Radio. His long-time secretary Asha Dokre mentioned his stories from the same time – of the white horses he rode in Abbottabad, the age-old banyan tree under which he dreamily sat, the post office he visited at the start of every month to send a money order to his beloved Amma.

The grandchildren recalled tales of his 'travelling salesman days' and how when they were together in New York he took them to his inspirational Waldorf Astoria, 'and, you know, he remembered the doorman's name'.

Hotel guests were bowled over by the tortuous journey of each of Captain Nair's properties, and no less by his own remarkable trajectory.

Like every consummate raconteur, the Captain would often spice up a narrative. Rajiv mentioned the small Shiva temple which existed on the Udaipur property which Madhu had reverentially restored. 'It was amusing how rapidly the antiquity of the temple increased at every telling. At the end of it, over a hundred years had been added.'

'Create the story.' He understood the power of this intuitively because he was quintessentially a marketing man. Wasn't that how he had won over his American buyers, starting with Jacobson and Bleeding Madras? Or even before that, Pandit Nehru, whom he had persuaded to impose a 1 paisa cess on every yard of machine-made fabric? Or the German minister who lifted the import duty on Indian handlooms?

Samyukta laughed indulgently. 'Yes, he'd be involved with the architecture and interiors, but when it came to marketing the hotels, he was right on top and centre.' A fact confirmed by the percentage of his time spent with the corporate communications department, long stewarded by Shobha Patel. And by his personal involvement at every stage of those audacious advertising campaigns pulled off by Mohammed Khan and his creative team at Enterprise. Or even by the way he immersed himself in the planning of Hardev's assignments, knowing that a photograph was equal to a thousand bookings. For the same reason, he assiduously worked the floor at every international travel and tourism conference.

The showcasing of his hotels was fundamentally about the showcasing of India, its past glory and its future possibilities. That said, the effervescent extrovert wasn't averse to showcasing himself. He revelled in the accolades and loved being centre stage even in the hotel ads. After all, Captain Nair *was* the Leela, and the Leela was Captain Nair. Like a marriage vow, 'in sickness and in health'.

Consider the Agra episode. How could a man who built hotels to showcase India not have one in the city of its greatest showpiece? The company had strained every sinew to fill the gap. Finally, in 2008, they found a 6 acre bonanza, right across the parking lot from where all visitors had to either walk the 1.1 kilometres to the Taj Mahal or take an electric vehicle. Which meant everyone would see the hotel much before they saw Shah Jahan's crown jewel.

HLVL president Rajiv Kaul had even been unceremoniously 'hoisted' up a contraption hired from Delhi to check the view of the monument above the tree-line. Just then, Captain Nair had a cerebral stroke. Mercifully, he was attended to immediately and the effect was minimized. After he was done with work in Agra, Rajiv rushed back to Bombay and went straight to meet him. The still-groggy chairman's first question was, 'How was the site? Have we got it?' And, right there in the ICU, with Vivek and the CFO also present, he held a mini board meeting authorizing them to 'Buy it now!'

You see, even some forty years later, nothing had changed from the time he had spotted a billboard while driving into town and said to his accompanying GM, 'This is an excellent position to advertise our hotel. Buy it now.'

As he approached his 90th birthday, the unquenchable Captain would arm-twist Rajiv and Vivek to visit yet unsampled restaurants, saying, 'This is my last trip abroad, so come on.' Like on a bitterly cold December evening in Paris, when he insisted on having dinner at the new Shangri-la, which had been the former mansion of Napoleon's nephew, Prince Roland Bonaparte. They walked there from their suites at the equally historic Mandarin Oriental, built on a 16th-century estate which had housed a monastery, a theatre and a royal riding school.

Among the Captain's 'last trips' abroad was Switzerland in his late 80s. At Lake Geneva, he said to Rajiv, 'Let us sit out in the winter sun, it is so special. We'll have a coffee. No, it's 12 o'clock, let's have an aperitif.' He enjoyed life to the last.

Recalled Rajiv, 'Even towards the end, in the hospital, when he was fading and had lost all that weight, what hadn't faded, what he hadn't lost was his joie de vivre. He wanted to laugh, to remain connected to life. At our last meeting days before his passing, I tried to cheer him up with some spicy anecdotes. He was too weak to laugh, but he did flash me a broad smile. That memory will always stay with me.'

44

A Heart for All Seasons

Captain Nair had a 'size XXXL heart', to use his secretary Minal Srivastava's choked phrase. Examples of his caring generosity abound. When Rajiv Kaul needed cardiac intervention in 2010, the chairman wanted the American surgeon Dr Nick Smedira – whom Madhu had researched and found – to fly to Mumbai. When he was finally persuaded that the procedure was better performed at the doctor's Cleveland facility, he insisted on Dr Ashok Shetty, the Leela medico, going along. Okay, Rajiv was the company president, but the chairman's generosity went down the line.

Bhaskar Massini, a civil engineer at the Leela Palace Bangalore, had asked for an extension of leave. He wanted to be by the side of his father who was under serious mental strain. Within two hours of hearing about this, the chairman had Rs 20 lakh transferred into Massini's bank account, no receipt vouchers signed. Some seven months later, he met him in the lobby and his first question was, 'How's your father, Bhaskar?' Massini's annual salary then was Rs 18 lakh; he paid back the money over three to four years, and no one reminded him to do so.

When the monumental Bangalore hotel was finally ready, the chairman summoned his favourite photographer. Hardev Singh declined, saying his father had just been diagnosed with cancer of the kidney and needed surgery. Captain Nair characteristically insisted, arguing that surgery was now simple, recovery-time fast, etc., etc., and he should come in three or four days. He threw in the lure, 'This is my best project and it will be your best assignment.' Hardev stood his ground, saying he felt equally bad about letting him down and passing up this opportunity, 'but my father comes first'.

The ace photographer recounted the aftermath of this dingdong battle of nerves. 'Six weeks later, his secretary Asha called me at 7 a.m. asking if my father was home because "chairman is taking the morning flight to Delhi to meet him." Sure enough, he arrived and roared from the gate of my house, "I haven't come to see you. I've come to meet the great man who has such a dutiful son." He invited my father to his Bombay hotel whenever and as often as he wanted. Then, finally turning to me, he said, "Hardev, the assignment is still waiting for you."'

That wasn't all. When the photographer lost his wife and his father, Captain Nair offered him a stay at any of his resorts because 'you and your family need time to heal'. Hardev declared emotionally, 'I would give my life for such a compassionate, generous man.'

The chairman was a master of the touching gesture in different ways. Once, Kunal Chauhan was the GM at the Trident Cochin when he got a 6.30 a.m. call from reception, saying, 'A Captain wants to meet you.' Thinking it was an airline pilot with a complaint, he went down to find his former boss, who greeted him with, 'Hello, Kunal. I knew you were working here so I thought of seeing how you were doing before catching my flight.'

Chauhan was taken aback. 'I had been a mere F&B manager. How did he even remember, let alone take the trouble?' No prizes for guessing that Kunal would be back at the Leela. 'You don't feel like you are working in a corporation. You feel like family.' Many simply didn't leave.

Sometimes, his warm-hearted gestures had an awkward aftermath. On a trip to New York, he heard that his lawyer Mike Rosenberg's mother had been hospitalized. He marched off to visit her with a basket of two dozen red roses. As flowers weren't allowed in the room, the nurses kept the dramatic arrangement in the reception. The lawyer reciprocated by sending him opera tickets. During the performance, while the coiffured audience listened enraptured, for the Captain the Italian being trilled was double Dutch. He promptly fell asleep right there in the very expensive, very visible front stalls.

More often than not it was an embarrassment of riches – for the seeker of favours. Captain Nair never turned down a request for rebates on room rates or banquet functions; instead, he always upped the petitioner's expectations. It didn't bother him that sometimes he was taken undue advantage of. His style was epitomized by the phrase 'Do it and forget it!'

This approach towards life was casually revealed to Dr Shetty, who could not mask his serious concern during one of Captain Nair's medical setbacks. The patient told the doctor, 'Ashok, why are you getting so tense? My friend, the only certainty in life is death. It comes at the time of its own choosing, and there is nothing we can do about it. All we can choose is the way we live our allotted span. We can do good or we can do bad. No need to overthink. We just have to listen to the voice of our conscience.'

Another indication of his caring was the energy this busy man expended on keeping in touch even with those who no longer had any bearing on his life. He would call up old friends, acquaintances and businessmen just to say 'Hello' and enquire about their health and family. Sometimes, it was more direct. Like the way he eased R.K. Seth out of his hard times, remembering how, decades earlier, the textile trader had helped him pay the hospital bills for his wife's third delivery.

Or take this incident recounted by Mithu Basu, who headed PR and marketing communications at HLVL. 'On spotting a name on the VIP list of the Leela Bangalore, the Captain promptly called the GM instructing him to "serve piping hot idlis soaked in sambar to the guest in Room ##. Make sure it is in a large white bowl, and surprise him before he goes down for breakfast." Then he explained why.

'"That man is my old friend, though we have lost contact now. Some thirty years ago we both were walking the streets of New York, lugging heavy suitcases packed with textile samples. Suddenly, my companion's eyes lit up on sighting a south Indian restaurant. 'Ahh, time for some hot idlis soaked in sambar served in a large white bowl,' he had said excitedly. I want him to relive the memory."'

The next morning, the long-lost friend called. Mithu added, 'And I sat listening to the chairman having the happiest conversation in Malayalam punctuated by gleeful laughter.'

Another long-time, but continually lubricated, friendship was the one between Captain and Mrs Nair and Kempinski chairman Guenter Berendt and his wife Anna. It was as warmly reciprocated. Anna said, 'There was barely a day when my late husband and I did not mention Krishnan and Leela. The number of stories that come into our mind are really endless. We have shared these with our German and European friends on many occasions.'

Not surprisingly, Captain Nair remained emotionally attached to his long-ago defence services connection. One morning, his secretary found him uncharacteristically morose. He explained, 'I could not sleep last night. I kept thinking about the poor boys who perished on the Sindhurakshak.' On 15 August 2013, eighteen crewmen were killed when this key submarine exploded in Mumbai's high-security naval dockyard.

In practical terms, he always put retired army officials in charge of hotel security, with the guards smartly dressed in Gorkha uniforms. Noting this, Berendt had added, 'During the reconstruction of the Leela Goa, he appointed none less than a brigadier general as construction supervisor.'

Of course, Captain Nair would continue to keep in touch with the sons of his old army boss who, as kids would run through the little gate separating Lieutenant General Kuldeep Singh Brar's Gun House and the villa allotted to his ADC and his bride. The General's wife, Meena , who had initiated young Captain Nair into the finer points of hospitality, had a standing invitation to stay at the Leela in Bombay or Goa when it got too cold in Chandigarh where she later lived.

In fact, considering the number of people to whom this 'be-my-guest' generosity was extended, it is a wonder that he had room for paying customers at all. The redoubtable Kokilaben Ambani fondly recalled the long friendship Captain Nair shared with her late husband, Dhirubhai, an even more audacious industrialist. 'Every time a new Leela opened, we would receive one of his green-inked letters asking us to come experience it. I will never forget the care lavished on me at the Udaipur hotel en route to the Shreenathji temple which I regularly visit.'

But such royal treatment wasn't just for the rich and powerful. Prabha Prabhu, who later rose to director at Sam Balsara's Madison India, was a junior accounts executive at Mudra Advertising Agency when she first met Captain Nair in 1989, and came to 'admire and adore him'. She appreciated how 'he would get the hotel car to drop me home because we were working on a campaign, even on weekends. My children, seven and nine, would have a ball because he insisted I bring them along. All these years later, they still think of the Leela Bombay as home.'

What truly touched Prabha was how, when her daughter was critically ill, Captain Nair summoned an Ayurvedic *vaidya* from Kerala and instructed him to do everything to save the child. It worked. 'And Captain paid for the full year's treatment.'

In fact, he spread his faith in Kerala's celebrated Ayurveda remedies to several others, among them Dr Vinod Chandiramani, whom he called his 'nephew' because 'he was my father's friend. We were all in awe of this man who had built Bombay's first five-star hotel NOT overlooking the Arabian Sea.'

Dr Chandiramani went on to become an eminent surgeon. At one time he himself was hospitalized. 'Not only did this warm, generous man call daily to check on my progress, he went to the extent of contacting his Kerala *ayurved*s who sent a special massage oil to rebuild my strength. Captain Nair followed up till I had made a complete recovery.'

45

In the War Room and Trenches

Since Captain Nair was the Leela, and the Leela was Captain Nair, it is impossible to separate the man from the hotelier. Some stories help illustrate his leadership style and also explain how he built such a global reputation despite his late arrival.

By now it should be clear that he never measured his success in dollars and cents, but in terms of ranking, of 'how can we be better the next morning'. Therefore, however big his heart, however bright the twinkle in his eyes, he was demanding and exacting.

The gentleman was an officer who led from the front. He was always the first to be in office and at meetings. By constantly and ardently sharing his goals with his teams, he conveyed the high expectations he had of them – at all levels. That was also how he delivered his oft-repeated ambition, 'I want the best of the best for my guests.'

Consciously or independently, Captain Nair had arrived at the same conclusion as J.R.D. Tata: 'Always aim at perfection, for only then will you achieve excellence.'

He was particularly impressed by the perfection of the Japanese, fascinated by the oriental balance of yin and yang. He would thrill to the perfect little box that packaged a Japanese confection or the fan from a temple that his granddaughter Aishwarya brought back for him. She recalled from their travels together how, examining the customized cutlery at a French restaurant, he once said, 'We must do this at our Fiorella.' In a small Italian café which served a very good espresso, he persuaded the owner to tell him exactly how they did it so it could be replicated in his own hotel coffee shops. He diligently noticed everything and made notes. Then he would reconfigure what he liked and stamp his own personality on it.

But she pointed out, 'Demanding perfection can be abrasive. He was blunt in telling you off straight and square till he got the results he wanted. He got in full what he paid for.'

Rajiv Kaul spent eleven years working closely with Captain Nair, and his biggest learning was 'failure may be a comma, but it is never a full stop. Also that nothing is unachievable.'

A better summary of the boss's mantra lies in the stack of identical Adidas tees he bought for his teenaged grandson, Aushim. They were emblazoned with the catchphrase 'Impossible Is Nothing'. Amruda, Aushim's oldest sibling, said, 'Achacha absolutely owned that slogan.'

Well, he personified Nike's too: 'Just Do It'. In Mohammed Khan's creative phrase, 'He was no air-conditioned chairman.' He got down and dirty. Literally too. He'd prowl the corridors late at night. Catching the unseemly – and unhygienic – sight of room service trays left out by guests, he would pick them up himself. Khan's agency even did an ad on it titled 'The Night Raider'. This hands-on involvement is typical of founder-hoteliers. Later generations give their marching orders to a different drumbeat.

He nutshelled his impetus to Kunal Chauhan, who was about to take over as GM of the new Leela Delhi. 'No one else even imagined there could be a grand hotel on that desolate Goa beach. When we build, we are fulfilling a vision, making something unthinkable – and memorable. I never think of the cost.' True, GMs don't have the luxury of ignoring the bottom line, but in the boss's scheme of things, making memories had to rank at least on par with making profit. That really is the true hotelier's credo. Even if it drags him under.

Chauhan received more indirect indoctrination on the chairman's expectations. Walking him through the exquisite grounds, he said, 'This garden may be the responsibility of the horticulture department, but anyone is free to make a suggestion.' The subtext was: 'Bring everyone together on the same platform; don't pigeonhole staff and issues.' Next came his obsessive 'P' word: 'My GMs should be people-oriented. Not only guest delight, they should aim as much at employee delight.'

He aimed at it as well. When a junior manager got a job at the Bangkok Mandarin, the chairman called to say, 'I understand your aspiration, but you can be part of the biggest story in Indian hospitality.' Sure enough, he assigned him to the next grand property that was taking shape despite others having more project experience. He had understood the young man's need to grow and satisfied it. He also believed that the faith placed in him would make him deliver.

He instructed the HR manager in Bangalore to 'locate a building and make very good accommodation for all our people. They can't come from some modest home, put on a uniform, and start running a palace.' It calls to mind the Infosys founder Narayana Murthy who, ruing the same city's terrible infrastructure, despaired, 'My people have to drive through Third World roads and then deal with First World expectations.'

Among Captain Nair's many inspirational sayings was, 'You are bigger than your problem. Believe in yourself, and you will find a solution.' He had walked that talk, refusing to be battened down by too little cash or too much controversy. Instead, he had upped the ante, buying more land.

He could also take the pressure off his people. One year in Goa, the staff had gone all out to dress up the beachside garden for the Leela's renowned alfresco 31 December party. The bottles and buffet tables were already laid out. Then, just before the revelry was to start, unseasonal rain came crashing down and showed no sign of relenting.

The chairman always brought in the new year here with his closest friends. He appeared on that sodden ground, pressed the GM's hand,

and said, 'Don't worry. Move the food and dancing to the banquet room. Tell the guests that the bar is open, and drinks are on the house.' Not the first drink, but all drinks! On New Year's Eve! In Goa! You can imagine the scale of that gesture.

Still, you could be sure that a guest staggering to the venue the next dawn would find no detritus of revelry. He couched an important ask in another story he loved to tell his people. 'Many years ago, I had been at a huge, late-night party at a Sri Lankan resort. Early the next morning, I had gone for my usual walk to the same garden, dreading the mess of the previous evening. Instead, it was already spick and span. I want my hotels to be like that.'

Sameer Sud was a management trainee when the chairman, looking out of his window, saw him pick up something small from the grass and bin it. He walked into the morning's training session, singled him out, asked his name and told the assembled group how pleased he was by what he had seen Sameer do earlier. He then repeated the Sri Lanka story. He would also always remember Sameer's conscientious act, make public mention of it wherever Sameer was posted. If you had done something that caught his sharp eye and approval, or even if he'd heard something good about you, you subtly became part of an empowered circle.

He would call for Chef Aungshuman at the Leela Bombay and tell the guests at his table, 'This is my boy.' Or, spotting F&B's Abhisek, who had been borrowed from Bangalore to help with his 90th birthday gala dinner, the boss called out to him by name, adding how happy he was to see him here. To underline the importance of the juniormost employee, he would give the analogy of a classic Swiss watch: 'It has hundreds of moving parts; each one of them has to work perfectly for the whole to keep ticking.'

Captain Nair had direct access to the kitchen from his bungalow, and he would check everything on his way up to his suite. He had the eye of an eagle as well as its daring. A trolley or a pan out of place, he would move it himself. A spoon not polished to mirror finish, he'd want it buffed – now! If something couldn't be fixed right away, he expected the person concerned to report to him when the job was done. And done ASAP. Like Biki Oberoi, he knew, 'The devil, not god, is in the details.'

He loved the Germans for their sense of discipline. He drummed in the fact that a business hotel especially had to be run like a military operation because the guest had to get everything on time, and the staff had to get it right every time.

One morning, he told his Bangalore GM, 'You must up the game. What are you doing about the coffee?' The guy anxiously asked if he had heard any complaints about it. The chairman said, 'No, none at all. But we are so happy with what's not broken we never strive for the next level.'

Every GM endeavoured to 'up the game'. At Leela Ambience Gurugram, they took the cue from Delhi's wedding caterers, bringing in food trends that people enjoyed instead of merely chasing Western trends.

Breakfast is a comforting start-of-day meal. So, if you are used to having just-off-the-griddle 'paronthe' for breakfast, the hotel should give you a perfect one. Similarly, realizing that at home the kids had Cheerios, Dad had muesli and Mum had bran and raisins, a whole 'cereal wall – like a supermarket' was created at the Gurugram hotel. Pick up the brand you want. It was one of several retail ideas picked up from food halls.

This was in keeping with the Captain's diktat: offer something new, not just the best. Fulfilling this quotient, the Leela Mumbai was the first to set up a cybercafé in 1996 with the help of Vijay Mukhi and Pritish Nandy. School parties flocked to it. The Leela Goa was the first to have top-end tennis (and squash) courts hosting serious tournaments. Remember, they had the powerful serve of Vijay Amritraj. The Leela Bangalore became the first self-reliant, energy-positive hotel in the country via windmills in the Western Ghats.

If memories are a hotel's currency, they come in many denominations. To the best and the new, the consummate marketeer adds the 'Wow!' of the different. Guests at the Leela Bangalore didn't just salve their work-weary senses with its waterfall-splashed glades, they were encouraged to photograph the birds they spotted. These were turned into personalized takeaway postcards.

'Don't give a 2 kg cake, but one worth taking a picture of.' The prescient hotelier had sussed this out before Insta-gratification began measuring every experience in 'gram-worthiness'. So, to their eye-widening delight, a couple of Messi-manic kids were welcomed with a chocolate-filled praline football when they checked into their room at the Leela Mumbai – the creation of pastry chefs Rashna Elavia and Cawas Cama.

Also consider the fuzzy feeling when this hotel's gardener, having noticed a guest pick up fallen plumeria blooms, greeted her the next morning with a leaf-cup filled with these pink-tinged beauties. No one had trained him to do so. Another example of the warmth that seems to spring up spontaneously, naturally, at the Leela.

46

For Guest and Country

The only negative memory Captain Nair had from his childhood was caste prejudice. So, was he trying to vindicate this by building these massive, opulent hotels in the same way that a 'backward' caste chief minister would flash her diamonds to assert Dalit empowerment? 'No,' Amruda emphasized, 'he enjoyed hospitality for its own sake, and its access to people and places. It was the perfect fit for his personality. His ambition wasn't to put a pin on multiple places. What he wanted was to put Indian hospitality on the map because he was so passionate about India.'

This last sentence is unanimously voted the double engine that drove him – the ancient Indian doctrine '*Atithi devo bhava*' and his deep belief in the coming of the golden age of India. Sam Balsara's punchy advertising agency, Madison, even did an entire campaign with the theme 'guest is god'. It featured authentic guests, not models, as confirmed by Shobha Patel. Among the most fetching of the Leela's lovely ads is one in which the beaming chairman bends to hand one more lotus to the armful held by a clearly thrilled young woman.

Captain Nair would stand in the lobby of his hotels engaging guests in more than just polite conversation. He would listen intently, offer them a cup of tea at his table in the lounge and/or take them on a guided tour of his precious garden. He did all this not as a practised hotelier, but as a gracious host. Sometimes he had to play both.

At one of the Leela Mumbai restaurants, he had been observing a clearly inebriated guest create an increasingly ugly and unfounded scene over the wine he had been served. The chairman went across, suavely introduced himself, and told the obnoxious fellow that the meal would be complimentary – and so would his entire stay.

Customer is king even when he's being an insufferable knave. More so in the service industry where the product is pampering. Every book on great hoteliers is replete with examples of such personal touches.

What set Captain Nair apart was the second part of that double engine. His larger agenda was to showcase India itself, not only its deep-rooted hospitality. He built his hotels on the lines of the past empires of the region; filled them with the country's rich craft traditions. But that was only half his story. It was equally about showing off a modern India which could take luxury and service to international standards.

Amritraj, no mean example of global Indian excellence, savoured the long evenings over fine wines, spent talking about the country's past glories and future promise. 'He was Indian to the core. For instance, when Jet Airways started, he persuaded Naresh Goyal to set up office at the Leela Mumbai, and he only flew on that airline whenever possible.'

Captain Nair believed, 'When I win, India wins'. He made a full production of flag-hoisting at the Leela Bombay's sylvan poolside on Republic Day and Independence Day. He gave a speech in the imposing banquet hall, and led 'freedom walks' from Sahar to Santacruz. Guests were welcome to join. The family was expected to.

Remember? The money and effort he had spent on greening the whole of Sahar was because he didn't want the foreigner's first sight of India to be of a stretch of slums.

He didn't celebrate only India, he celebrated Indians. He wrote long, detailed, congratulatory letters to a person who had achieved anything of note, where he would talk about the honour awarded, the milestone reached. He drafted these with great care, knowing that they would be read by several of the recipient's business and personal circles. Some were also handwritten in his distinctive green ink. Yes, that was a signature colour. The one that set apart his verdant hotels. Even his wardrobe.

47

Trailblazer in Parrot-Green Blazers

If the Leela hotels were a bird, they would be a peacock. The chairman too was given to flashy plumage. He would team a cream-coloured suit with a polka-dotted shirt and green tie, always a pocket square, and often that preppy affectation, suspenders.

'I want the best of the best' applied to his choice of labels. He sported Brioni, the Birkin bag of men's suits. But he would also have about three made every month by 'Charlie Tailor', whom you might find getting the measure of the man while the boss was tailoring his strategies at a meeting.

His favourite US haunt was Bijan, self-anointed as 'the costliest men's clothing shop in the world' on Rodeo Drive, Beverly Hills. A wealthy immigrant from Iran in the 1970s, Bijan Pakzad had bought a parking lot and turned it into a building store. He had famously said he was confident of custom because in LA, 'I saw brilliant men earning thousands of dollars dressed in the most ridiculous clothes'.

Captain Nair was such a regular that his photograph featured in the store window along with royalty and US presidents. Once, when Dinesh, Madhu and Samyukta stopped by to pick up a gift for him they were snootily informed that this was an 'appointments only' store. They mentioned the magic 'N' word, and 'the assistants hurried to open all the double-storeyed wardrobes'. If further proof were needed, a counter of mementoes in Captain Nair's suite at the Leela Bombay holds a signed birthday card: a photograph of the great Bijan himself flanked by all his staff, including a lapdog.

When Madhu and Dinesh lived in New York, they would regularly get cuttings in the mail. They were from the *Financial Times* column 'How to Spend It'. 'Dad wanted us to go over to the featured store and buy whatever fancy piece of apparel or expensive accessory caught his fancy.'

After the chairman's passing, Mrs Leela Nair insisted on preserving his hotel suite in an 'as-was' condition, complete with rows of suits, stacks of silk shirts, tie racks festooned with Hermès and Ferragamo, and his beloved red cashmere sweater.

He had no compunctions about teaming one of his linen suits with a Miami Cruise print shirt, carrying off his outrageous combinations because of his self-confidence and inborne flair. The child stands out among his siblings in faded family photographs. Recall how A.K. Gopalan noticed the secondary schoolboy on account of his physique and bearing. Or, for that matter, the assurance with which he marched up to the Chirakkal Valiya Raja and recited the verse that secured him the education to which a Vaniya village child could never otherwise have aspired.

His shoes were Italian and hand-stitched, but in later years problem feet forced him into Birkenstocks or sneakers. One year he surprised Samyukta by asking her to get him the Alexander McQueen brand from New York where she then lived. Or maybe it wasn't surprising at all. The grandchildren's unanimous verdict: 'Achacha combined grandeur with cool.'

It followed that he loved shopping. On the way from Shanghai to the garden city of Hangzhou, he spotted a Paul & Shark store – the label's tees are priced at an obscene $1000. Moth to flame. 'So expensive!' he exclaimed, adding, 'Let's buy ten.' But such extravagance had a flip side too. In Beijing, he began bargaining over the price per yard of silk. Rajiv recalled his embarrassment since they had been accompanied by an interpreter from the Hyatt. The chairman said coldly, 'I have been a textiles man for decades. I know their worth, and no one's going to make a monkey of me.'

He always did remain a textiles man, prioritizing the touch and feel of fabric even in his hotels. Shopping with him abroad, the teenaged granddaughters were initiated into 'really fine silk and 400-thread-count cotton'.

He would quote Churchill, 'My tastes are simple. I want only the best.' Though surely the bulldog prime minister would rather 'preside over the liquidation of the British empire' than be seen in one of Captain Nair's parrot-green blazers.

Harsh Goenka wouldn't either. In a memorial piece in the *Economic Times*, the industrialist wrote of his frequent visits to his long-time friend and fellow gourmet during his last months in and out of Breach Candy Hospital. 'When I commented on his style of clothes, the Captain asked me to give him my suit measurements, and as soon as he got out of hospital he would buy one for me. Then I did wonder how I would carry off a yellow or a pink suit.'

Our man not only had the panache with which to do so, he also had the necessary grooming. He was regular with his manicures and pedicures, even facial treatments – spared from being labelled a dandy thanks to his army bearing. He pampered his skin daily with his favourite $480 50 ml jar of Orchidée Imperial face cream and Shalimar body lotion, rounding it off with Samsara Eau de Toilette, all from the House of Guerlain. No wonder he exuded that 'mesmerizing aura'.

Leela Nair accompanied him on many of his international conferences, and he would insist on her buying designer handbags by the armful. Amruda said her Amamma had the whole line of Louis Vuitton, 'not big bags, just clutches to hold her spectacles and keys'. She gifted Samyukta 'her green snakeskin pochette which never fails to get oohs!' From Thailand and the Philippines he brought back fistfuls of South Sea pearl bracelets for his wife and granddaughters.

Amruda accompanied him to a PATA conference in Morocco when

she was sixteen. More than the gala dinner at the fabled La Mamounia where they stayed, she remembered 'the fun we had scouring the local markets of Marrakesh, buying rugs and handicrafts. On other trips we went to quarries to select marble, and of course, the must-stop was at nurseries. We always came back home with two suitcases full of cuttings and seeds.'

And as if he hadn't shopped enough, he would swoop down excitedly on the duty-free stores at airports, hoovering up more shirts, bags, watches and perfumes. Usually losing track of time. Once at Frankfurt airport there was the frantic, white-mopped Rajiv Kaul preceding a ramrod-straight octogenarian Captain Nair marching like an army general, with his inseparable butler Aneesh bringing up the rear while hanging on to half a dozen duty-free bags. It was so riveting a sight that, when they made it to the gate just as it closed, they received a round of applause.

Shopping was for dressing up. After he'd Windsor-knotted his Hermès tie with the cherry print, ensured the perfect fall of his canary linen jacket, adjusted his satin pocket square and patted on his Samsara, his valet would hand him the most important part of his attire. A small gold stud, no bigger than a button. It was the medal inducting him into the United Nations Environment Programme's (UNEP) Global 500 Laureate Roll of Honour. It was presented by Emperor Akihito in 1999 for his gigantic greening efforts. 'For me the recognition was about achieving the impossible,' said Captain Nair. Once he had pinned it to his lapel, the chairman was ready to take on all the possibilities – or googlies – of the day.

A week after his passing, Amruda spotted a blue and yellow sunbird flashing through the bungalow groves. 'Ah,' she smiled to herself, 'Achacha is back.'

48

The Captain's Table

Each of his hotel restaurants had a 'Chairman's Table' where Captain Nair loved to entertain friends, associates, even random hotel guests. Mohammed Khan savoured the memory of lunch at Fiorella's on the eighth floor of the Leela Bombay, which became an extension of his advertising campaign meetings. 'The restaurant was open only for dinner, but he would have it laid out only for me. We would discuss with the chef what masterful creation he would whip up that day. The Captain would order the best wine to pair with it. Then he would call the Malayali chef and ask for an Alleppey fish curry and appam for himself.'

But his culinary tastes certainly did not begin and end with his native Kerala cuisine. Rajiv Kaul, who travelled a great deal with him in later years, spoke of the difficulty he had in getting the boss the fabled bird's nest soup he fancied one evening in Beijing. Granddaughter Samyukta illustrated the same point when she said, 'He had appams with caviar.' Rajiv added, '. . . along with scrambled eggs, his favourite breakfast. He loved angel-hair pasta with crab, Chinese fried rice, always with extra crab, and he adored lobster Thermidor.' Not much of a chicken man, he didn't eat red meat at all, which left him hungry and grumpy at a Leading Hotels of the World gaucho lunch in Argentina.

His secretary, Asha Dokre, recalled that occasion: 'Wine and champagne flowed freely at the horse ranch party for all the attending hoteliers, and everyone excitedly gathered round a big spit on which a whole cow was roasting. Hon'ble Chairman expressly forbade me to see it. A buffet was laid out in what looked like a warehouse. We wandered up and down those loaded tables with no luck. Finally, in an obscure corner, he found a small tray of cold fried rice topped with crumbled boiled egg. He picked up a few spoonfuls, and munched on them indifferently.'

The chairman's Girl Friday added, 'Even the brave-hearted Chinese delegates could not face the blood sausages, with the red smearing their plates. These eating habits would seem bizarre to a common Indian.' Even to her boss, who was anything but a common anyone in the culinary department. Or any other.

The trip the Captain organized for his wedding anniversary on 30 April 1995 was far more to his and Leela's taste. No surprise that he tied it up with a PATA annual conference in Auckland, New Zealand. Since he would inevitably combine pleasure with work, Asha went along too. He may or may not have planned the itinerary specifically around his favourite food, but there was fish, fish, more fish, and when they tired of that, there was shellfish.

En route to Auckland, they made a stopover at Hong Kong. The Regent Hotel's exclusive seafood restaurant expectedly had a wall-sized 'live' menu. From the unsuspecting fish swimming around, the Captain selected a fine specimen of his favourite garoupa, and ordered it steamed whole, Chinese style. There was nothing gingerly about the way he relished it, finally putting down his chopsticks to pick out every juicy morsel from the large head with his fingers.

After Auckland, no slouch in the freshest fare, they flew to Tahiti, a place which Captain Nair had always wanted to explore. More than him the Polynesian paradise seemed to stun Asha, who would later gush equally over the 'blue-green, crystal-clear waters and the huge, bare-chested men with just a small sarong tied round their waists'. Her eyes widened further over the fact that the islanders made even more than 100 per cent use of the coconut palm than the Malayalis.

When in Tahiti, eat like the Tahitians. So they tucked into fish grilled or cooked in coal-bottomed pits covered with banana leaves; munched through sweet, tender, mostly raw prawns with a dash of lemon; gorged on an ocean trove of crabs, lobsters and crayfish, and, of course, the Pacific star, mahimahi.

Captain Nair, always demanding the full sensory experience, had booked a villa which was literally in the ocean, built on stilts. The hotelier couple's heads must have swum with the possibilities of what they could incorporate into their own hotels as they looked down to the ocean floor and the multi-splendoured water world on display.

Captain Nair's preference in wines was Italian, especially the coveted Super Tuscan Sassicaia from Tenuta San Guido. Factoid: the 75,000 acre estate came as part of the dowry of the Marchesa Clarice della Gherardesca when she married Marchese Mario Incisa della Rocchetta in 1930. Valuing it more than Charles II had his Bombay dower, the marchese planted its first vineyards in 1944, daringly with Cabernet Sauvignon and Cabernet Franc rather than the traditional Italian grapes. He wanted to produce wines akin to the Bordeaux reds to rival the nearby prestigious Chiantis and the Barolos of Piedmont.

Nair's granddaughter Aishwarya, Graduate Chef from the Culinary Institute of America, would train as a sommelier and design the Leela cellars. Her choices at Le Cirque Signature won the internationally acclaimed *Wine Spectator* magazine's Restaurant Award for Excellence six times in a row, from 2015 to 2020. These awards recognize establishments whose wine lists offer interesting selections; are appropriate to their cuisine; and appeal to a wide range of wine lovers. To qualify, a wine list must present complete, accurate information, including vintages and appellations for all selections.

Incidentally, while the Michelin guide awards stars, *Wine Spectator* ranks with 'glasses'. A single glass denotes an Award of Excellence – for those with more than ninety and less than 350 labels. Two glasses is a Best Award of Excellence, won by properties with more than 350 and less than 1000 labels. More than 1000 labels puts you in the running for the Grand Award denoted by three glasses.

With the boss being such a foodista, no prizes for guessing that he took personal interest in what went into and out of his hotels' kitchens. At the Leela Goa, lavish breakfast buffets would be laid out. On a minute examination of the spread one morning, the boss asked for a perfect-looking dragon fruit replaced by an even more perfect one. He had said, 'Add so and so, add this and that. The cost is not the issue. My guests must eat absolutely the best.'

At the Kovalam poolside, he once called out to photographer Hardev Singh, 'Come join me for breakfast. I've ordered crab curry and puttu. I only dare to have it here. Leela doesn't want me to eat all this now.' Like she could stop him. Madhu laughed while describing dinner time at home. 'He would stare balefully at his soup, declare he was on a diet, but by the end of the meal, he had more than sampled all the different things that everybody else was eating.'

Elaborate meals were not just the privilege of guests and friends. Shobha Patel still salivated over meetings fuelled by a procession of mini idlis, tikkis, sandwiches, tartlets and his favourite dal vadas. 'The chairman loved food, and he loved feeding everyone even more.'

It goes without saying that you still get the best south Indian food at the Leela – the whole banana leaf, not just the standard idli–dosa–upma breakfast. Executive chef Aungshuman Chakraborty proudly reeled off the diverse repertoire of the five (including Telangana) states of the region at the fine-dine Jamavar or even the all-day Citrus.

If Kerala crowned the list, it was not only for reasons parochial. The distinctive curries of Malabar, Alleppey and Calicut evoked salty adventurers in boats with wind-puffed sails. Authenticity was assured, more so because of the personal attention of Captain and Mrs Nair, who hand-picked cooks from modest Kannur eateries. People like Chef Babu – enticed from Chovva Café in 2000 – whose nadan fish curry the couple had particularly relished. 'Amma stopped eating fish in Kerala for years after the tsunami in 2004,' he said. He also revealed, 'Sar loved dal chutney and the one with Kashmiri red chillis', and that 'the bungalow lunch-time sambar has urad dal and lots of vegetables'.

Chef Babu also mentioned home favourites which segued into the hotel menus. Many of them were 'Madam Leela's own family recipes, such as the prawn curry cooked in an earthenware chatti' – which had so enthralled Jivajirao Scindia of Gwalior at the Nairs' old Vatcha Gandhi Road flat. Samyukta, who is now a restaurateur in hard-boiled London, recently introduced 'Leela's Lobster Neerulli' at her own Jamavar in Mayfair. Served (dramatically) 'on a bed of tiny onions and coconut milk'.

Other migrants from the family kitchen were the various Moplah-style biryanis made with the thicker, fragrant Kannur rice. Arguably the same variety that Madhavi Amma gave Mrs V.P. Menon while persuading the lofty lady to play courier for that far-reaching prawn pickle.

The Leela at Sahar was the first five-star this side of the Vindhyas to serve appams, and south Bombay foodies would drive all the way across town for them. They still do. It is masochistic to have to choose between these fluffy temptresses and the distinctive Kerala Maharaja dosas, whose secret is a bit of sugar plus a mix of butter and ghee which makes them crisp yet spongy. In fact, the idli, chutney and sambar would go to the bungalow at 6 a.m., and only if it met the chairman's approval, could it be served at the hotel breakfast.

Abhisek Basu of F&B narrated this had-to-happen story: There was an unlabelled extension no. 4455, which connected Captain Nair's bedroom to room service. One dawn, newbie Namrata, two days into the night shift, sent the samples instead to Room 455. Abhisek, then the private dining manager, was summoned at 7 a.m. by a livid chairman impatiently pacing up and down, demanding to know why he hadn't got the stuff. Equally irate was the guest who had groggily answered his doorbell to find a waiter holding a tray of idli, sambar and chutney.

It was the private dining manager's duty to go to the chairman's suite while he was having lunch to discuss present and future businesses and

VIP guests. Detailed answers were expected. You couldn't wing it.

Chef Aungshuman added, 'Mr Dinesh, like Madam Leela, has a very sharp palate. You cannot get anything past him either. Because of this family's great respect for food, I have never been asked to cut corners.'

With the whole ocean beyond the Kerala coast, Malayalis know their fish, and the Nairs of the Leela wear this knowledge like a badge. Aungshuman explained, 'The west coast has a fishing ban during the June–August breeding season; the east coast, April–June. Other hotels might stock up on 5000 kg to circumvent this, but we fly in fish every day from Vizag; our sourcing vendor is very strict with quality.'

In his assessment, 'Only Captain Nair and Mr P.R.S. Oberoi truly understood the core of hospitality. They aren't just businessmen. Even in the café, our side plates are from the Thomas Rosenthal Group. Unlike elsewhere, the quality of flatware, cutlery and ingredients is the same as in the fine-dine restaurants. The room service crockery is Bauscher. Before the pandemic shut it down, there was always black truffle at Le Cirque, the fabled Franco-Italian restaurant that Captain Nair brought to Leela.'

A tray of the staff cafeteria lunch always went to the bungalow. Mrs Nair wanted to check that the food there was as good as it was for the hotel guests. A telling and touching practice, but then the staff was almost family.

Dinesh Nair is the true heir to his parents' palate. Here's an amuse-bouche. He is very particular about which veggies respectively spike his sambar and ishtew; the latter must have 10 per cent less coconut milk and 10 per cent fewer chillies. Inheriting his father's legendary hospitality, he likes as much to entertain as to eat. A long discussion precedes his dinner parties. Including the time and the temperature at which each carefully selected dish is to be served.

It should come as no surprise that the Captain's 90th would be marked by the grandmother of all parties, organized by his children at the Leela Mumbai. A beaming birthday boy stood under a canopy below a large tree at the poolside along with Dinesh, who introduced him to each of the

500 hand-picked guests who came up to wish him. He continued to greet them with unflagging energy right till the celebrations ended at 1 a.m.

It was a night to remember, befitting the man who had been the master of memorable hotel experiences for the past three decades. Prem Joshua's band, invited by Madhu, livened up the tempo. Cristal Champagne added to the effervescence. Everyone had stretched every fibre to ensure that nothing was wanting. The choicest fare from the world's cuisines was served. From groaning buffet tables and live kitchens, the top chefs from all the Leela properties were at hand.

The party wasn't over even when it was over. Around 1.30 a.m. a still bubbly Captain Nair joined his beloved Leela and Mr and Mrs Guenter Berendt for dinner at an elegant candlelit table. Close friends are the cherry on the cake of hospitality.

49

I Ever Promised You a Rose Garden

'I think that I shall never see
A poem lovely as a tree.'

Joyce Kilmer's wonderment could well have been that of Captain Nair. Hadn't he rejected the blueprint for his first hotel simply because it meant felling a centurion banyan to create the entrance?

Indeed, what is the one feature that sets his hotels apart? It is not the monumental architecture or the sinful luxury that hospitality brochures gush about. It is the fifty, or 500, shades of green – the softscape into which one's very soul can escape. It is also what sets the man himself apart from any other hotelier anywhere.

Would Conrad Hilton have clambered over an 8 foot wall to cajole a bemused Brazilian farmer to give him a sheaf of exotic cuttings?

Would Isadore Sharp consider a handful of lotus seeds the most precious gift a Thai princess could give him, a man for all Four Seasons though he was?

Asked if he had anything to declare on his return from Central America, would J.R.D. Tata have said, 'Only my *Pseudobombax ellipticum*', the shaving-brush tree?

And if at a WTTC convention Captain Nair had smoothly reeled off '*Archontophoenix alexandrae*, *Latania verschaffeltii*, *Dypsis decaryi*, *Bismarckia nobilis*, *Chamaerops macrocarpa*, *Wodyetia bifurcata*' wouldn't all the assembled delegates wonder why they were being subjected to an irrelevant Latin lesson? All he was doing was listing some of the sixty exotic palms in the 7 acre sprawl of the Leela Bangalore.

His horticulturist, Shambhu Sitaram Naik, said, 'The chairman brought back rare species, many of which we had never heard of. He insisted on us marking every plant with its proper botanical name as well.'

'Brought back' did not mean the odd cutting. Nurseries were a compulsory stop on his itinerary on any trip abroad, and there would be two suitcases full of seeds and grafts in his matching designer luggage. They'd be planted and propagated at the huge Bangalore nursery, then sent on to green all the other properties or grace their indoor flower arrangements. The horticulture department's proud boast was, 'Once we procured a plant, we never had to buy another of the same species.'

Captain Nair's own green and soil-smudged thumbprint is the signature scrawled across the flower beds, coppices, shrubberies, glades and rock gardens he created and communed with – and caught the culprit who dared move even one pot from the place he had personally allocated to it. The managers would be waiting for a meeting, but he'd be talking to his malis, each of whom he knew more than just by name, and whom he considered to be as much the executors of his vision as the VPs and GMs.

A man who planted over a million trees across his properties, who turned Mumbai marsh, Bangalore dirt and Goan scrubland into verdant acres could justifiably say he was 'born with a green spoon in my mouth'. To which one must add that he married a woman who may have been born with the proverbial silver one, but who had marched with him every grass tuft of the way. Some say, 'bent every leaf to her will, bade every bud to bloom'.

When Vivek's bride, Lakshmi, arrived in her new home, she was mesmerized by the fragrance emanating from the terrace filled with

Leela Nair's treasured rose plants. Greening was an innate passion for this couple, long before ecology became a buzzword.

Vijay Amritraj realized that 'nature was the god Captain Nair worshipped'. Naik quoted his boss, 'Land is Mother Earth. It has nurtured us. We have to protect her. However high our achievement we cannot forget her.' The child of Kerala's groves had written in his Malayalam autobiography, 'My childhood friends were trees. Not only do they have life, they have a soul.'

His eyes would sparkle even brighter when speaking of his gardens. And as with everything, he would tell the story of how he acquired this or that botanical specimen on his global outings.

In Bangkok, the princess may or may not have known his green passion when she gifted him the seeds of the sacred lotus. Even without his close association with the Dalai Lama, Captain Nair was fully aware of its importance in Buddhist symbolism. The Thai seeds were of the rare standing lotus. He planted them in a raised, fountain-centred pond at the Leela Mumbai. Sitting in his reserved 'chairman's corner' of the lobby lounge, he would point them out as they swayed gently just beyond the near-invisible plate glass.

Nelson Mandela gifted Captain and Leela Nair five saplings of South African mangoes. The distinctive red, yellow and green fruit joined the procession of curiosity arousers.

But it was the plumeria flower story that everyone loved. On a visit to Sao Paulo in 1996, something caught Captain Nair's eye while the car was winding up a mountain road. He told the driver to stop, and ran across to a high, rocky compound wall, which he managed to climb over. On the other side was a grove of brilliant plumeria trees. These were akin to India's ubiquitous champa, but the blooms were of shapes and hues he had never seen. In excited sign language, he pleaded with the lad tending them to give him some cuttings. The bemused boy agreed, his surprise and eyes widening when the stranger handed him a hundred-dollar note.

Today, plumerias in nine gorgeous hues blaze from trees at the Leela properties. The scatter of blooms on the grass is a visual windfall for the guest. And at the Leela Mumbai, offering a reverential handful to the small, stone Buddha seated under a canopy was the endnote of the chairman's morning walk.

The Goa resort was chosen as the venue of the World Spice Congress in 1992. The pièce de résistance of the preparation for it was a spice garden, for which the Captain ordered truckloads of pepper, clove, cardamom and cinnamon saplings from Kottakkal, Kerala. Their fragrance still infuses the air.

Samyukta summed up her grandfather with a simple, telling anecdote. 'We were driving through Central Park [New York], when he told the chauffeur, "Stop, stop!" We thought he had left something behind at the hotel. He explained: "I want to see the daffodils in full bloom."' Wordsworth would have understood.

After his passing, on every birth anniversary, the Leela group plants a total of one thousand trees on its hotel grounds and the gardens it has adopted. Could there be a more appropriate tribute?

50

The Spiritual Sensualist

The child Krishnan was inculcated into the rituals with which the Vaniya community worships its goddess, Muchilot Bhagavathi. He had dutifully participated in the temple ceremonies, and felt his little heart beat to the rising frenzy of the Theyyam drums.

The older Krishnan bent towards the spiritual rather than the overtly religious. He said his god was nature. He propitiated it in ways that would turn a professional horticulturist green with envy. Still, he found place in his rational mind for several gurus. He delved deep into their wisdom, and engaged them in informed discussion.

He also made his banquet rooms available free of charge to their followers for lectures and events. Mata Amritanandamayi, 'the smiling godwoman', would be a guest not of the hotel, but invited to stay at the bungalow itself. 'My father-in-law was drawn to anyone who had the energy,' said Lakshmi Nair.

The Kerala connection may or may not have been instrumental in drawing him also to Swami Sivananda Saraswati, who had been Dr Kuppuswamy in his previous secular avatar. This was way back during Krishnan's first army stint in Abbottabad. He and a colleague from the wireless office, a fellow Malayali called Balakrishna Menon, had gone in search of this proponent of orthodox Vedanta.

Finding him on the banks of the icy Ganga, they had begged to become his disciples. The yogi signalled his acceptance of Menon by reaching out for his hand. He turned away the twenty-something Nair, telling him that his destined path was that of a karmayogi, one who achieves a higher state through action rather than meditation.

Having more than lived up to that prediction, the successful entrepreneur would seek out his army colleague years later. To find that Menon had immersed himself in Vedanta and emerged as the revered Swami Chinmayananda Saraswati. One who revels in the bliss of pure consciousness.

Arguably, the most glowing niche in Captain Nair's heart was reserved for the Dalai Lama, who was as much a down-to-earth friend as spiritual guide. The two developed a remarkable camaraderie over the thirty years they knew each other. They would sit together talking of matters sacred and secular. Often holding hands. Granddaughter Amruda revealed that the duo with twinkling eyes and full-throated laughs also had a running gag, ribbing one another with 'I am older than you!'

Each time His Holiness arrived at the Leela Bombay the chairman would be waiting in the lobby to welcome him with a bunch of lotuses. When the Dalai Lama visited the hotel soon after Captain Nair's passing, he went straight up to his framed photograph in the lobby and placed a lotus garland over it. The two old friends exchanged their usual twinkling smiles.

Thanks to this bond, the lotus is the leitmotif at so many Leela hotels. In Buddhism, it symbolizes purity of body, speech and mind, since it floats above the murky waters of material attachment and physical desire. Legend has it that these blooms miraculously sprang up wherever the toddler Prince Siddhartha placed his tiny feet. Think too of the padmasana in which the Enlightened One sits. Or the haunting Bodhisattva Padmapani at Ajanta.

Hundreds of Tibetans in traditional robes would reverentially throng the garden of whichever Leela hotel His Holiness was visiting, and await the benediction of the Being whom they worshipped as a god. No one would ever think of objecting when they streamed into the plush lobby.

Captain Nair and the Dalai Lama were so comfortable with each other that the hotelier thought nothing of asking His Holiness to perform as mundane a task as inaugurating the staff cafeteria, simply because his visit coincided with the date of its scheduled opening. The aghast Leela team scrambled to make a worthier event of it.

In his suite on the eighth floor of the Leela Bombay, along with framed photographs of the Captain with his Hindu gurus and the statue of his tribal deity Muchilot Bhagavathi, sits a small Buddha. It is swathed in the ceremonial white silk *khata* scarf presented by the Dalai Lama to his dear, devoted friend and unstinting host.

Captain Nair lived the good life, whichever way you look at it. He had enjoyed it to the full, but his spiritual bent had influenced him to spread his goodness in equal measure. His surgeon friend Dr Vinod Chandiramani recalled the familiar smile that played on his lips in his last days. To him it seemed to say, 'I have attained nirvana and no one can take that away from me.'

51

Friend, Guide, Wife

The astrologer got it only half right. Asked to check if the stars approved of the match between a young army captain and the daughter of Kannur's illustrious mill owner, he had foretold that she would bring great wealth to her husband. She did. But she also gave him much more. Companionship, strength, counsel – and he gave her name to all his ventures, from lace to luxe hospitality. Arguably, these are the world's only hotels named after a woman. Real, living, prosaic, not a creature of legend or poetry.

In Hindu mythology, a woman's merit becomes the good fortune of her husband. This unapologetically patriarchal view was also only half true with this couple. While Mrs Nair was morally upright, her brownie points weren't earned through fasting and prayer. They came from the 100 per cent secular qualities of a practical mind and an astute understanding of opportunity. Yes, like Rider Haggard's heroine, Leela was 'She Who Must Be Obeyed', though in her case this wasn't a command. The obedience emanated from the respect she had earned by virtue of being right, doing right.

Leela was seldom the woman *behind* Captain Nair's success; she was often at its centre, sometimes even leading from the front. Without her push, he would never have left the army. Without her clear line of vision from airport to hotel, his last and grandest venture would never have taken off. Without her, those storied groves would have been a less vibrant shade of green. Finally, and perhaps most importantly of all, without her, the family would never have had the rooting that helped sons, daughters-in-law and grandchildren branch and flower the way each did.

To everyone in the hotel she was 'Madam Leela', as admired and deferred to as the 'Hon'ble Chairman' because everyone knew she was, in Madhu's words, 'the wind beneath his wings'. Samyukta, more familiar with the time when her grandmother wasn't such a public presence, called her the company's 'secret legend. The world knows her through his life and her brand name.'

In the family, while the grandfather was referred to as 'Achacha' in traditional Malayali fashion, the grandmother was 'Ma'. She saw all the girls as the daughter she had yearned for ever since she lost her own infant. That vacuum was filled by the wives and children of Vivek and Dinesh.

The couple was yin and yang, opposite in several ways and yet true kindred spirits, living for each other, doing things for each other with unstinted devotion. This could be seen in the introvert Leela's willingness to attend all international conferences because Captain Nair wanted her at his side. In Mumbai too, they would regularly go shopping – and even to dental appointments – together. All the way into town. Both were each other's world. Aishwarya was touched by the way the chairman 'ran so many of his business ideas past her, and she did the same about the home, even changes in the kitchen'.

Leela stopped travelling abroad in later years, but she continued to arrive at the Mumbai hotel at 5.30 p.m. for their daily tea date long after. Her busy, busy husband never missed it, and his eyes never stopped twinkling several watts more at every mention of her. If she was his closest friend, she was also, like a true one, his severest critic. No one ever saw him argue or ignore what she bluntly said. Simply because he never did.

How close he felt to her is illustrated by a story told by Dr A.S. Shetty. When the Captain was in his 80s, the Leela doctor got a frantic call at

9.30 a.m. from Captain Nair's secretary, Asha, saying, 'Something is very wrong. Chairman's speech is slurring.' Dr Shetty was fortunately in the vicinity. He sped there, checked his vitals and said, 'We need to take you to hospital.' Captain Nair didn't waste time asking questions, and simply said, 'Let's go.' They were exiting from the hotel's back gate when he asked to make a short halt at his adjacent bungalow.

As Dr Shetty recalled, 'He must have thought, "This is it!" Still calm despite fearing the worst, Captain's uppermost desire was to bid goodbye to Madam Leela. He spent a few private moments with her, and then we rushed him to Hinduja, where everything had been prepped to attend to him. Happily, it was nothing serious and he was soon back to his normal bubbly self.'

Truly, Captain and Mrs Nair were yin and yang. Unlike her dynamo husband, Leela was a very private person; her bearing was reserved. Unlike his OTT ones, her sartorial tastes were sober. None of his flamboyance, she wore fine Chanderis with narrow borders which they bought together from a small shop in Charni Road in the crowded heart of Mumbai; she kept her rich southern silks for conferences and other formal occasions. 'There was a sense of aristocracy about her,' said Samyukta. But wasn't that the same self-assured bearing which had attracted the schoolboy Krishnan to the illustrious A.K. Nair's youngest daughter?

When Lakshmi came into the family as a bride, her mother-in-law advised her to be at breakfast at 8 a.m., bathed and in a crisp sari – just as she was. She ate at 1 p.m. sharp, had a nap, and then would refresh herself, wear a different sari and go to meet her husband at the hotel.

It might be stating the obvious to mention that she was always dressed for dinner, with a matching blouse, and even coordinated jewellery – well, maybe not the diamond pendant which features prominently in all her photographs. While she was always understated, she would thrill to see the girls in all their party finery.

Needless to say, both adored the grandchildren. Apart from showering them with gifts, Achacha would be as excited when he took them round the menagerie in the Leela gardens: deer, two peacocks which had come as gifts from admiring friends, exotic fish, and an aviary full of colourful delights.

When the grandchildren were babies, Leela would give them Kerala oil baths, and wean them on traditional porridges of home-ground millets. When the first grandchild, Amruda, arrived, she ritualistically fed her a smear of a paste made from a gold nugget embedded in an Ayurvedic root; when she began crawling, Amamma covered the floor with yellow satin so as not to graze those tender hands and knees.

Leela Nair's home was her empire, acceded without asking. 'Her every breath, every dream was for her husband and sons,' said Madhu, who, thanks to her meticulous mother-in-law, never had to worry about any domestic tasks as she went about creating hotels that were several notches above 'a home away from home'.

Amruda was impressed by the detailed notes her grandmother kept of everything that was served to the guests her gregarious husband was always inviting over. She never repeated dishes for successive visits. Amruda's mother, Lakshmi, modified this statement to: 'If someone had particularly relished one of her celebrated fish curries but hadn't been able to take the heat level, she would serve it to him or her again, duly adjusted.'

That dining table was the nerve centre of both family and business – in truth, there was no line between the two. Plans would be discussed, and Leela would be an active participant, not just the passer of the payasam. Which, by the way, she tailored to each one's taste. When Aushim, the youngest, came home for his holidays, there'd be his favourite 'brown payasam' made with jaggery. Or with mango from the bungalow's lush orchard.

From the same garden she would pickle the giant, elongated Kerala limes. She also pickled grapes, keeping that rare recipe close to her chest. On Aishwarya's visits home, Amamma kept ready her favourite flower-shaped achappam wafer biscuit. When her grandmother came over to Singapore, 'she made a ton of her fabulous biryani and portioned it so neatly that I could live off it for months'.

Again unlike her husband, Leela Nair had little use for godmen or organized religion. She never went to temples. Her faith instead was in rock-solid values. And yes, she did believe in a higher power. 'She knew every shloka,' marvelled Samyukta. Her father's story vouched for this.

Dinesh had rushed back from London when his mother's long illness took a turn for the worse. She had hung on till he returned. He went straight to her room at Breach Candy Hospital, held her hand and began reciting her favourite Malayalam shloka: 'Strength is your life . . .' Then, to the teary amazement of her son, 'even in that barely conscious state, her lips moved to complete it'. Then she gently passed on. It was 18 May 2021, seven years and a day after Captain Nair's passing.

They cremated her in an exquisite Banarasi silk from her go-to shop for formal saris, the fabled Indian Textile Company at the Taj Mumbai. Like everything in life, in death too, she had planned this. Madhu found the sari in her mother-in-law's wardrobe, neatly wrapped and clearly labelled for her final outing. The meticulous Leela Nair had chosen it before her faculties began letting her down.

The family took Leela's ashes to their parents' sea-lapped Kannur home, and immersed them in a solemn, flower-bedecked ceremony. There, her soul mingled with that of her husband in the next life as it had in this.

52

Kerala Boy

Nair may have been a consummate man of the world, but at heart he was a Kerala boy. He looked cool in his bespoke Bijans and Brionis, but he chilled in his silk *jubba*s and mundus made of fine cotton with their thin gold borders. He loved his caviar, but if it were a choice between that and crab curry with puttu? Ah, no-brainer!

When Captain Nair spoke, as he often did of his early Kannur years, it wasn't out of an affected inverted snobbery. He was simply as comfortable in his own skin as in the accoutrements of power. Asked what she learnt from her amazing father-in-law, Madhu Nair did not mention some honed secret of hoteliering. Instead, she unhesitatingly zeroed in on 'the importance of home, family, roots. We believe in our Kerala culture. We carry out all the rituals with the traditional votive utensils.' She added, 'What's at home is in the hotels.'

Onam, the Malayali New Year, and the harvest festival of Vishu were equally celebrated in the Leela hotels before they were sold to Brookfield in 2019. In the Leela Mumbai (which alone remains with HLVL), the staff cafeteria is still laid out with the elaborate *sadhya* on banana leaves. It features plain boiled rice served with a minimum of twenty-four savoury dishes collectively called koottan, comprising curried vegetables, sambar, rasam, papads, pickles and banana chips. The feast is rounded off with buttermilk and at least three types of payasam.

While Onam would be ushered in with reverence at the Nair home and hotels, it was too much to expect the three-day affair to be as elaborately celebrated as it is in Kerala. The *pookakalam* flower rangoli was always there, but even Captain Nair's resourcefulness would falter when it came to putting up traditional events like the boat races (*vallam kali*) and tiger dances (*pulikali*). He may on occasion have organized an Onathallu martial arts display or even an Onam Kali tug-of-war.

On Vishu, the bungalow portico and the Leela Mumbai's lobby alike are colourfully decorated with the auspicious items which traditionally should be viewed first thing in the morning. Chief among these are a small image of Lord Krishna, flowers, fruits and vegetables, all artistically arranged on a silver platter. A must-have are the golden blossoms of the Indian laburnum (*Kani konna).* Little wonder then that the gardeners point to this tree at the Leela Bombay as being specially valued by 'Chairman and Madam Leela'.

Elders give the traditional token blessing of *kaineettam*, and the chatelaine of Leela Baug always had a wad of crisp currency notes to hand out to children or hotel staff who came to wish the Nairs. On Vishu, everything is about welcoming prosperity to the home – which, for this family, extends to the hotel.

More quotidian features of Malayali culture were naturally reinforced thanks to the materfamilias. Family dinner together was non-negotiable. The kids were indulged with Chinese food on Fridays and Italian on Saturdays, but the rest of the time the fare was regular home food. And why not? For, Kerala cuisine is like the beauty of Helen of Troy – custom never stales 'its infinite variety'.

Familial bonds were cemented by work, relaxation, and yes, shopping, which Captain Nair revelled in. Travel also tightened togetherness. The teenage grandchildren were sometimes taken along to international conferences to elasticize their minds and expose them to the finer things in life. His accolades burnished family pride as much as the brand.

Madhu made it a point to describe how the extended family was equally nurtured. Leela's two older sisters, Parvati and Nani, and her brothers, Bala and Ravi, along with their families, would often visit, as well as the Captain's niece, Jayashree. They were caringly looked after. Vivek's wife, Lakshmi, said, 'They all looked up to my parents-in-law, also because they were leaders in our society.'

Captain Nair counted the world's good and great among his acquaintances. He was on first-name terms with global celebs, but at the end of the day he liked nothing better than a long chinwag with his Malayali buddies. He always brought in the New Year at the Leela Goa with Anna (nee George) Malhotra, Madhavan and Mohanlal, no excuses entertained.

Mohanlal was heartbroken that he could not be with Captain Nair during his last moments because he was away on a cruise in Sweden. The icon of Malayalam cinema sent a long emotional tribute to the daily *Mathrubhoomi*. Here are a few lines from it : 'A 28-year-long relationship has ended. A generous host, a bosom friend, a guide, even a protective father is no more. It's an irreparable loss. The last time I met Krishnan Nair was when, along with Madhavan, I had gone to Mumbai to visit him in hospital. There, he held my hands and said, "Yesterday I saw you in my dream." When I heard that, I was so overcome that I could not speak.'

His childhood pals from Kannur, Rairu and Sankaran, would regularly arrive at Kottakkal to lighten the rigours of his annual Ayurveda retreat. They would talk nostalgically of the old days and excitedly about contemporary politics. They weren't enamoured of that other Malayali obsession: football. Lakshmi said her father-in-law wasn't much of a sports follower. 'But he would definitely have sent one of his detailed congratulatory letters to all the Indian achievers at the latest Olympics.'

Having fed on that same Kannur breakfast gruel, this duo too remained fit, all faculties intact. 'Rairu passed away at ninety-nine in 2021; Sankaran, of the same age, still practises yoga, eats only the Kerala congee and is as thin as a rake,' said Lakshmi.

Yes, Captain Nair gave wings to his dreams, but never forgot his roots.

As was said of hockey goalkeeper P.R. Sreejesh, who won for India its redemptive bronze at Tokyo 2020, our man embodied the son-of-the-soil spirit that each Malayali treasures close to his heart however far he travels. Speaking of travel, he gave all those globetrotting NRIs an international (and domestic) airport in their own Kannur. Here's the unrelenting effort that went into making it a reality.

In the old days, you had to land in Mangalore, then drive for almost an hour into and through the city to catch a train which took three hours to reach Kannur. This was the tedious journey Captain Nair and Leela had to make twice over annually ever since they settled in Mumbai. Some years later, the Calicut airport came up, but it still took a three-hour drive to get home. The new prosperity of Kerala was fuelled by Gulf NRIs and Captain Nair rightly considered it a shame that those from Kannur were saddled with such a tortuous route.

However, since Kerala already had airports at Calicut, Cochin Trivandrum and at Mangalore on the northern border of Karnataka, it would be a tad audacious to ask for one at Kannur. But, as we know by now, audacity was Captain Nair's middle name. So, with his own finances and contacts in the civil aviation ministry he managed to persuade key officials to make the trip here from Delhi to take a look. Of course, he had already done the groundwork, making several visits home to locate two possible sites for an airport.

The big hurdle was to convince the political heavies. He lobbied at the Centre, and tried to do the same at the state level. Till the 2021 elections, Kerala had a predictable pattern of ruling parties. The government alternated between the United Democratic Front (UDF) and the Left Democratic Front (LDF). Most of the UDF's leaders were from the south, so when they were in power none of Captain Nair's persuasive arguments worked. They simply weren't interested in sanctioning an airport in north Malabar as it would be of no use to their constituencies (read 'voters').

We've also seen how, over the course of many setbacks, Captain Nair honed the quality of patience. He waited for the next cycle, and sure enough, it brought in the LDF, more receptive because this coalition was dominated by communist veterans from north Malabar such as E.K. Nayanar, who became the chief minister in 1987, and the younger Pinarayi Vijayan. Both of them revved up the Captain's dream, helped by his network at the Centre. Then the airport project flew into rough weather.

The CPI(M), assuming a favourable climate, called for early elections and lost. Nayanar resigned from his party post, and was replaced as leader of the Opposition by V.S. Achuthanandan. Remember, he had been a thorn in the sand during the Kovalam Beach Resort transfer, and he was a bitter rival of Captain Nair's patron, Pinarayi Vijayan.

The unhelpful Mr A became chief minister in 2006. So, once again, impasse. But also a sure way to spur our man onwards, more so because the now-octogenarian warrior didn't want his airport dream to die with him. Luckily, a friend and admirer had landed at the Centre. The suave bidi baron Praful Patel had become civil aviation minister in 2004.

Captain Nair 'air-dashed' to Delhi and said, 'Praful, Kannur needs an international airport, and I have worked towards it for fifteen years with the help of bureaucrats in your department.'

The minister said, 'Uncle, rest assured that during my watch the foundation stone will be laid and land acquisition will start.' Patel was as good as his word, and Achuthanandan had to go along. The foundation stone was laid in December 2010.

Alas, Captain Nair passed on four years before the first commercial flight, Air India Express to Abu Dhabi, took off on 9 December 2018. Pinarayi Vijayan, who had become chief minister by then, acknowledged in his speech, 'This airport would not have been a reality without the efforts of the Late Captain C.P. Krishnan Nair.'

Validating his dogged persistence, the Kannur International Airport ferried 1 million passengers in its first nine months, and doubled the figure by 2020 despite the pandemic. With three terminals, it is the biggest airport in Kerala, and the first in the world to be powered entirely by solar energy.

Kannur's son brought more benign sunshine to his home district. He grandly renovated his mother's revered Katalayi temple, also paying for the rituals and for the Theyyam dances which had held the toddler in thrall. Amidst the framed accolades and celebrity mementoes in his still-preserved suite stands a primitive statuette of his Vaniya deity, Muchilot Bhagavathi.

Captain and Mrs Nair retreated whenever they could to their sylvan bungalow, Krishnan Leela on the northern Malabar coast. Designed by Didi Contractor, it incorporated Laurie Baker's principles of mud and vents that put air-conditioning to shame. From here, in 2014, his sons immersed his ashes and then those of their mother seven years later. From here this dedicated couple had come into the world, and their earthly remains departed from the same unwaveringly treasured Kannur font.

53

Till Debt Do Us Part

The higher the climb, the harder the fall. Captain Nair, master of new beginnings, suddenly found himself staring at the endgame. Of course, he was no stranger to dream projects turning into nightmares courtesy a combination of best and worst. In Bangalore, for example, he refused to downsize his insistence on 'the best of the best' even when the non-payment of the refund legally due from HUDCO had squeezed his financial jugular, blocking the Rs 200 crore he had paid for the auctioned plot in New Delhi's Friends Colony.

Yet, he had always managed to convert dream to reality. Now, however, the alarm bells began clanging more stridently, and the wake-up call could no longer be silenced. That old duo of internal and external forces reared its head more forcefully than ever before. This time, Shakespeare and W.B. Yeats conspired towards his downfall. 'Vaulting ambition, which o'erleaps itself' from the playwright's *Macbeth* and 'Things fall apart; the centre cannot hold; mere anarchy is loosed upon the world . . .' from the Irish poet's 'The Second Coming'.

A company's EBITDA (earnings before interest, taxes, depreciation and amortization) is the true measure of financial performance. On this matrix, in 2006–07, HLVL boasted almost Rs 264 crore against a borrowing of Rs 950 crore, a ratio which would not appear lopsided to anyone familiar with the way business works. The following year, its EBITDA had climbed to Rs 304 crore plus. It didn't matter that the borrowings had also jumped to Rs 2039 crore because the company's share price was soaring, and at Rs 73 crore plus, it was among the Indian hotel industry's highest taxpayers.

Then 'things' began to 'fall apart'. In 2009–10, the EBITDA almost halved to Rs 153 crore and the borrowings spiked to nearly Rs 2884 crore. Two years later, the former plummeted further to a mere Rs 35 crore, and then slipped into the red in 2014–15, registering a loss of Rs 84 crore.

Interest snowballed from a manageable Rs 35 crore in 2007–08 to a staggering Rs 501 crore by 2013–14; the borrowings had naturally kept mounting, and in that year they hit Rs 5047 crore. What on earth was happening? How did a company bursting with health end up on life support barely eight years later?

The robust health of HLVL in 2006–07 had prompted Captain Nair to go in for FCCBs to bankroll his 'vaulting ambition'. These added up to Rs 750 crore in US dollars and euros, and would be converted to equity with 0 per cent interest. The company went ahead with the construction of the Leela Palaces at New Delhi, Chennai and Udaipur.

In 2011, HLVL had been forced to sell the gorgeous Kovalam Beach Resort. However, against all financial prudence, the Rs 500 crore from the sale wasn't pumped into retiring some of that huge debt, but was instead siphoned into the upcoming Chennai hotel with all its Leela-grade luxury. This took the interest cost on borrowings to Rs 321 crore in 2011–12, snowballing to nearly Rs 502 crore by 2013–14. So, instead of borrowing from Peter to pay off Paul, this was tantamount to adding one more creditor, Philipose.

For Captain Nair, always the great gambler, this was the last throw of the dice. His eternal optimism assured him that he would be back in the game once the Chennai hotel was up and running, because this south Indian capital city was already giving Silicon Plateau Bangalore a run for its money. Banks knew that it was untenable for companies to sustain such heavy borrowings, but played ostrich since writing off loans would look bad on the books.

Now comes Yeats's 'anarchy' being 'loosed upon the world'. The chairman's otherwise dependable instinct met its nemesis in a financial catastrophe two continents away. Markets being dominoes, the Lehman Brothers' declared bankruptcy of 15 September 2008 led to collapses across the world. The investors who had bought HLVL's once-win-win FCCBs were now spooked. They spurned the option to convert them into equity, and instead chose to back out – with the redemption premium ranging from 25 to 40 per cent.

What hit the company even harder was that to pay out it had to borrow from Indian banks where, in that same domino effect, interest rates had gone up from 8–9 per cent to over 12 per cent. HLVL had to return nearly Rs 1000 crore against the Rs 750 crore it had gained from the FCCBs.

As if Lehman Brothers hadn't done enough damage, another whammy followed two months later. This time, a domestic blow punched the economy's solar plexus: the 26/11 Mumbai terror attacks.

Was the king's gambit doomed to a checkmate right from the start? No. Considering the company's earnings, the debt snowballing to even Rs 5000 crore would not have mattered. The KO came in that fatal cliché: 'factors beyond our control'. By the end of 2011, the New Delhi and Udaipur hotels had opened, but were not generating the expected profit because the market was subdued. Oversupply had lowered room rates, even though occupancy was high. The gung-ho fell with the room rates.

Now there was no option. The Godzilla loans having made it an NPA, the company had to go into corporate debt restructuring (CDR) mode in February 2012. Under this, not only was it allowed to defer the payment of interest, it was given an additional loan of Rs 375 crore to redeem the remaining $40 million FCCBs plus it was permitted to complete the Chennai hotel. In return, HLVL was required to sell one of its properties, but it was 'unable' to do so.

Thus, in June 2014, the ineffectual CDR had to make way for the next step. The lenders assigned the debt to an asset reconstruction company:

JM Financial. Why did the CDR fail? Insiders concede that the bankers were 'window dressing'. No one wanted to take a 'haircut' even though everyone knew that the interest was unsustainable.

The company sold the fabulous 75 acre Leela Goa for Rs 725 crore. This time, unlike Kovalam, it perforce used the money to service part of its debt. However, it did succeed in retaining the precious brand name by securing a management contract from the new owner.

What had changed was that Captain Nair had passed away on 17 May 2014. With him had gone the clout which had enabled him to hold on to his painstakingly nurtured dream hotels. He could say, 'Don't sell off Leela New Delhi. Wait for the market to pick up and thus get a better price.' He could call in favours. He could persuade higher authorities to lean on the lenders not to force a sale with the argument that 'This chairman isn't running away, the asset is not going anywhere.'

Then came the inevitable coup de grâce. Keeping in mind the other interests – those of the lenders, employees, etc. – the promoter company divested itself of the four hotels it owned: Bangalore, New Delhi, Udaipur and Chennai, plus the five it managed on contract. Thus absolving itself of the entire debt. For the sum of Rs 3950 crore, ownership of the four hotels passed on to Brookfield Asset Management Inc. on 17 October 2019.

Hiving off the family silver piece by piece might have added more to the overall kitty, but this way the precious Leela brand remained intact and safe in the hands of a strong and long-term investor. Indeed, just before the sale, *Travel+Leisure USA* had crowned it the World's Best Brand, and would do so again for 2020–21. With this historic deal, the Canada-based Brookfield entered the Indian hospitality industry with a resounding splash. It bought the properties, contracts and the business – but not HLVL, which continues as a separate listed company in which Brookfield has no equity interest.

By the way, the brand itself was the property of a promoter company and not HLVL. Brookfield paid the former for the brand and certain support services. Brookfield understood the value of the legacy and the promoter family was confident that the new owners would nurture it. However, ITC Limited, a minority shareholder of HLVL, filed cases in various forums such as the SEBI and National Company Law Tribunal (NCLT) objecting to the entire transaction including the payment to the promoters. Since it could not succeed in obtaining a stay, the transaction was concluded. However, to date, ITC has continued to pursue the matter in higher courts.

This was a time of cataclysmic crashes in the travel trade. Jet Airways and Kingfisher Airlines disappeared into thick air. Jet's Naresh Goyal tried to play hardball with the bankers, which backfired. The company went bust; a great brand got splintered; and the employees were hung out to dry. As for Vijay Mallya, the self-styled 'king of good times' flew off to London's high life, leaving a Rs 7000 crore debt compared to HLVL's Rs 5000 crore.

Amidst this opprobrium, the Nairs stood out. Not only did they not run away, their conduct was transparent, respectful of their creditors and mindful of their employees. For the founding father, it had always been more about showcasing India and giving the best to the guest, whatever the cost. If this double-minded pursuit was at least partly responsible for the collapse, his heirs ensured that the loss of empire was not also a loss of face or trust.

For Vivek and Dinesh Nair too, it was more than a business; they would not treat their legacy cavalierly; after all, it bore their beloved mother's name. And it was not just in name. For 'Madam Leela' had left as strong an imprimatur on the hotels as she had on her husband, her sons and their families.

54

Where's the Crisis?

Remember Mark Twain's (misquoted) riposte? 'The reports of my death are greatly exaggerated'? So, could HLVL say the same about the imminent sale or liquidation of the Leela hotels which had set the media abuzz right from 2013? Well, yes and no. Sale, yes. Death, no. More to the point here, how did the company manage to weather the storm?

Full-page advertisements that appeared in the *Economic Times* put the official seal on the media's doomsday predictions, announcing asset reconstruction company JM Financial's 'expression of interest' in selling the Leela Palace Delhi and Chennai hotels on behalf of the lender banks. The ads were virtually an obituary notice.

No surprise, then, that the competition amplified the death knell. Even more expectedly, this shook the confidence of the two pillars which had helped the Leela edifice attain such heights: the rich 'guest experience' and the highly motivated staff which provided it.

If the precious brand was to survive, guests had to be islanded from the 'market noise', and the staff needed serious hand-holding. More so since the jungle drums had also unleashed a frenzy of headhunters wanting to scalp the best talent.

Rajiv Kaul outlined how the top management went into overdrive to ensure that no evidence of the company's financial stress leached into the guest experience. The fastidious standards continued to be adhered to as meticulously. The service remained as sleek and warm, the amenities were as luxe, the restaurants as lavish, the brass as gleaming, the gardens as manicured. The corporate expenses may have been given a 'haircut' by the asset restructuring company but the impeccable grooming remained.

Guest feedback confirmed this. The 'Leela experience' had created a loyal fan base, and those who returned during this financial maelstrom found no signs of fraying at the edges. In fact, the tenacity with which appearances were maintained won both admiration and a competitive edge.

However, there would have been none of that edgy guest experience if the staff was equally on edge. It would be like the cliché of performing *Hamlet* without the Prince of Denmark or serving chicken a la Kiev without the ensconced herb butter. Therefore, as much attention and energy went into shoring up employee morale. Any marketing manual will tell you that internal customers are as important as the external; those you pay are as much to be cared for as those who pay you. A two-pronged strategy swung into action, concentrating on self-belief and esprit de corps. These had always been the warp and weft of the Leela fabric; now they were consciously reinforced.

The self-belief was strengthened by the constantly emphasized fact that the heights achieved by the brand were the result of a group effort. The esprit de corps sprang from the daily evidence that the staff were part of the Nairs' extended family. Now, special effort went into inspiring them with the conviction that 'we are all in this together', that the whole rank and file was in the battle to safeguard the citadel, not just the generals in the corporate office.

The way everyone rose to the occasion endorsed the Harvard study which found that productivity increased by as much as one-third when propelled by a 'higher cause'. In this case, it was the drive to be the best in class. It certainly helped that the brightest light shone on the group during this darkest hour. Individual properties kept being ranked among the Ten Best Hotels in the World, rated by the industry Oscars, the *Travel+Leisure USA* awards.

Indeed, the Leela Palace Udaipur soared to No. 1 in 2018–19, followed by the Leela Group being voted the Best Brand in the World in 2019–20. With much the same staff extending the highest standards of service, it wrested the same honour the following year when ownership had passed on to Brookfield.

But the rah-rah pep talks would have a hollow ring without palpable on-ground evidence. To allay the genuine fears of instability and job losses, the top management sharpened HR best practices. A double dose of reassurance was given by carrying out routine salary reviews for the year, and, more importantly, paying salaries on time throughout the period of financial duress.

This was backed by sustained formal and informal employee interactions by GMs of each hotel and multiple HR-supervised employee engagement initiatives. More effectively, queries and doubts were routinely addressed face to face via 'town halls' conducted by GMs.

Such hand-holding was also important as a preamble to the sale. Naturally, team members across hotels and the corporate office were apprehensive about their own future being thrown into an abyss along with that of the company. Much brainstorming by the top management resulted in the messaging points to be communicated through the respective GMs.

These were: (1) The Leela hotels were transiting into the safe hands of Brookfield, which respected the brand and would aim to sustain its rich legacy; (2) The new owners shared the same values and philosophy that the Leela Group cherished; (3) Day-to-day functioning would remain unchanged and the new group would continue to provide stellar guest experiences with the help of the old team members' well-honed expertise; (4) Staff were encouraged to look ahead with optimism, and to focus on elevating standards of excellence instead of being gnawed at by negativity.

What made all this actually work was the family feeling and a deep trust in management, mutual respect, even bonhomie built up by Captain Nair's open-minded, open-hearted style. Without these foundations, it could all have been scoffed at as eyewash, and led to a toxic unrest which would be as detrimental to the sale as to the valued guest experience. The charismatic paterfamilias had passed away in 2014, but his passion and values were a powerful rallying force, the glue that held everyone together in tough times.

There was a third 'customer', and arguably the toughest in those tough times. This composite entity comprised the creditors in their many avatars, from bank consortium to corporate restructuring tribunal to the asset restructuring company, JM Financial. The Leela management promised this 'customer' that it would eliminate wastage and pare down expenses provided none of this diluted or diminished guest experience. A caveat that made good business sense since the brand's luxury quotient remained in focus, thereby retaining the premium value of the assets.

Trust played a great part here too because the debt managing parties saw that HLVL was putting its mouth where the money was. Most importantly, it was adhering to the budget targets set by the corporate office in tandem with the GMs. This was to persuade the lenders and JM Financial to allow the hotels to operate as freely yet frugally as possible without compromising excellence.

What was remarkable was that despite the company foundering on these gigantic, jagged rocks of debt, most of the individual hotels remained market leaders with high operating profitability. So it was not difficult to convince lenders and key stakeholders to permit a free hand to the Leela management.

Still, some expenses had to be trimmed, and all that could be avoided or postponed done. There were four key areas where reducing investments could withstand curtailment or where effective alternatives could be found.

One, the company restrained capital spending on hardware to bare essentials. Two, marketing budgets were trimmed and more cost-effective digital media was used to showcase the company. Three, traditional academy learning expenditure was reduced and greater allocation made towards e-learning modules. Four, expensive refurbishing of hotels and upgrading of interiors were postponed.

Convinced of the bona fides, JM Financial and the board extended its concurrence and support. The hard-nosed 'third customer' understood that maintaining the ultra-luxe quotient was necessary to get top dollar from the sale. Indeed, the ultimate buyer, Brookfield, was on the same wavelength; it shelled out the 'earnings multiple' premium for this lavishly nurtured brand.

55

Epilogue

One man created a proud Indian brand that came out of nowhere, set its signature standards of luxury, and challenged the industry's entrenched aristocrats right from the start. Thirty-two years later, Captain Nair's sons had to let go of all the hotels they owned or managed, barring the Leela Mumbai which had thrown down the gauntlet in 1987. But the invaluable brand lives and continues to bear their mother's name. The new owner, Brookfield Asset Management Inc., will respect and further burnish it. Five years after his passing, Captain Nair could finally rest in peace knowing that his legacy remains. Mrs Leela Nair lived to see the full and final settlement which closed the painful last chapter – with honour untarnished.

Where did all this leave the Captain's sons, Vivek and Dinesh? The Nairs unwittingly snatched victory from the jaws of defeat. The sale actually saved them. When the economy began spiralling downwards, ultimately to be pushed into free fall by the pandemic, when the travel and hospitality industry imploded, they had paid their dues, collected their money and exited the fray. At the end of the day, if not laughing all the way to the bank, they certainly went smiling into the sunset.

Put it down to inherited good karma. For hadn't their parents passed on to them a bequest which was as much about values as velvet?

56

The Inheritors

> 'My message today is simple. Whatever dream you choose to pursue, take pride in it. Aim at being best of the best. Nothing is guaranteed, and everything is possible. Go forth with courage and resilience. Life will not be necessarily smooth – but its script is yours to write.'

This was part of Captain Nair's speech when Jodhpur University conferred an honorary doctorate on him in 2013. Eight months later, he passed away. There's no way of knowing how deeply these wise words impacted his audience, but his family members have certainly taken them to heart as they carved out their own niches.

Vivek Nair

Captain Nair's elder son is CEO of HLVL, which runs hotels and resorts. The company owns the Leela Mumbai which has – apart from guest rooms – a spa, salon, restaurants, wedding banquet halls, a fitness facility, a swimming pool and meeting rooms. He chaired the WTTCII forum in 2011 and continues to be a member of the executive committee.

He was a two-term president of the FHRAI, which represents 50,000 hotels and 5,00,000 restaurants across the country, and recommended several policy changes of immense bottom line and brand value to the hospitality industry; he remains on the executive committee. He is also the chairman of Leela Lace Holdings Pvt Ltd, which is in the business of developing real estate for commercial purposes, including a state-of-the-art IT business park for ITES.

Vivek is married to Lakshmi and they have three children, Amruda, Aishwarya and Aushim.

Dinesh Nair

Captain Nair's second son is co-CEO of HLVL and co-chairman of Leela Lace Holdings Pvt Ltd. The company is in the process of building the 1 million sq. ft Leela Business Park II, as a sister to its first one on Mumbai's prime Andheri–Kurla Road. Dinesh, along with his daughter, Samyukta, founded LSL Capital in London. It opened the first Jamavar restaurant outside India in 2016 in London's tony Mayfair, followed by the more relaxed Bombay Bustle. Both restaurants have featured in *Conde Nast Traveler*'s list of 27 Best Indian Restaurants in London. MiMi Mei Fair, a restaurant serving gourmet Chinese cuisine, is the company's most recent offering. The father–daughter duo plan to expand their collection of restaurants in London's Mayfair. In spring 2022, they will open a modern Japanese restaurant on 1 Grosvenor Square, among the world's most expensive residential addresses. In summer 2022, they hope to have a casual French bistro on South Audley Street in partnership with a two–Michelin Star French chef Claude Bosi. More openings are planned for 2023, again at toff Mayfair locations.

Dinesh is married to Madhu, and Samyukta is their only child.

Lakshmi Nair

Vivek's wife is an active board member of the family's holdings. She has been a hands-on patron of young artists, from curating art camps at the

Leela Goa in the 1990s to currently showcasing their work in a gallery at the Leela Mumbai. Believing in the impact women can have on their community, Lakshmi is a founding committee member of the Sahachari Foundation, which works towards the upliftment of women and children, plus an active member of several women's groups such as INDUS. She also sits on the advisory board of the Gateway School, Mumbai, a not-for-profit dedicated to empowering children with disabilities. Lakshmi is a dedicated animal lover who regularly supports rescue, feeding and adoption programmes in animal-centred NGOs. She completed her master's degree at St Xavier's, Mumbai, and studied hotel management at Cornell University, New York.

Madhu Nair

Dinesh's wife packs in multiple roles and professional commitments.. She has spent thirty-two years infusing the soul of India into the interiors and service standards of the Leela Palaces, Hotels and Resorts. Amalya and Dandelion are the high-end labels of LSL Holdings Pvt Ltd, which she owns in partnership with her daughter, Samyukta. Amalya draws on Madhu's vast experience in sourcing and recasting traditional artefacts for the hotels; in the process, she has uplifted both craft and craftspersons for decades. Her signature collectibles have found homes across the world. Dandelion is Samyukta's baby, offering bespoke nightwear and clothing. Madhu is also a great resource for her husband and daughter's London-based LSL Capital. After the passing of her inspirational 'Mummy' in 2021, Madhu formalized her 25-year-long philanthropic activities by creating the Leela Nair Foundation for Women and Children. She hopes to extend its welfare work to her native Kerala, especially Kannur.

Amruda Nair

Vivek and Lakshmi's eldest child has over fifteen years' experience in hospitality and asset management in twelve countries on four continents. After graduating from Cornell's School of Hotel Administration in New

York, Amruda worked at the Mandarin Oriental, New York, before joining Jones Lang LaSalle Hotels, Singapore. In 2019, she set up Araiya Hotels and Resorts, a hotel management company specializing in boutique resorts in India and operating upscale dining concepts in Europe. Amruda has received the Generation Next Award for Hospitality (2011) given by the All-India Association of Industries, the Young FICCI Ladies Organization Women Achievers Award (2012) and the Rising Star – South Asia Award at the Hotel Investment Forum (2016). As vice president of Apne Aap Women's Collective, the globally acclaimed anti-trafficking organization, she works towards eradicating second-generation sex work.

Aishwarya Nair Mathew

Amruda's younger sibling headed corporate food and wine merchandising at the Leela Palaces, Hotels and Resorts, which wrested top global awards six years in a row. She is the only woman in India to have been felicitated with a Diplome d'Honneur by the Comité Interprofessionel du Vin de Champagne, based in the iconic and eponymous French region, for her efforts in creating dynamic wine lists. Aishwarya was chosen Business Woman of the Year 2014 by the Indian Leadership Conclave for her work with wine for the Leela Group. In 2020, she was ordained as a chevalier by the Confrérie des Chevaliers du Tastevin, an exclusive fraternity of Burgundy wine connoisseurs. Currently based in Singapore, she has developed her own online retail fashion label, ALIGNE. She continues to consult with corporate clientele, helping them build private cellars of high-end wines.

Aishwarya is married to Nishant Mathew.

Samyukta Nair

After completing her education in the UK, Dinesh and Madhu's only daughter apprenticed with her dynamic mother, working on the project development, design and operations of the Leela Palaces, Hotels and

Resorts at Udaipur and Chennai. This led her to Ecole Hoteliere de Lausanne and an executive MBA in hospitality management. Next, her entrepreneurial genes took her down a different but still familial path. Assessing the gap in aesthetic yet comfortable sleepwear for Indian women, she filled it with her own lifestyle label, Dandelion, in 2014, encouraged by her father, who had earlier built a highly successful garment export business. In 2016, Samyukta went on to partner with Dinesh to open the first international chapter of Jamavar on Mount Street in Mayfair, London, where she now lives and helms a clutch of design-led restaurants under LSL Capital that include Jamavar, Bombay Bustle and, since September 2021, MiMi Mei Fair, with more equally exclusive openings under her belt.

Aushim Nair

Vivek and Lakshmi's youngest, and Captain and Leela Nair's only grandson, is also the only family member who has veered away from hospitality – or even the textiles which fuelled the hotel dream. True, Aushim graduated with honours from Chicago's Kendall College with a degree in hotel and sports management, and then earned a diploma in hotel management from Les Roches Bluche, Switzerland. True, he worked with such luxury hosts as Kempinski and Peninsula in Switzerland, Prague and Chicago. But then he found his true metier: music plus digital brand building. He is tech-savvy and, like his sisters and cousin, sharply creative. Aushim is based in New York where he consults for independent record labels and media companies. He also directs and designs campaigns for the food and beverage industry in the US and Europe.

Acknowledgements

Writing non-fiction is akin to working at an archaeological site. Or similar to a Michelangelo chipping away at a block of Carrara, revealing the awesome David existing inside. Most of all, it is a carnival of many participants, compared to the loneliness of the long-distance writer of fiction. In that sense, and with no offence, it is more a collaborative democracy than a dictatorship filtered through a single mind.

So it was with this biography of Captain C.P. Krishnan Nair. Since he was not one life but several, there was a corresponding number of sites to dig. Since he had passed on seven years before I took up the task, I had lost access to this singular first person. Since he would have been 100 in February 2022, there also weren't too many who would have known my subject from his childhood in north Malabar's Kannur. However, the absence of chronological contemporaries was compensated for by Captain Nair being such a gregarious, generation-bridging figure. Grandchildren apart, even thirty-somethings had memories to share.

First off, my thanks to Vivek and Dinesh Nair. For the stories they recalled of their father – from his trudging through the lint-choked textile mills and markets to braving the heartburn which almost killed each of his hotels at birth. If they described his monumental showcasing of India's past and present, they did not shy away from detailing the debt-ridden path to the collapse of empire. Much more than their time,

I'm thankful for the free hand. A halo should never be a biography's must-have accessory.

The goad was Rajiv Kaul. Closely familiar with my book on M.S. Oberoi, he suggested I write on another hotelier, one who had entered hospitality's velveted arena some forty years later, but was no less a pioneer. Rajiv was archive, facilitator, hand-holder – and soldier on the front-line who took all my impatient bullets. So, an apology as well as a thank you.

Alas, 'Madam Leela' also passed away before I could get her valuable insights into the man she walked with every step of the way, the soulmate who was totally dedicated to her. It was a devotion that went far deeper than the name he gave all his ventures, from lace to deluxe hotels. However, their daughters-in-law and grandchildren provided all the deep, rich shades of a remarkable couple who were yin and yang, perfectly counterpoised.

Thank you, Lakshmi, for sharing your experiences of entering Leela Baug as Vivek's young bride and the strong influences of your mother-in-law. Madhu, it was you, Dinesh and Samyukta who lived with Captain and 'Ma' Leela in all those later years; moreover, you created all those fabulous interiors and service standards. So, my gratitude for your particularly helpful contribution.

It was such a warm, fuzzy feeling listening to Amruda, Samyukta, Aishwarya and Aushim, all of whom recalled so many touching details of their loving, caring Amamma and Achacha.

Team members past and present rose to the occasion. The GMs, HR department and F&B guys, housekeepers, bellhops, executive chef Aungshuman Chakraborty and Balu, whom Captain and Mrs Nair picked up from a modest restaurant in Kannur and made master of the Leela's unique Kerala kitchen. Also, Rajeev Kumar Mangalad and Shambhu Sitaram Naik, the horticulturists who shared the boss's passion and gave shape to the signature gardens of the Leela Palaces and Resorts.

Their variegated anecdotes complemented those of the family. Together they helped me create the man in full: demanding and generous, paterfamilias at work as much as at home, patriot to the core – and sartorial buccaneer.

A special thanks to Shobha Patel, who handled the group's PR, and returned to help me. Hers was the ringside view because Captain Nair intuitively understood the power of the story, and devoted a great deal of his time to convey how he wanted it told. He was himself the master communicator, the face of the brand like few other head honchos. Shobha also trawled through a zillion photographs to choose the ones in this book. By her side was Minal Srivastava, filling in details, and bearing with my last-minute tech demands.

Vijay Amritraj gave me the first inkling of the many lives of Captain Nair via the succinct audio-visual he did on his long-time friend. He then fleshed it out at an ungodly hour on a long call from LA.

Priya Dutt was my first interviewee, and thanks to her I knew it would be a rewarding exploration.

Adman Mohmmed Khan of Enterprise recalled his role in the telling of the Leela story, as did ace photographer Hardev Singh. They were the professionals who ended up getting not just lessons in their own field, but a masterclass on life and how it should be led.

A different perspective came from media maven K. Madhavan, who, along with Kerala superstar Mohanlal, was among the closest of Captain Nair's buddies. He too was from Kannur, but thirty years younger, an example of my subject's eclectic range – across fields and generations.

I have to mention my long-time friend Geeta Doctor and my former colleague Suresh Nair. It was to them I turned at the start to get a context of Nair culture. Geeta pulled out her own prodigious writing, ranging from young Krishnan's 'door-opener', V.P. Menon, to the food of north Malabar. Suresh rolled out his academic contacts.

I am grateful to Parth Mehrotra of Juggernaut for his continued trust in my ability to turn in a worthy manuscript – in the promised time. And for telescoping his schedules so that this biography could be Amazon-ready for Captain Nair's birth centenary. Arani Sinha, the Managing Editor of Juggernaut, held the necessary gun to my head, for which, too, a grudging gratitude.

Finally, I must thank my partner, Dinyar Modi, for his painstaking review of my manuscript, and more so his patience with the prima donna excess which is the divine right of every author. Right?

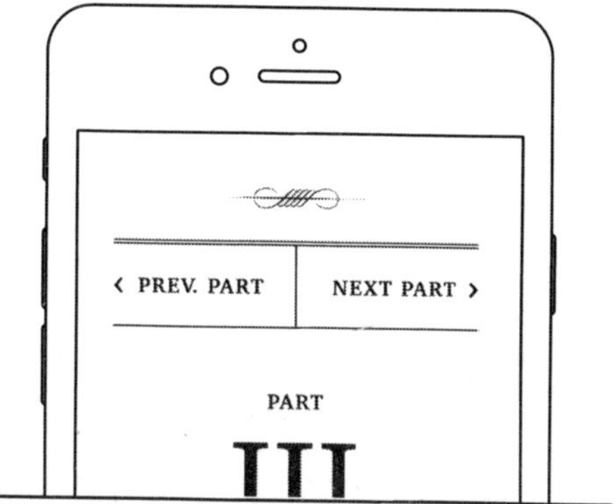

Beautiful Typography

The quality of print transferred to your mobile. Forget ugly PDFs.

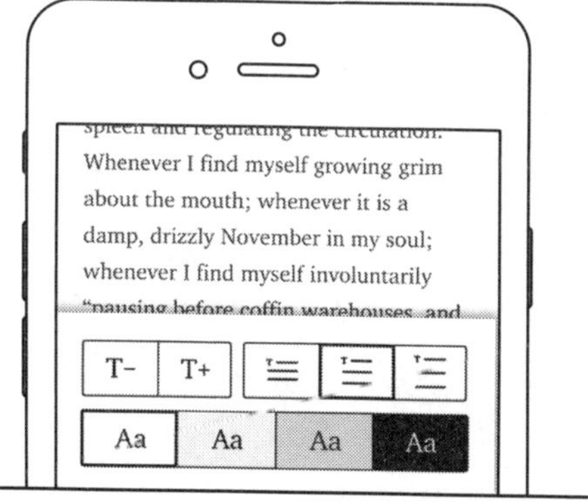

Customizable Reading

Read in the font size, spacing and background of your liking.

AN EXTENSIVE LIBRARY

Including fresh, new, original Juggernaut books from the likes of Sunny Leone, Praveen Swami, Husain Haqqani, Umera Ahmed, Rujuta Diwekar and lots more. Plus, books from partner publishers and loads of free classics. Whichever genre you like, there's a book waiting for you.

CRUCIBLES OF SIN
HITESHA
Can a Geek ever find Love?
Finding Juliet
Toffee
Mary Shelley
Frankenstein
A FAROOQ RESHI INVESTIGATION
COLD FLAKE
PRAVEEN SWAMI
How to Heal Your Broken Heart
A Psychiatrist's Guide To Heartbreak
DR SHYAM BHAT
MOIN and THE MONSTER
ANUSHKA RAVISHANKAR
Stories of women from the ganglands
S. Hussain Zaidi
with Jane Borges
Foreword by Vishal Bharadwaj
Pakistan's Queen of Romance
UMERA AHMED
Nowhere Girl
A Story of Love & Forgiveness
THE BEHEADING
This Is How He Will Bless Her
ABHEEK BARUA
THE Peshwa
The Lion and the Stallion
THE INVISIBLE WOMAN
SAURBH KATYAL
ANGRY BIRDS FAN? READ THE BOOK...
ANGRY BIRDS TOONS
TOONS TALES
ARCHANA SABOO
ADIKOOL
in
#AfricanAdventures
Tarana Khan
She hates me, he loves me not but...
DON'T FALL IN LOVE
Vandana Shankar
KHUSHWANT SINGH
WE INDIANS

DON'T JUST READ; INTERACT

We're changing the reading experience from passive to active.

juggernaut.in

Ask authors questions

Get all your answers from the horse's mouth. Juggernaut authors actually reply to every question they can.

Rate and review

Let everyone know of your favourite reads or critique the finer points of a book – you will be heard in a community of like-minded readers.

Gift books to friends

For a book-lover, there's no nicer gift than a book personally picked. You can even do it anonymously if you like.

Enjoy new book formats

Discover serials released in parts over time, picture books including comics, and story-bundles at discounted rates. And coming soon, audiobooks.

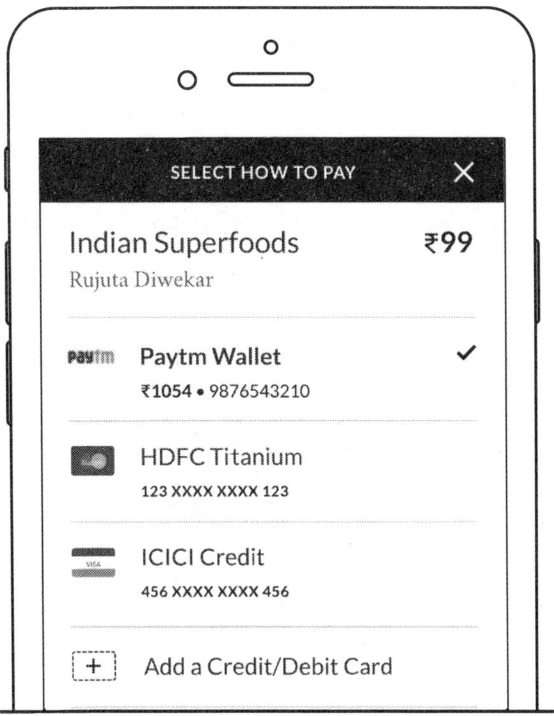

Paytm Wallet, Cards & Apple Payments

On Android, just add a Paytm Wallet once and buy any book with one tap. On iOS, pay with one tap with your iTunes-linked debit/credit card.

Click the QR Code with a QR scanner app or type the link into the Internet browser on your phone to download the Juggernaut app.